ECOLOGY,
LITURGY,
AND THE
SACRAMENTS

ECOLOGY, LITURGY, AND THE SACRAMENTS

Kevin W. Irwin

Paulist Press
New York / Mahwah, NJ

Cover design by Joe Gallagher
Book design by Lynn Else

Library of Congress Cataloging-in-Publication Data
Names: Irwin, Kevin W., author.
Title: Ecology, liturgy, and the sacraments / Kevin W. Irwin.
Description: New York / Mahwah, NJ : Paulist Press, 2023. | Includes index. Summary: "Concern for the environment is a traditional Catholic stance based on the goodness of creation and our belief that God created heaven and earth. The liturgy and the sacraments use elements of creation—fire, water, oil—to help us discover God in the world. Respect for creation is thus related to sacramental and liturgical practices"— Provided by publisher.
Identifiers: LCCN 2022027542 (print) | LCCN 2022027543 (ebook) | ISBN 9780809155194 (paperback) | ISBN 9781587689147 (ebook)
Subjects: LCSH: Catholic Church—Doctrines. | Creation. | Catholic Church—Liturgy. | Sacraments.
Classification: LCC BX1751.3 .I79 2023 (print) | LCC BX1751.3 (ebook) | DDC 264/.0208—dc23/eng/20221104
LC record available at https://lccn.loc.gov/2022027542
LC ebook record available at https://lccn.loc.gov/2022027543

ISBN 978-0-8091-5519-4 (paperback)
ISBN 978-1-58768-914-7 (e-book)

Published by Paulist Press
997 Macarthur Boulevard
Mahwah, New Jersey 07430
www.paulistpress.com

Printed and bound in the
United States of America

To Patricia Bauman

CONTENTS

CONTENTS

Contents

PREFACE

As is my custom, I write this preface as I conclude the writing of this book. It turns out that today is Ash Wednesday 2022, when literally millions of Christians of all denominations will be signed with ashes, most on their foreheads. As I note throughout this book, the church's liturgy is always *primal*—of, belonging to, and from the earth that God created and saw that it was "good."

Today's liturgy is as primal as it gets. Like all liturgy it contains "rites and texts."

The *rites*:

- the leftover palms distributed on Passion (Palm) Sunday last year are burned, literally, to death;
- most often the burning of the palms is done outdoors to remind us of gathering outdoors for the Easter Vigil "under the stars";
- the ashes are blessed with holy water, which always brings us to baptism;
- water and air are the only elements we need to live life and without them we die;
- in baptism we are immersed in water to signify entrance to eternal life through the water that sustains life itself both earthly and heavenly;
- immersion brings us back to the water in the womb of the mother;
- it conveys the primal sense of belonging to what we often call "mother" church because it nurtures and sustains;

- these rituals are the liturgy's ways to acknowledge the numberless ways we drink water in life and engage water in sacraments.

The (ancient) *text*: "Remember that you are dust and to dust you will return."

- the biblical reference is to Genesis 3:19, which comes toward the end of the banishment of Adam and Eve because they disobeyed God;
- it begins the season of being restored to new life in Christ, the second Adam;
- when accompanying the imposition of ashes, the text reminds us of the wood of the cross "on which hung our salvation" (Good Friday);
- Adam and Eve ate the fruit from the wood of the tree that God forbade them to eat;
- on Good Friday we venerate the triumphant wood of the cross that brought our salvation.

A major part of this book explores the theological meanings of what we do and say in the liturgy. I regard these as premier sources for delineating liturgical and sacramental theology. It explores the liturgy through the lens provided by primal elements and the works of human hands. In effect, it is an example of the importance of linking ecology with all liturgy, including sacramental liturgy.

From time immemorial Christians have gathered on Ash Wednesday to engage in these ancient rituals that are also ever new. The deep tragedy of Ash Wednesday 2022 is that it is celebrated within the first week of the unprovoked, illegal, and unimaginable destruction undertaken by Russia on Ukraine. Negotiations, sanctions, retaliation, killing, migration, and, yes, the destruction of the earth herself are occurring daily. Masses are being celebrated utilizing the Mass texts "in time of war," for "exiles and migrants," and "for justice and peace" and rightly so. The *contents* of the liturgy of Ash Wednesday are celebrated in the *context* of indescribable horror, loss of life and loss of the earth. The spark that makes the liturgy the liturgy is the perennial and daily combination of contents and context. Sadly, today the figurative use of *spark* is juxtaposed with the reality of fires that kill. Like all other primal elements, when we engage them in the liturgy all have the potential of meaning what is both positive and negative at the same time. On this Ash Wednesday the primal element fire was used to burn palms for today's ashes. That same primal element is bringing devastating destruction to the earth.

This book has been a "work in progress" since the early 1990s. It is the result of my having been involved in national and international dialogues and conferences on ecology, as well as liturgy and the sacraments. I thank Fr. Mark-Davis Janus for his invitation to write this book, which has allowed me to further and deepen research into these matters and the evolution of my own thought. I thank my "local editor" Dr. James Starke for his untiring and faithful work, coupled with enormous patience with the author.

In pride of place, I raise up my very close friend Patricia Bauman, whose initial promptings and sustained support have enabled me to venture into what was and is a new avenue of study for me.

Ash Wednesday, 2022

INTRODUCTION

This book is based on the principle that liturgy and sacraments enact and engage us in "the work of our redemption," through Christ's paschal mystery, in the communion of the church living and abiding in the Triune God through words, gestures, and the raising up of the cosmos and all our "fellow creatures" on "our common home" (phrases from Pope Francis's encyclical *Laudato Si'*).[1] It is a work of "liturgical theology," meaning that it is based on the classic principle that what we pray is what we believe, *lex orandi, lex credendi*, in both liturgical *texts* and liturgical *rites*.[2]

As far back as the early 1990s, I judged that much of what I was reading about "creation spirituality" and "earth spirituality" under the umbrella of Catholicism was broad but not deep. In addition to offering ideas about how to address this issue in previous articles and parts of books,[3] I propose here to offer an expanded method and argument from the depths of Catholic theology and practice. Specifically, it is based on the assertion of *Sacrosanctum Concilium* of Vatican II that the liturgy is the "summit and font" of the Christian life, and on the way sacraments and liturgy engage creation in any number of ways. While in some respects what I propose is meant to be timely I will not propose anything that is "trendy" or facile. In effect I want to recover and reestablish the importance of creation in appreciating sacramental theology through a liturgical lens.

This book is occasioned by what I judge to be the important and pressing cultural and theological contexts that converge on the issues of creation, ecology, and care for the environment. Part of the cultural context in which we find ourselves today is the very survival of the planet on which we live because of ecological and environmental devastation involving all created beings—including humanity and the whole earth. There is a contemporary urgency to act on behalf of the planet with both short- and long-term goals. These include fostering appropriate sharing of the world's resources and countering rampant pollution, hunger, poverty, and disease. It is documentable that especially the populations from Gen X to the present judge concern for environment to be a major life issue concerning not merely "quality of life" but "survival of life itself." While some have made it a major timely concern, others even wonder (not illegitimately) if it is too late to save the planet. This book is meant to put in dialogue the role of creation in theology, in liturgy, and sacraments with the deep concern we all (should) have for the earth and all who dwell together on it. It is also an invitation to contemplate the beauty of creation in all its richness and interconnectedness, to offer praise and thanks for the gift of "our common home" as we do regularly in and through the liturgy and sacraments and in particular the Hours, as well as to take responsibility for it.

A related and similarly urgent issue for the churches that celebrate the liturgy is the very survival of the liturgy in those churches. This is to say that the increasing number of the "nones" (not religiously affiliated) and the decline in church attendance even before the coronavirus pandemic in the liturgical churches (meaning at least the Orthodox, Anglican, Episcopalian, and Lutheran churches, as well as increasing numbers of Methodist and Presbyterian churches) indicates that there is at least a slow bleed in terms of church vitality and commitment to worship. The kinds of liturgies that were offered and celebrated during COVID-19 are not our concern here,[4] but those experiences deserve to be borne in mind as this book unfolds. The urgent pastoral question "Will they come back to sacraments after COVID-19?" will be answered only over time and likely in some ways that do not return us to the way we were. This book is meant to be a way of explaining how important the liturgy and the sacraments are in offering our communal thanks and praise to God through Christ in the Holy Spirit for our salvation, through these sacred actions through which we engage the world and then work with one another in reverence and love on and about our common home.

Many people eschew worship in community in church and prefer to pray on their own as they enjoy nature and contemplate the Creator God of all in heaven and on earth. When I am asked to explore the difference between the celebration of liturgy and sacraments and this kind of prayer, I reply that in fact creation is an inherent part of what constitutes the celebration of the liturgy and sacraments. I also note that praying on one's own is highly laudable, but that a major factor of the liturgy is that in and through it we pray with and for each other as a covenanted people of faith. In and through the liturgy we always pray to the God of creation and of redemption. In fact, in the liturgy we not only pray *to* God but through the liturgy we *abide* in a God of relatedness and relationship. An *apologia* for the liturgy and sacraments in all their fullness is an intended *leitmotif* in what follows.[5]

At the same time, a coincidental and urgent issue in the churches that celebrate liturgy and sacraments is that, in my estimation, liturgies of many of these churches have become too heavily weighted on words ("texts") and insufficiently attentive to liturgy's primalness and earthiness, which are enacted in the ritual of the liturgy always involving a multivalent experience with many effects and meanings. For example, baptism is about new life in Christ, washing, purifying, being made daughters and son of God, passing from death to life, being clothed in God's grace, and so on, through engaging in the multivalent element of water, which can both give life through hydration and cause death in drowning (more in chapter 5). Some of my underlying concerns are the unintended consequences as the Roman Catholic Church shifted from a liturgy celebrated only in Latin to the vernacular liturgy, where the translation process necessarily involved (and involves) enormous effort on the part of many people for a long time and for the foreseeable future. One unintended consequence may well have been that we came emphasize didactic and educative aspects of the liturgy through its vernacular "texts" so much that we may have eclipsed the "rites" of the liturgy. The rites engage us and all our fellow creatures on this good earth in multifaceted and nonverbal ways through our senses of sight, sound, smell, taste, and touch. This is where I have found the theology and experience of the Orthodox in the rituals of sacramental liturgy to be particularly insightful for us all (more in chapter 3).

In what I judge was a time of ecumenical and liturgical convergence from the 1960s on (not to say enormous ecumenical energy), Catholics were engaged in the reform of the liturgy, and many other liturgical churches, such as Anglican, Episcopalian, Lutheran, Methodist, and Presbyterian, were similarly engaged. One of the changes that took place pastorally was to encourage these (sister) liturgical churches to move from celebrating only a Liturgy of the Word on Sundays to celebrating the Liturgy of the Eucharist, at least on several Sundays. These initiatives met with much success even though for many congregations this was a "hard sell." (In fact, during an ecumenical conversation about proper liturgical practices during the coronavirus pandemic it was reported that some parishioners of these churches preferred to welcome back a Liturgy of the Word as the Sunday service. Old habits do die hard.) In addition, it was not so long ago that Lutheran pastors wore the academic gown of the university professor rather than the liturgical alb when they led services. My own Lutheran aunt would bring a notebook to the Sunday service (along with her Bible) to take notes during the sermon, as though it was a university lecture. But Roman Catholic worship was and is always primal and earthly, as well as verbal and textual, as we pray about creation and redemption through the words and works of the liturgy. A main part of this project is to recover these key aspects of both liturgical and sacramental practice, as well as liturgical and sacramental theology.

My hope is that this coincidence of the contemporary concerns about the environment and the way that the liturgical churches always engage "our common home" in worship can inspire a renewed appreciation for the liturgy and sacraments as sacred rituals that deeply ground us in engaging fellow creatures with reverence and respect, even as they draw us to a "new heaven and a new earth" (Rev 21:1, 4). Liturgy does not ask us to forsake or shun the world. Rather, liturgy engages the world at a deep level based on reverence, contemplation, and awe of all that exists. Part of engaging in liturgy and sacraments means that we need to take responsibility for our world and all our fellow creatures. I will argue that the traditional principles and practices of the liturgy can move us to an ever deeper and fuller appreciation of the earthiness of our worship and the consequences of a liturgy that is both heavenly, as an experience here and now of what we yearn for in heaven, and earthly, as we engage each other as brothers and sisters, including the earth itself, on our common home.

This book is grounded in research into the history of sacramental theologies (to be explained below) and the practice of the liturgy. These yield unfathomable insights about the cosmos, our place in the world and the contemporary challenge of concern for the environment. I will argue that concern for the environment is a traditional Catholic premise, as well as a premise of the churches that celebrate the liturgy based on the goodness of creation and that the God we worship is "maker of heaven and earth." Gratefully this concern has been revived in our day by significant efforts by the Ecumenical Orthodox Patriarchate, the World Council of Churches, statements of numberless religious bodies and, for Roman Catholics, by national bishops' conferences of bishops and by statements and actions of recent popes (more in chapter 3).[6] I will also argue that an ecological approach to sacramental theology can help to understand underlying factors and principles in the enactment of the liturgy of the sacraments about how and where God is discovered in the world in general and in the liturgy and sacraments in an intense and focused way. In effect, the very celebration of liturgy in text and rite reminds us again and again that we do not live in "two different worlds," the "sacred" and the "secular." We live in one graced world for whose very survival we bear responsibility.

FOUR PRESUPPOSITIONS

1. One of the characteristics of the Catholic Church is that it is a *theological tradition*. Among other things, this means that Catholicism engages the contemporary world in all its vitality yet complexity, especially the questions that evolve in our culture and deserve to be addressed by the Catholic tradition. Catholic theology does not repeat answers from the past or reiterate definitions or insights from the past that simply do not respect the contemporary contexts in which the Catholic community has found itself and finds itself today.

This means that the worldview and ways of communicating theological ideas in the patristic era were found to be unsatisfying in the early medieval period.[7] Similarly, the precision and arguments put forward by St. Thomas Aquinas were not the same as those put forward by St. Bonaventure, yet both find themselves as revered monuments of the Catholic theological tradition—but not the only ones. Many of the reformers (e.g., Martin Luther) argued forcefully against what was regarded as a Catholic theology that was too philosophical and not sufficiently biblical. The canons of the Council of Trent were intended to correct Protestant "errors," but the fathers at Trent never intended to provide a comprehensive theology of liturgy and sacraments.

The intent and language of the documents from the Second Vatican Council were quite different because the conciliar fathers wanted to assess and address issues facing the church in the modern world. In much of their work the fathers of Vatican II returned to the sources of the Catholic tradition, and they gave them new life. They expressed Catholic truth differently from Trent and looked to engage the modern world in teaching and witness. Tried and true answers to questions and issues of the past are to be respected, but they need not be repeated in a different societal and Church contexts.

2. One of the features of the Roman Catholic liturgy is that through it we engage words, actions, gestures, signs, singing, and silence as an assembly gathered in the Lord's name. One thing that the liturgy does not invite us into (and cannot by its very nature) is a "personal relationship with Jesus." Many may wish for that to happen in their spiritual lives. If that is the case, it needs to be nurtured by personal prayer and group events other than Roman Catholic liturgy. By its nature liturgy and sacraments are not designed to do that. Liturgy and sacraments presume nothing less than engagement in the triune God through "fellow creatures" of our common home and each other "through Christ our Lord."

The prayers of the Roman liturgy never name Jesus without a theologically refined modifier (e.g., "Christ our Lord" or "through our Lord and Savior Jesus Christ"). All those modifiers carry rich theological meanings. Each of them reminds us that we do not call upon or experience "Jesus." In the liturgy and sacraments, we experience God by way of the mediation made possible by the incarnation of the Son of God and by raising up elements of our common home. God engages us in and through the liturgy in nothing less than the resurrected Christ sitting at the Father's right hand in glory interceding for us. The purpose of the liturgy, therefore, is not to foster a personal relationship with Jesus. Among other things, the purpose of the liturgy is to foster the unity of the church in the Triune God and then sent forth to serve others in the world. The inherent dynamic of liturgy is that the assembly is gathered together by the Lord at his gracious invitation so that the church may experience anew the paschal mystery of Christ through the action of the Holy Spirit and then be sent forth to glorify the Lord with our lives (adapted from one of the dismissals from the Eucharist).

We experience the triune God by way of liturgy, the "summit and source" of the whole Christian life, by a "mediated immediacy." This is to say that our *immediate* experience of God is always *mediated* through the texts and rites of the liturgy engaged in by the gathered assembly. Liturgy and sacraments are the closest we can come to a direct engagement in God as mediated, organized and set in order by and through the liturgy. We were "not there when they crucified my Lord" at Calvary. If we were, then we would have had immediate access to watching the passion, crucifixion, and death of Jesus. In God's providence, what we know of and experience through the liturgy is the entirety of the paschal mystery, involving Christ's death, resurrection, and ascension, and waiting "the blessed hope and the coming of our Savior, Jesus Christ" (embolism of the Our Father, Order of Mass). In the words of Leo the Great, what Christ accomplished has passed to the liturgy and sacraments.[8] This means that in and through liturgy we experience all that Christ has accomplished "for us and for our salvation." The words and rites, the texts and symbols of the liturgy engage us in the work of our redemption through means that reflect our humanity and our intrinsic connectedness to the earth.

3. When reflecting on the liturgy as a foundation for the sacramental theology argued here, the revised Roman Catholic liturgy will be the principal source. The revision of the "texts and rites" took place under the direction of the Second Vatican Council by a number of committees and subcommittees (called *coetus* groups) over a number of years. This work is presumed to be normative and is the basis for the assertions in this volume.

In what follows there will be no additions to or deletions from these revised rites. Any suggestions made for celebration are *from* the rites, they are not "add-ons" thought to be helpful. I first learned this from Sofia Cavalletti in Rome in the late 1970s.[9] She was a disciple of Maria Montessori, for whom this was a major premise as she argued against adjusting the liturgy to different age groups.[10] The liturgy is. No more, no less. A Lutheran colleague, Benjamin Stewart, argues this principle from one of the liturgical churches engaged in a similar retrieval of the ecological dimensions of the liturgy and sacramental theology.[11]

4. The focus of this book will be methodological. It is intended to put forth ideas that raise consciousness about several contemporary (and very pressing) issues about ecology and how to understand its relationship to Christian theology in light of liturgical practice. It is intended to be a comprehensive vision of how to go about understanding the liturgy and sacraments today, especially considering issues of ecology and the environment. It is meant to incorporate and complement much of what I and many other Catholic and ecumenical colleagues have endeavored to offer in teaching and writing on the liturgy, especially issues of method and how to go about determining a proper theological approach to study the liturgy. This book is meant to be a reminder of the wealth of theology contained in the celebration of the liturgy, a wealth that has not always received the attention it deserves in delineating the theology of the sacraments. The basis for what is put forward here is the officially approved and normative rites of the Catholic Church. It will not include or address issues of the tone of liturgy ("high church" and "low church," monastery and parish, etc.), preaching, or music. I judge these variables to be of great importance in the actual celebration of the liturgy, but because they vary so much, my focus will be on the established liturgical rites in which are engaged despite the variables noted above.[12]

TERMINOLOGY AND CONTENTS

There is a disciplinary complexity that we need to bear in mind when offering a method for articulating the theological depths and the many meanings of liturgy and sacraments. An indication of the contours of current sacramental theology may be seen from a brief inspection of the bibliography published at Gregorian University Press (Rome) by Maksimilijan Zitnik.[13] A look at the indices in the fourth volume shows how intricate the discipline has become and how much it draws on other fields of research. Under "Sacraments in General," alongside traditional issues such as matter and form, institution and causality, one finds such items as rite and ritual, festival, symbol, liturgical year, and iconography, as well as the anthropology and sociology of sacraments. The general index of entries contains headings on women, feminism, family, and popular religion, as well as on liturgy and each of the seven sacraments of the Catholic tradition.

Such a bibliography witnesses to the fact that the study of the phenomenon of the revised liturgy after Vatican II has added a number of elements and factors into a rich conversation. To take but one example, one cannot study the sacraments of initiation in a complete way without reference to the liturgical year and to the rites of the catechumenate as revised after Vatican II. In addition, manuals of the study of liturgy, such as *L'Eglise en Priere, Gottesdienst der Kirche, Anamnesis, Handbook for Liturgical Studies*, and *La celebración en la Iglesia* consider historical contexts, liturgical contexts, and liturgical contents for theological reflection on sacraments.[14] Furthermore, along with historical, liturgical, and theological considerations, attention is given to rituals in which there is a considerable interaction of corporal, visual, and verbal expressions, all having a relation to cultural experience and custom.[15]

From my own perspective, issues of ecology and the environment loom large in any contemporary articulation of what sacraments are and what they accomplish. At the same time, at least two areas that are lacking in this survey (and in chapter 2) are any additional voices from feminist theologians other than Susan Ross[16] and African and Asian voices.[17] These require strict attention to the disciplinary complexity of the study of liturgy and sacraments today. Feminist theology highlights respect for women's voices and their critique of church and sacramental structures. Asian and African voices will continue to emerge, especially regarding our specific topic of ecology and sacraments. I defer to others to enlighten us all on these emerging and challenging conversations.

In what follows, I offer an approach to the reality of sacrament that is celebrated in the liturgy and that what is said and done in the liturgy is the primary source (in all its many facets as will be seen below). I judge that by default we may "straitjacket" the possibilities for a liturgical-sacramental theology if we continue to separate liturgy—what we say and do in ritual—from sacraments—if limited to the parameters set by the Council of Trent. In liturgical celebrations, creation and "all creatures great and small" are engaged in a public action, a major part of which is to raise up "fellow creatures" of "our common home." In effect I argue a liturgical theology inspired by the classic phrase *legem credendi lex statuat supplicandi*.[18]

I have also decided to retain the linguistic distinction between "liturgy" and "[the seven] sacraments." I do this well aware and with due respect to those theologians (some of whom are noted in chapter 2) who have made inroads into deepening our appreciation of the word *sacrament* (e.g., Semmelroth, Schillebeeckx, Rahner, and Osborne). However, if I were to follow the very intriguing thesis of Kenan Osborne in *Christian Sacraments in a Postmodern World*,[19] I would end up so widening the meaning of *sacrament* that would go far beyond the teaching of seven sacraments in the teachings of the Council of Trent, specifically "no more and no fewer" (see chapter 1). While one sees in Trent a reaction to Luther's teachings about the number of sacraments, there are two additional and important reasons to keep to the number *seven*.

The basis for choosing the number seven is the biblical precedent established as early as the Book of Genesis (seven days of creation), codified in Jesus's admonition that we are to forgive "seventy-seven times" (Matt 18:22) and throughout the Bible. The number seven becomes an increasingly important number for medieval theologians, who capitalized on the number and separated three from four. The number three signified the Trinity (three persons in one God); the number four signified the earth, either the four seasons (summer, fall, winter, and spring) or the directions of the compass (north, south, east, and west). The divine number three is combined with the number four to give us seven, meaning that each sacrament was a combination of the divine and the earthly. If I were to ignore the number seven for sacraments, I might undercut my argument from the start by ignoring the numerous ways that "seven" can contribute to appreciating the role that creation plays in sacraments.

In addition, if I were to collapse the distinction between liturgy and sacraments, I would be unable to include theological reflections on the Liturgy of the Hours as an essential part of the daily liturgy. I do this for two reasons. The first is that the Hours were called the "Roman Breviary" after it was codified in 1568 and was used in monastic and mendicant communities, as well as by diocesan priests daily on their own. Because the revised Liturgy of the Hours is intended to be celebrated by all the baptized—not just priests and religious—it invites articulating its many theological meanings, including a rich theology of creation. That the Hours are now in vernacular translations (in numerous formats) has invited a much larger number of the baptized to participate in and them and to ruminate on their theological meanings and richness. Put differently, to articulate the meaning of the liturgy of every feast and season requires that we allow the Hours their rightful place along with the Eucharist as a main pillar for articulating that theology.

The second (hopefully remedial) reason for incorporating the Hours is that in the revised *Liturgia Horarum* there are several hymns about the days of creation (see Evening Prayer). These were not included in early vernacular translations, but they will be included in the revised translation. The contemporary world needs ways to raise up the value and concern for the environment that classically comes through Christian rituals (among others). This means allowing the enacted liturgy and sacraments to be the very basis of our investigation. What we do in liturgy and sacraments is done at God's invitation as we engage each other and all "our fellow creatures." The wealth that the Psalms and canticles contain as celebrated in the Hours deserves close attention to form a proper attitude toward and, yes, reverence for every element of creation, especially in the context of what Pope Francis has called "a throwaway culture."[20]

A STORY

Almost immediately after final exams at the Catholic University of America, especially in my earliest years of teaching, I would regularly go to Rome for several weeks of research at my alma mater, the Benedictine University at Sant'Anselmo.

In May of 1993 I was staying at Santa Sabina, the mother house of the Dominican Order, at the invitation of an American member of the community, Fr. Chrysostom Finn, OP. The churches at Sant'Anselmo and Santa Sabina are linked liturgically because recent popes (from John XXIII on) begin Ash Wednesday at Sant' Anselmo and walk in penitential procession to Santa Sabina for the Eucharist and the imposition of ashes. John XXIII revived the custom of observing the "stational Masses," which was an ancient traditional way to observe Lent in Rome—meeting at one church, called the "station," and processing to another for the Eucharist.

Santa Sabina houses the international offices of the Dominican Order and often hosts visiting Dominicans from throughout the world. (Such is life in Rome: mother houses and generalates of religious communities in close proximity, not to mention universities, academies, and libraries.) One morning at Mass I spied a recently arrived Dominican friar who was concelebrating the Mass. After taking a second look, I realized that the guest was the famous systematic theologian Fr. Edward Schillebeeckx, OP. By then, Fr. Schillebeeckx was eighty years old and had had two skirmishes with the Congregation for the Doctrine of the Faith, largely about ordained ministry. My interest was not in those controversies but in his writings on sacraments, specifically his seven-hundred-page book published in 1952 in Dutch. (Many of us know the book from a very short abridgement published in the early 1960s entitled *Christ the Sacrament of the Encounter with God*; more in chapter 2.) I immediately decided that I would place myself near him at the noon meal and shamelessly engage in "research by interview." (The noon meal in Italy is called *pranzo*, which is really the eighth sacrament—a time for food, wine, conversation, and relaxation.)

That day at *pranzo* and for the following three days we were across from each other at table discussing his view of sacraments from 1952, as compared with his understanding of sacraments four decades later. The original book began with how humans seek God, as guided by the writings of St. Thomas Aquinas, followed by an extremely comprehensive study from the scriptures through the Catholic theological tradition. This leads to the last part of the book containing Schillebeeckx's work relating phenomenology to sacraments and the importance of using encounter as a way to describe what happens in sacraments and as a way to move beyond the category of causality. During one of those lunches, Fr. Schillebeeckx leaned over to me and said, "If I were to write a book on sacraments today, I would begin not with St. Thomas or the Bible. I would begin with creation."

May I suggest that my table companion was both ahead of his time and basing himself on something of a "back to the future" approach to theological method. I suggest that he was ahead of his time given the way that Pope Francis speaks in *Laudato Si'* about how liturgy and sacraments raise up and revere "fellow creatures" in creation as we humans worship God. Pope Francis himself engages in a "back to the future" method in *Laudato Si'* by reaching back to the Scriptures, to patristic sources, and the rest of our theological tradition to reflect a rhetoric and reality of relatedness and relationships with all creatures on this good earth.

One of the three main sources for church teaching on the environment (see chapter 1) is the Roman Catholic Church. The others are the Ecumenical Orthodox Patriarchate (Istanbul) and the World Council of Churches. When it comes to examples of the method proposed, the data will be from the officially approved Roman Catholic liturgy (chapters

4—6). Here, ecumenical colleagues can follow their own texts and rites to shape their own theology of sacraments based on liturgy. It is hoped that the final chapters can find deep resonance today among churches across denominational lines.

An observation that is often made about the scope and the craft of liturgical theology is that is less systematic than some would like. I can well appreciate this and admit that one of the reasons is the multidimensional and multifaceted reality that is liturgy. The rites and prayers of liturgy and sacraments reveal a wealth of interconnected images and ideas, actions and gestures, words and silences, which together make up a specific and unique *act* of theology here and now. While the texts and rites of the liturgy may be used again and again, there is no such thing as a repeated liturgy. The celebration of the enacted liturgy is impacted by numerous factors in the church (e.g., sex abuse crisis), in the liturgical calendar (e.g., the Paschal Triduum in the Northern and Southern Hemispheres), in the community that celebrates (e.g., diminishing number of parishes and parish "consolidations") and in the wider world (e.g., during a pandemic).

This can make for an untidy theology compared to other methods. But the method employed and exemplified here is meant to raise our consciousness precisely to the "multivalence" inherent in liturgy. This multivalence is ever to be encouraged because liturgy is something in which we are immersed and are doing among, with and for each other. Even as we "name God" through the texts in the liturgy, we also experience the God we name in and through the liturgy. Liturgical theology is meant to raise up and indicate how we can view the liturgy always through wide-angle lenses so that we can experience the Triune God and the Trinity's sanctifying action among us as fully and as richly as possible this side of heaven. Part of the liturgy is also experiencing, not just understanding, "our common home" in ever richer ways. From my point of view, liturgical theology is always an invitation to "go deeper" into the very mystery of God, "in whom we live and move and have our being" (Acts 17:38, Sunday Preface VI in Ordinary Time).

CHAPTER ONE

OFFICIAL CHURCH TEACHING ON SACRAMENTS FROM TRENT TO THE TWENTIETH CENTURY

To set up the discussion of contemporary approaches to ecology, liturgy, and sacraments, I begin by summarizing official Roman Catholic teaching on the theology of (the seven) sacraments as determined by the Council of Trent (1545–1563). I then comment on developments in the late nineteenth and early twentieth centuries.

The Council of Trent was called, in large part, to deal with the teachings of Reformers like Martin Luther, John Calvin, Henry VIII, and Ulrich Zwingli. The work of Catholic theologians in the centuries preceding this council were very influential on Trent's teachings, exemplified by the writings of Peter Lombard (bishop of Paris), Thomas Aquinas and Melchior Cano (both Dominicans), Alexander of Hales (Franciscan), and many others. On the one hand, theologians helped to prepare the teachings adopted at Trent. On the other hand, the teachings from Trent helped to frame the categories, rhetoric, catechesis, and official church teachings on the sacraments for the Catholic faithful and framed the teachings of (many) theologians following Trent. Following the council, Pope Pius V issued the revised Roman Breviary (*Breviarum Romanum* 1568) and the Roman Missal (*Missale Romanum* 1570). The major concern at the time was to unify liturgical celebration, meaning the precise observance of the rubrics. It is only subsequently that the liturgy became the subject of church teaching (more below).

CANONS OF THE COUNCIL OF TRENT (1545-1563)

The teachings of the Council of Trent on the sacraments concern both "sacraments in general" and individual sacraments. In what follows, I focus on the thirteen "canons" on sacraments in general.[1] The canons are the highest-ranking teachings from Trent, and all Catholics must believe what is contained in them. They were and are the definitive teachings of the church. However, these official magisterial teachings have served and continue to serve best as a baseline from which to articulate the meaning of sacraments, rather than to delimit such work. Again (as noted in the introduction), the fathers[2] at Trent never intended to offer a comprehensive theology of the sacraments.

Canon One

If anyone says that the sacraments of the New Law were not all instituted by our lord Jesus Christ; or that there are more or fewer than seven: namely, baptism, confirmation, eucharist, penance, last anointing, order, and matrimony; or that one or other of these is not truly and in the full sense a sacrament: let him be anathema.

The determination of seven sacraments of the New Law resulted from theological reflections and systematic presentations of the faith in the twelfth century. Prior to Peter Lombard, authors did not judge it necessary to define or confine the number of sacraments to seven. For example, St. Augustine refers to over two hundred sacraments, including "holy water" and Lent, which he called a "venerable sacrament."

In addition, the number symbolism of *seven* (three plus four) is important. For some medieval authors three signified the Trinity, hence the divine part of the sacraments, and four delineated the cosmic, either the seasons (summer, fall, winter, and spring) or the directions (north, south, east, and west). Thus, the divine and the cosmic were combined to reflect on the nature of "seven" sacraments.[3]

Interpretation of the number seven recalls that seven in the Bible is the perfect number, signifying completion and totality: thus, the seven days of creation.[4] Other biblical examples include Matthew 18:22 (Jesus replies to Peter about forgiveness, "Not seven times, but, I tell you, seventy-seven times"). If seven is the number for combining the divine and the earthly, as well as the number of completion, then we can argue that expanding on seven means not a literal number but an infinite number. While for some authors the number seven can be restrictive, this numerology can also be understood in an expansive and inclusive way to include all the sacred rites that humans need to celebrate at all stages of life, such as funerals and weddings outside of Mass and rites of religious profession.

At Trent, the fathers of the council were concerned about the Reformers' insistence that only sacred ceremonies found directly in Scriptures be considered sacraments. For example, Luther counted different numbers of sacraments based on his evolving understanding of the Scriptures—two or three. The obvious ones were baptism and Eucharist. His concern for competency in preaching and in leading the liturgy caused him in some places to regard "the ministry" as "sacramental." In response to the Reformation controversies about the number of sacraments, the fathers at Trent decided to define seven sacraments instituted by Christ.[5]

Not surprisingly, theologians differ about *how* to describe Christ's instituting the sacraments, for the work of theologians is to debate, discuss, probe, and amplify teachings. Commonly, theologians distinguish between "explicit" and "implicit" or "immediate" and "mediate" institution. In these categories, the New Testament evidence of baptism in water and sharing the eucharistic bread and cup are taken as evidence of "explicit" and "immediate" institution. The other sacraments are deemed "implicitly" and "mediately" instituted by Christ. That is, the church was responsible for delineating how these sacred rites derived from Christ. Thus, canon 1 asserts *that* there are seven sacraments instituted by Christ, but it does not specify *where* or *how* they were instituted.

This is but one example of the way church teachings can be debated among theologians about possible ways to explain and interpret them: hence, the value of calling Trent's teachings "laconic" and "open ended."[6]

Canon Two

If anyone says that those same sacraments of the new law are no different from the sacraments of the old law, except by reason of a difference in ceremonies and in external rites: let him be anathema.

This canon reacts to Luther's assertions about ceremonies and words that the church came to use to celebrate the sacraments. Luther rejected such ceremonies unless they were evident and found in the Scriptures.

Canon Three

If anyone says that these seven sacraments are so equal to each other that on no ground is one of greater dignity than another: let him be anathema.

This canon concerns the assertion of Thomas Aquinas, among others, that some sacraments are more important than others. For example, baptism, as necessary for salvation, is more important than marriage and orders, which one need not receive. At the same time, Eucharist has often been called "the sacrament of sacraments."

Canon Four

If anyone says that the sacraments of the new law are not necessary for salvation but are superfluous, and that people obtain the grace of justification from God without them or a desire for them, by faith alone, though all are not necessary for each individual: let him be anathema.

This canon helps to explain the previous canon and reacts to the more "spiritualist" strain among some Reformers who denied the necessity of the sacraments outright (despite the biblical warrant about being "born again" in John 3).

Canon Five

If anyone says that these sacraments have been instituted only to nourish faith: let him be anathema.

Again, the necessity of sacraments for salvation is at issue here.

Canon Six

If anyone says that the sacraments of the new law do not contain the grace [*contenere gratiam*] which they signify; or do not confer [*conferat*] that grace on those who place no obstacle in the way, as if they were only external signs of the grace or justice received by faith, and some kind of mark of the Christian profession by which believers are distinguished from unbelievers in the eyes of people: let him be anathema.

This formulation was influenced by the writings of Thomas Aquinas, Melchior Cano, and Alexander of Hales. Aquinas argued that sacraments cause grace by being "efficient" (meaning they do what they are intended to do). He also argued that sacraments are "instrumental" because the principal cause of grace is God himself. Cano argued a kind of causality (sometimes called "moral causality") whereby through the sacraments we plead with God to give grace. Alexander of Hales argues that sacraments themselves do not produce grace but they are occasions when God himself produces grace. In the end, the canon from Trent says that sacraments "contain the grace" (*contenere gratiam*) that they "confer" (*conferat*). These words were carefully chosen in order not to overstate the role of sacraments as "causing" grace (God does that). The use of "confer" lessens any kind of rhetoric that would make the sacraments automatic. Provided that when speaking about the causality of sacraments theologians use the words *contain* or *confer* or other such words that reflect this nuanced teaching, they could describe *how* sacraments confer grace in ways that reflect the thought world, culture, and pastoral needs of their own time and place.

The use of "who place no obstacle" in the canon means that the emphasis is always on God's graciousness being overwhelming and never exhaustive. Sacraments function unless a person places an obstacle in the way, such as admitting lack of faith in Christ or in the functioning of the sacrament. Behind this canon is the delicate balance between *ex opere operato* (literally, "by the work worked") and *ex opere operantis* ("by the work working"). These are two sides of one coin, and the sacraments are not so automatic as to constitute magic.[7]

5

Canon Seven

If anyone says that grace is not given by the sacraments of this kind always and to all, as far as depends on God, even if they duly receive them, but only sometimes and to some: let him be anathema.

God's initiative and the giving of grace in and through sacraments are at issue here. We do not "earn" grace from sacraments; we receive it.

Canon Eight

If anyone says that grace is not conferred by the sacraments of the new law through the sacramental action itself [*ex opere operato*], but that faith in the divine promises is by itself sufficient for obtaining the grace: let him be anathema.

Trent taught that sacraments are conferred *ex opere operato*. By the fact that the sacrament is celebrated according to the prescribed texts and rites, we believe and know that sacraments happen. The issue here is that God is always present and active in and through the sacraments. This canon reminds us of God's covenant relationship with the chosen people in the Scriptures, despite their infidelity and sin, and it reminds us of God's fidelity to us despite our failures and sin.

Canon Nine

If anyone says that in three sacraments, namely, baptism, confirmation and order, a character, namely a spiritual and indelible mark, is not imprinted on the soul because of which they cannot be repeated: let him be anathema.

This assertion goes as far back as St. Augustine, with "irrepeatability" a key element in describing the sacramental character. Baptism, confirmation, and order cannot be received twice. This is drawn out by Thomas Aquinas to refer to one's being deputed to worship God after one receives baptism and confirmation. This is but one way to understand what Trent meant by "character," and it is another example of believing in the content of the teaching of Trent but having the ability to interpret what it means. Recalling the medieval debates about the nature of sacramental character from ordination, it is notable that Trent simply asserts "order" (*ordine*) and makes no other specification about which order. At the time, the presumption about the term *order* would have been "priesthood." However, one contemporary application of the way the singular term can now refer to diaconate, presbyterate, and episcopacy is evident in the revised rites of ordination.

According to Aquinas, baptism and confirmation conferred *passive* characters and orders conferred an *active* character. The more recent teaching of the papal magisterium on the active participation of the laity in the liturgy mitigates the separation of the "active" from "passive" characters.[8] The contemporary emphasis on the essentially communal nature of the liturgy (*Sacrosanctum Concilium* 27[9]) mitigates any interpretation of "character" as about an individual without understanding sacramental characters in the context of the whole church.[10]

Canon Ten

If anyone says that all Christians have the power to exercise the ministry of the word and of all the sacraments: let him be anathema.

Among the issues that lie behind this canon is the nature of ordination as conferring a sacramental *power* to administer sacraments. In other words, it is tied to the sacrificial nature of the Eucharist and the priest's power to concentrate. A more egalitarian notion of church belonging and ministry is evident in the assertions of some Reformers. However, one nuance in Lutheran practice is that one needed to be credentialed and have the requisite theological and scriptural background to preach.

Canon Eleven

If anyone says that, when ministers effect or confer the sacraments, they do not need the intention of at least of doing what the church does: let him be anathema.

Two of the issues here concern having the right "intention" so that sacraments are not regarded as (quasi-)magical or automatic. Sacraments are acts of human beings requiring heart, will, and mind. The other issue is the use of the word *confer* to describe how ministers of the sacraments are precisely that—ministers. Also, the word *effect* suggests that God "confers" the grace through his Son and through human instrumentality.

Canon Twelve

If anyone says that a minister in a state of mortal sin, even if he observes all the essentials which belong to the effecting or administering of a sacrament, does not effect or administer it: let him be anathema.

This assertion has its origin in the Donatist controversy in the time of St. Augustine. While a minister's lack of virtue should never be countenanced, the personal unworthiness of the minister cannot be a barrier to receiving grace in the sacraments. Put differently, who would decide, on what basis and how could one tell? In the end, it is the overarching graciousness of God that is always at stake in sacraments.

Canon Thirteen

If anyone says that the received and approved rites of the catholic church in customary use in the solemn administration of the sacraments may, without sin, be neglected or omitted at choice by the ministers, or can be changed to order new ones by any pastor whatever: let him be anathema.

Liturgical rites matter. In the sacraments, "matter" and "form" need to be respected and kept intact in celebration. This is to say that elements from creation are the "matter" for sacraments; the "form" is the words used. From our point of view, matter matters.

Summary: Council of Trent on Sacraments in General

In a very circumspect way, the fathers of the Council of Trent state that sacraments do not confer grace simply because of "human faith" (canon 5). Sacraments do confer the grace they signify (canon 6). Indeed, the conciliar fathers clearly state the reason for such conferral of grace: God has ordered this "on God's part" (*quantum est ex parte Dei*, canon 7). The Council emphasizes this free action of God in its use of the term *ex opere operato* in contrast to the human good work, the human side of faith (canon 8). On causality, the conciliar fathers simply state that God acts through the sacraments to give his grace; humans can set obstacles (i.e., mortal sin). The sacraments confer the grace they signify (based on Augustine's approach to the conferral of grace). How these three areas are put together in detail is left to theologians.

Thus, in interpreting the canons on sacraments, as well as the accompanying explanatory decrees, one should carefully recall that the teachings are laconic and open ended. They are also "reactive" to "specific" teachings of the Reformers, which teachings the fathers at Trent sought to correct.[11] The fathers at Trent never intended to produce a full theology of sacraments, either in general or about specific sacraments. After Trent, however, catechisms and other works summarized and repeated Trent to the extent that directives were given to priests to give sermons taken from catechisms based on the teachings from Trent (I avoid the word *homily*, which is a different genre). The intention was to be both instructive and apologetic.[12] As the centuries evolved, theologians judged the teaching of Trent as a base and frame for additional theories and theologies about sacraments.

Among other things germane to sacramental theology and practice is that the primalness of sacraments (i.e., their "matter") was eclipsed after the Council of Trent (1545–1563), partly out of concern to disseminate the defensive and apologetic teachings of the canons decreed by Trent. This meant a loss of attention paid to the robust, fulsome, and pluriform teachings about sacraments from earlier eras of the church's life. After Trent, "matter" was reduced to the absolute minimum so that the sacraments could be understood to take effect. For example, infant baptism was regularly practiced by the pouring of water on the head of the infant or adult, as opposed to immersion, as presumed in the patristic era. Notably the revised rites for infant and adult initiation place "immersion" before "infusion" when describing the way we engage water in the sacrament.[13]

LATE NINETEENTH AND TWENTIETH CENTURIES

The work of nineteenth-century historians, biblical scholars, and theologians on then newly discovered manuscripts and texts from much earlier centuries influenced scholars of the liturgy and some sacramental theologians to take a longer historical view. Data from the biblical and patristic eras through the early twentieth century called for study and reflection that was not limited to Tridentine teachings. Provided that an author does not contradict a canon from Trent, he or she can develop theologies and theories about sacraments that respond to contemporary needs. Theologians need not simply repeat or imitate Trent's dogmatic statements, which met the needs of the sixteenth century. A prime example of such an approach is the compendium by Pierre Pourrat (France, 1914).[14]

The papal magisterium itself evolved, especially beginning in the early twentieth century. In 1903, Pope Pius X (1835–1914) published a letter given motu proprio (i.e., "on the pope's own initiative") entitled *Tra le Sollectudini*. The letter addressed active participation in the liturgy and the revival of Gregorian chant in order that the gathered assembly could participate vocally in the liturgy.[15] This document helped turn a corner regarding the content of papal teaching on issues related to the sacraments and "active participation" in them.[16] This led to three watershed encyclicals from Pius XII (1876–1958, papacy 1939–1058):[17] *Mystici Corporis* on the mystical Body of Christ (1943), *Divino Afflante Spiritu* on the importance of scriptural study and biblical translations (1947), and *Mediator Dei* on the sacred liturgy (1947). (As will be discussed in chapter 3, a papal "encyclical" is the highest ranking authoritative statement a pope can issue on his own. What ranks higher are the decrees from a church council like Vatican II.) Pius XII's triad of church, Bible, and liturgy revived much of the content of earlier eras in the church's life when these were enacted together in liturgy and sacraments (e.g., the patristic era). The revival of this triad—church, Bible, liturgy—provided an essential framework for the revival of the liturgy from the mid-1950s on (as well as the content of some of the writings of theologians summarized below in chapter 2).

These encouraging and open-ended papal teachings gave permission and even encouraged the work of theologians to focus on some long presumed but often neglected aspects of Catholic teaching on sacraments. In other words, there has never been *one* theology of liturgy and sacraments. The work of theologians is to offer appropriate theologies based on culture, controversy, and continuity with the church's teachings.

CHAPTER TWO

ISSUES OF METHOD
FOR CONTEMPORARY
SACRAMENTAL THEOLOGY

From my perspective sacramental theology may be understood as the systematic study of the sacraments based on reflection upon the liturgical celebration of these rites throughout history and on the insights of theologians and other teachers in light of the magisterium. At given historical periods certain theological points came to be emphasized, sometimes for polemical reasons. At other times assertions of the magisterium clarified issues of conflict.[1]

In this chapter I argue that there is not now nor has there ever been *one* theology or *the* theology of the sacraments in the history of the Catholic Church. From the patristic period through the early medieval period, the Scholastic period, the Reformation, the Council of Trent, the modern era, and to the present (what I call the "contemporary" period) different historical, theological, and pastoral *contexts* in the church's life required different methods when articulating the *contents* of sacramental theology.[2]

This chapter contextualizes and summarizes what several contemporary theologians have said about sacraments. Often these authors respond from the depth of the Catholic magisterial and theological tradition to face into new opportunities and situations that required and continue to require a response. From the very beginning humans engaged "fellow creatures" of "our common home" (again to use the language of Pope Francis in *Laudato Si'*) in the act of sacraments. A shorthand way to say this was to assert, as was done at Trent, that sacraments contained "matter" (materials from creation or human work) and "form" (words). Because of our contemporary cultural and theological context, I will argue that the basis for sacramental enactment is through engagement with elements from the earth, both primal and manufactured, words and rites. Sacraments themselves are therefore inherently ecological statements about the goodness of creation and our responsibility for a damaged creation. While aspects of ecology and environment (to use words familiar to us today) have been embedded in descriptions of sacraments throughout history, they deserve to be raised up and placed in the forefront today. As noted above and addressed in detail in chapter 3, we are all indebted to the Greek Orthodox Patriarchate since 1989 for the steady and abundantly rich commentaries about "sacramentality" that reflect liturgical and spiritual depth.[3]

The study of sacraments from the mid-twentieth century onward should not and cannot be limited to the authors whose work is discussed in this chapter. Recall the assertions made in the introduction about the "disciplinary complexity" involved in the study of sacraments today. These summaries are meant to serve as examples of expanding parameters for sacramental theology from the mid twentieth century on.[4]

EDWARD SCHILLEBEECKX (1914–2009)

Edward Schillebeeckx published his monumental study of sacraments in the economy of salvation, *De Sacramentele Heilseconomie*, in 1952.[5] The breadth and depth of this book shows the author's profound respect for an historical study of sources of theology and church teaching, as well as a concern to offer new ways of thinking about sacraments in a contemporary context (e.g., phenomenology over Aristotelianism). In the book, Schillebeeckx begins with a thorough review of the meanings of the Greek *mysterion* ("mystery"), the Latin *sacramentum* ("sacrament"), and related terms from the New Testament that have come to influence our understanding of what the term *sacrament* (and its derivatives) mean. He continues with an equally careful study of the patristic era, the Scholastics (with special treatment of Thomas Aquinas), the

Council of Trent and then modern theologians, such as John Henry Newman (1801–1890), Matthias Scheeben (1835–1888), Maurice de la Taille (1872–1933), and Anscar Vonier (1875–1938). The real bridge from the thorough historical review to a more liturgically focused study of sacraments by Schillebeeckx himself is the work of Odo Casel (1886–1948), a Benedictine monk of Maria Laach, specifically Casel's theology of the "mystery presence" of Christ and the church in the liturgy.[6]

Casel argued that it is not simply grace as the fruit or effect of the redemption that is present in the liturgy (*Kultmysterium*, "the mystery cult") but engagement ("encounter") with the redeeming acts of Christ themselves. Casel does not say "Jesus" because we are interpreting the paschal mystery from the perspective of the resurrection and ascension of Christ as we await their fulfillment. We do not theologize about the passion and death of Christ only. Until the second coming we experience these saving acts themselves in and through the "mystery" presence and action of Christ. That is, both the person and saving acts of the Lord must be made contemporaneous in some way with all generations of Christians, since salvation can be effected only according to the economy (pattern) established by Christ as known in the Scriptures and tradition. Therefore, the death and resurrection of the Savior are made present in the action of the liturgy itself. Otherwise, no real participation in Christ by Christians can take place. According to Casel, this position is not simply a retrieval of tradition, which would be a value in itself. This position provides a response to alienation by positing the coactivity of the members of the Body of Christ in the offering of the sacrifice of praise.

Among other texts, Casel based his mystery theology on Romans 6:1–11, which is very important for the Catholic liturgy when proclaimed annually at the Easter Vigil and as an option for funerals and baptisms. Paul asserts that in baptism, the Christian dies to sin with Christ and rises with him *now* to new life. Casel claimed that in baptism we have a sacrament, a liturgical-mystery (*Kultmysterium*) in which the death and resurrection of Christ are reactualized in order that the Christian may experience justification (being set in right relation to God) by union with the Savior. So, Casel questions, unless the saving acts of the Lord are somehow re-presented, how can anyone die together with Christ?[7]

Schillebeeckx appropriates Casel's method and sources. He discusses baptism, confirmation, *anamnesis* (memorial of the paschal mystery) in eastern and western eucharistic liturgies, and *epiclesis* (invocation of the Holy Spirit), which is less obvious in the history of liturgy in the West as compared with the East. Schillebeeckx's particular contribution to the understanding of sacraments is influenced by his personalist philosophy and the notable use of words such as *encounter* as a possible replacement for the classical phrase that sacraments "cause" or "confer" grace.[8] His treatment of sacraments functioning *ex opere operato* follows his treatment of the importance of the community's expressing faith in and through the liturgy of the sacraments. He argues that *ex opere operato* means that God is always present and active in the sacraments; it is a certain divine "guarantee" and assurance that God will always act in and through sacraments. Schillebeeckx's contribution is especially impressive and nuanced given that *ex opere operato* had come to mean, in the minds of many, that God acts automatically, requiring no response of faith by the participants.[9] Some authors, however, parallel *ex opere operato* with *ex opere operantis*, with the latter emphasizing those who are engaged in the sacrament.[10]

One of Schillebeeckx's contributions to language about sacraments is the phrase "Christ is the Sacrament of the encounter with God." Here, theology from Pius XII's *Mediator Dei* (Christ as "mediator") is taken up by a systematic theologian to emphasize that sacraments are acts of Christ in the church, typified by every prayer in the liturgy ending "through Christ our Lord." The seven sacraments are thus seen as intrinsically interconnected and are unable to be understood without a clear emphasis on Christ, who is the mediator between God and humans and who is the fundamental or ground sacrament through which the seven sacraments are to be understood. Sacraments are also to be seen as intrinsic experiences of the church. This emphasis is especially important given the prevailing emphasis at the time on "individuals" and "private" celebration of some sacraments: for example, (infant) baptism, "private" Mass, and extreme unction. This ecclesiological emphasis is fully in line with Pius XII's *Mystici Corporis*.[11] In light of Schillebeeckx's writings, subsequent theologians often refer to the *ursakrament*, that is, the "primordial," "foundational," or "fundamental" sacrament.

KARL RAHNER (1904–1984)

Karl Rahner's writings are many and profound, often succinct in length yet impressive in depth, complementary yet not systematized.[12] If one were to attempt to generalize, Rahner begins with an anthropological starting point and his notion of *Realsymbol*.[13] As a comprehensive notion and method for all theology, this clearly had special relevance to sacrament. Rahner grounds his concept of symbol in its capacity to realize what is essential in a being. Without symbolic acts and their revelatory character, human persons would not be able to actualize their human nature.

In the very act of transcending their limits, human beings are engaged in an existence shaped by symbolic activity. In turn, the human encounter with God is premised on the symbolic possibilities of created reality. The church, recalling Christ's humanity as the perfect symbol of God's redemptive love and action, continues this symbolic presence, especially in its sacramental life. It is the church as the visible manifestation of grace that provides the understanding of the sacramental sign as a cause of grace because grace is given by being signified. Rahner's small volume *Kirche und Sakrament* reflects all the above characterizations.[14] For a proper interpretation this book should be placed in relation to the rest of Rahner's corpus on sacraments.[15]

Recalling the nuance at the end of the discussion of Schillebeeckx—that his contribution to an emerging sacramental theology was both christological and ecclesial—the same is true for Rahner. *Kirche und Sakrament* specifies one part of his contribution, namely, that the church is the "fundamental sacrament."[16] However, other aspects of his theology come to bear in interpreting both the sacraments and the church, including his Christology, trinitarian theology, eschatology, and anthropology. He intends his consideration of the church in sacraments to emphasize the church's role in the "actualization of the seven sacraments generally."[17]

Like Schillebeeckx, Rahner explores the way sacraments can be understood to function *ex opere operato*, although he prefers the phrase *opus operatum*. He argues,

> God has linked his grace once and for all to the making of this sign [i.e., a sacrament] and that through this connection established by God himself between sign of grace and grace signified, any objection that the sacramental *opus operatum* is being understood in a magical way *ipso facto* vanishes, all the more so as the grace conferred is not only not excluded but is expressly taught by the Council of Trent. If the sacrament is

> to be received with fruit by an adult, of a right disposition:
> active co-operation in the reception of the sacrament with
> faith and love. in the reception.[18]

Rahner gives a particularly penetrating series of observations about the
role of "the word" in sacraments, which are especially significant because
he wrote prior to Vatican II and the liturgical reforms that came from it.
Rahner argues that the word of God constitutes the basic essence of the
sacrament. With this as a foundation, symbols used in sacraments have
the secondary function of illustrating the significance of the word.[19]
Here the exhibitive and performative nature of the word is emphasized;
that is, words *do* something. Sacraments can be said to effect what is
signified (to adapt an adage from conventional sacramental theology)
in the proclaimed and enacted word.[20] This line of argument can help
contemporary authors appreciate the structure of Word and Sacrament
proper to all sacraments and help them argue the power and effective-
ness of the proclaimed word in sacraments.

After Rahner but before Vatican II, Otto Semmelroth drew out
many of Rahner's arguments about the word in sacrament. In *Wirkendes Wort* Semmelroth describes the way the word exercises its power in
the church.[21] He argues that the word not only disposes one for the fit
reception of sacraments but that it also possesses an "efficacious causality" (a term used of sacraments themselves) and possesses the power
of sanctification.[22] The preaching of the word is the actualization of the
incarnation, even as sacraments are the actualization of the sacrificial
life, death, and resurrection of Christ.[23] Semmelroth argues that Word
and Sacrament, incarnation and paschal mystery need to be understood
as integral parts of each other.[24]

Raymond Vaillancourt and Kenan Osborne have also followed
Schillebeeckx and Rahner. Vaillancourt's modest book includes three
succeeding chapters on "Christology and the Sacraments," "Ecclesiology
and the Sacraments," and "Anthropology and the Sacraments."[25] Kenan
Osborne distinguished between "Jesus as Primordial Sacrament" and
"The Church as Basic Sacrament" in his utterly lucid introductory work
on sacraments.[26]

Other theologians, such as Edward Kilmartin, have nuanced the
understanding of the church as the continuation of the incarnation.
Kilmartin makes a clear distinction between the incarnate Logos and
the church because the church is the gathering of the new people of

Christ in the Spirit.[27] Most important here is the emphasis on the presence and role of the Spirit in the church, an understanding that has been notably absent or underemphasized in many Western ecclesiologies and sacramental theologies.

At the same time, some have critiqued Rahner and Schillebeeckx for an overly optimistic appreciation of the world in which sacraments take place. They are also critiqued for a notion of the way church and sacrament relate that does not emphasize the church's prophetic and active involvement in the world. Political and liberation theologians, especially, have moved beyond such passive notions of the church to those more politically attuned.

Hans Urs von Balthasar offers a very different approach as compared to Rahner. Balthasar's approach is most fully addressed in the first volume of *Herrlichkeit*; there are also some pertinent pages in *Theodramatik*, to say nothing of articles scattered throughout his writings.[28] Two aspects of his understanding of sacrament continue to exercise an influence. First, Balthasar's soteriology focuses on the cross of Christ as the manifestation of divine love in its very concealment of the Godhead and on the kenosis of Christ's descent into hell. From this, Balthasar explains the sacraments as the church's communion with Christ in this mystery. Second, in explaining the mystery of the church, he turns to the bride and bridegroom imagery of salvation through Christ. Thus, he finds the church's form in the complementarity of Mary's spirituality to the pastoral office, expressed especially in the office of Peter. All Christians are called to model their lives on that of Mary in her relation to Christ, and through him to the Father and the Spirit. On the other hand, the continued presence of Christ, the bridegroom, is represented by ordained ministers, who act *in persona Christi* in their teaching, sacramental, and pastoral charge. The starting point is the exact opposite of the anthropological. The role of the aesthetic in revelation and the Word's disclosure of the inner life and love of the Trinity are fundamental to a discussion of sacrament.

It is no coincidence that both Rahner and Schillebeeckx imitate much of Thomas Aquinas's teaching on the sacraments.[29] They also follow the teachings of Trent as they break new ground for Catholic thinking on sacraments. While subsequent authors refer to the "church" as the *ursakrament* (meaning "fundamental sacrament") taken from Rahner's book, both the church and the word can be considered the *ursakrament* in Rahner's sacramental theology.

EDWARD J. KILMARTIN (1923–1994)

Edward Kilmartin provides his most thorough work in discussing how the Triune God's self-communication to humanity grounds liturgical expression. He sees the effort to demonstrate how a theology of liturgy might be articulated as a theology of the economic Trinity as a crucial theological task.[30] Kilmartin first postulates the need for a trinitarian grounding of symbol, stating, "The Word is the 'real symbol' of the Father. A real symbol exists when there is unity of being between the symbol and the symbolized."[31] The articulation of such a theology also presupposes a trinitarian anthropology, Christology, pneumatology, and ecclesiology, since our knowledge of the Trinity is grounded in the work of the Spirit as seen in the Christ event.

After reviewing some contemporary models in trinitarian theology and Christology, Kilmartin asks, If God has indeed formed new personal relationships with creatures by which they are capable of personal communication with God, how does their response to God's offer of self-communication affect God? Ascending Christology and the bestowal model of the Trinity suggests that "the prayer of Jesus is the historical revelation of the trinitarian dialogue. The prayer of that High Priest for us elicits the Father's offering the Spirit to enable the response of faith, in and through a purely divine act."[32] In turn, the prayer of the church shows the union of the liturgical community with their High Priest. When the church implores the Father in union with Christ and in the power of the Spirit to bestow that same Spirit of sanctification, both the dialogical structure of liturgy and the "Christological-Trinitarian dimension of Christian liturgy in all its forms" are effectively manifested.[33] Kilmartin's ultimate position is that there is only one liturgy, that of the fully realized economic Trinity as the heavenly liturgy and its earthly realization in the worship of the pilgrim people of God.[34]

Kilmartin's starting point for developing the trinitarian implications of *Realsymbol* and symbolic causality is the original insight of Rahner that the Triune God is the foundation of all symbolic reality and efficacy. As with Rahner and others, it is important to assess Kilmartin's contributions from the variety of his published sources.[35]

Kilmartin takes the liturgy very seriously in the presentation of sacramental theology. While we are the poorer theologically because Kilmartin never left a systematic treatment of his thought, we are the

19

richer theologically because of the breadth of his mastery and wise use of the writings of German systematic theologians.[36]

KENAN OSBORNE (1930-2019)

Kenan Osborne was a prodigious and prolific Franciscan scholar who made important contributions to a number of issues having to do with sacraments and ministry (ordained and lay).[37] Two articles published before his writings on specific sacraments led to his modest yet very insightful summary in *Sacramental Theology: A General Introduction* (1988).[38] His scholarship in the intervening years yielded *Christian Sacraments in a Postmodern World: A Theology for the Third Millennium* (1999).[39] His last work, *Sacramental Theology: Fifty Years after Vatican II* (2014),[40] is a useful summary and assessment of how the teachings of Vatican II have influenced sacramental theology.

In his first book, *Sacramental Theology: A General Introduction*, Osborne offers brief summaries about then contemporary Catholic sacramental theology, methodology for studying the sacraments that is highly christological and historical, a very clear exposition of the teaching of the Council of Trent, and the relationship of sacraments and spirituality. Two key chapters deal with "Jesus as Primordial Sacrament" and "The Church as a Basis of Sacraments."[41] Not only do these chapters raise up salient points from Schillebeeckx's and Rahner's works, but these key christological and ecclesiological insights are found throughout the book. "Matter" and "form" are briefly mentioned in the chapter on the teachings from Trent.[42] When discussing God's action in the sacramental event, Osborne offers a lucid set of descriptions on how sacramentality "works" according to Thomas Aquinas, theologians who favor "moral causality," "occasional causality," and then Rahner and Schillebeeckx.[43] Overall, *Sacramental Theology* is a sound and useful book, marked by clarity in structure, scope and content.

Osborne's decided emphasis on Christology and ecclesiology is understandable and, especially at the time of *Sacramental Theology's* publication, very welcome. One notable advantage of *Sacramental Theology* is its clear translation of and commentary on the canons on sacraments from the Council Trent. Whether or not his treatment of expanding Christ and church into additional sacraments is useful remains a serious debate. There are a few limits to his arguments: scant reference to theologians other than Rahner and Schillebeeckx, to the liturgy of the way sacraments are enacted, to Christian anthropology or eschatology, and to official church teaching other than Trent.

Osborne's book on method that followed, *Christian Sacraments in a Postmodern World*, retains the emphasis on Jesus (chapter 4 is "Jesus and Primoriality") and on the church (chapter 5 is "Church as Foundational Sacrament"). Osborne's discussion of Jesus and the church contain rich new insights and nuances not found in the earlier book. The book's central arguments are placed within what he calls a "postmodernism"[44] that requires new and nuanced responses to issues surrounding the (seven) sacraments. His modest assertion that the book is "a possible basis for discussion"[45] should be borne in mind when assessing it as a work of a true theologian and not one who simply repeats official church teaching and the *Catechism of the Catholic Church* without nuance and appropriate critique. In fact, one such lacuna that he finds with the *Catechism* concerns the sacramentality of the world, a phrase also reflected in copious Orthodox presentations.[46]

As opposed to other presentations of the term *sacramentality*, Osborne chooses a pithy phrase from Louis-Marie Chauvet: "creation itself is charged with sacramentality." Osborne continues,

> I wish to make Chauvet's thesis far more explicit in my presentation on sacramentality. Therefore, this volume begins (in chapter 3) with the world and its possible forms of sacramentality. From there I move to the Incarnation, which means Jesus, in his humanness, as the primordial sacrament (chapter 4). I turn next to the church as foundational sacrament (chapter 5). Next I attempt to form a synthesis of contemporary sacramentality and postmodern thought (chapter 6). Finally I consider solemn statements of the magisterium and their meaning within this postmodern framework (chapter 7).[47]

As this key paragraph asserts, Osborne transcends the deficiency of only citing Trent in his former book and offers a fulsome treatment of the contemporary magisterium, including a copious treatment of the *Catechism of the Catholic Church* with some poignant critiques (e.g., on sacramental character and the way the *Catechism* leaves it vague, deliberate or not).[48] Among the most important contributions for our purposes here is Osborne's emphasis on the world as sacramental, as found in the work of Louis-Marie Chauvet.

Finally, *Sacramental Theology: Fifty Years after Vatican II* is a fine example of the distillation of Osborne's thought placed in dialogue with what he calls the Augustinian tradition, the Thomistic tradition, and the Franciscan tradition. His review of sacramental theology from 1896 to 2014 summarizes the work of several important systematic theologians whose writings were clearly influenced by both Trent and Vatican II. While this work breaks no new ground in Osborne's own thought, it does offer worthwhile synopses and syntheses of several interconnected and complex issues. Any imbalance in overemphasizing Christology or ecclesiology in understanding sacraments is countered here by very helpful insights about the work of the Holy Spirit in the liturgy of the sacraments.

JUAN LUIS SEGUNDO (1925–1996)

Already in 1971, the Uruguayan Juan Luis Segundo raised serious challenges to the conventional liturgical and sacramental practice of the time, particularly regarding triumphalism in cult and church life in the face of serious economic and social injustices. In *The Sacraments Today* Segundo argues for a more authentic sense of community in liturgical celebration, a chief means toward which is the formation and fostering of base communities.[49] He urges a positive interpretation to the "secularization" process to retrieve the necessary prophetic and life-challenging aspects of liturgy.[50] He thus rejects the dualistic separation of sacred and profane. In addition, he describes liturgy as truly liberating of persons from such "demons" as inequitable land and wealth distribution, which "demons" are regrettably inherent in the social structures of underdeveloped countries.[51] Segundo critiques consumerist approaches to the use of sacraments and demonstrates that a sacramental system can, in practice, support systemic social exploitation. Consequently, he argues forcefully for deeper exploration and appreciation of the prophetic dimension of liturgy as celebrating what has not yet been accomplished, in that all of life is not yet pervaded by Christ's liberative Pasch.[52]

The book's structure and use of magisterial sources clearly reflect the beginnings of the move from the conventional post-Tridentine concerns about the institution of sacraments, their efficaciousness, and the number seven. The magisterial sources on which he primarily relies are Vatican II's Constitution *Sacrosanctum Concilium* on the Sacred Liturgy and the Pastoral Constitution *Gaudium et Spes* on the Church in the Modern World. He also appeals to Paul VI's *Evangelii Nuntiandi*, documents from the Medellín Conference of the Latin American bishops in 1968, and the Final Document from the Puebla meeting of the Latin American bishops' conference in 1979.

LEONARDO BOFF (B. 1938)

Leonardo Boff of Brazil articulates the sacramentality intrinsic to sacraments and what might be called a sacramental ecclesiology. In the brief *Sacraments of Life, Life of the Sacraments: Story Theology*, Boff aims to disclose the way sacraments express the interplay among human beings (especially how they view life and communicate human life), the world, and God.[53] Boff writes to "recapture the religious richness contained in the symbolic and sacramental universe that inhabits our daily life"; since sacraments are "basic constituents of human life...faith sees grace present in the most elementary acts of life."[54] Throughout, Boff views sacraments as *sub specie humanitatis*. Sacramental language is essentially evocative, self-involving, and performance oriented. Sacraments refer to sacred moments and places to disclose the sacredness of everyday life and to engage participants in acts of redemption here and now. They also aim to induce conversion and to change human praxis. In simple language that is often autobiographical, Boff discloses how persons (his father and his schoolteacher), nature (light), and elements of human manufacture (bread, house) can be sacramental, often linking these narratives with principles of sacramental theology (such as their symbolic substructure). The concluding chapter summarizes in a systematic way what he has articulated for popular consumption.

Boff's style and purpose in *Church: Charism and Power; Liberation Theology and the Institutional Church* are similar.[55] In arguing for a "church born of the people's faith" Boff asserts that the base community is a new and original way of living Christian faith, of organizing the community around the word, around the sacraments (when possible), and around new ministries exercised by laypeople. His broad notion of sacramentality from the previous book informs his opinion that "the wider understanding of sacraments [views them] as signs of a grace that is offered constantly and [is] present to humanity, rather than as the instruments of a preexisting grace."[56] This allows for "the rise of a rich ecclesial sacramentality (the entire Church as sacrament) with much creativity in its celebrations and a deep sense of the sacred—all belonging to the people."[57]

In a pivotal section where he explores the meaning of *sacramentum* as uniting the dialectical notions of identity and nonidentity, Boff's reliance on Rahner and Schillebeeckx is apparent. He writes, "Identity is affirmed through the sacrament: grace is present in the mediation, the parousia of the mystery is made present...shining forth through a word, made symbolically corporeal through a gesture, and communicated through a community."[58] Yet nonidentity is also affirmed in sacraments because "God and his grace are not imprisoned within this or that sacramental expression. There is an absence in the sacrament, despite the presence of grace. Mystery is revealed in the sacrament, but it is still a mystery. One cannot identify the mystery with the sacrament; there is nonidentity."[59] For Boff, the category *sacramentum* serves to sustain his dialectical thesis throughout the book. From this most traditional Catholic category he is able to articulate the role of sacraments in one's faith life and the role of the church as serving the kingdom in the world.

ANTONIO GONZALEZ DORADO (1928-2013)

Antonio Gonzalez Dorado's *Los Sacramentos del Evangelio* is a substantial contribution to the series of basic theology textbooks for Latin American seminary and university students (whom he calls "future evangelizers").[60] The synthesis it achieves is framed within the contemporary Latin American context, and it listens seriously to the Puebla conference's plea for a theology of liturgy and sacraments that takes into account the human and ecclesial context of Latin America, the preferential option for the poor, and the contemporary church project of what he calls "liberating evangelization" to bring the church to a new birth.[61] For Gonzalez Dorado, this involves engaging in direct criticism of decadent sacramental practice, evaluating the link between church renewal and the liturgical reform, and examining the relationship between sacraments and the contemporary culture, popular religiosity and ecumenism. He does not separate or oppose evangelization and sacramentalization. Rather he prefers to emphasize that liturgy and sacraments are to be celebrated in the context of pastoral life lived in harmony with the liturgy, especially its evangelizing function.

Gonzalez Dorado's work is comprehensive. In ten chapters he deals with sacraments in history, sacraments as symbols of faith, the origin and evangelizing mission of the sacraments, sacraments for the upbuilding of a more evangelizing and evangelized church, sacraments and the witness of the gospel, sacraments and the evangelizing cult, the purpose and effects of sacraments in history, ministers as dispensers of the mysteries of God, the relationship of sacraments to the commitment to witness to the gospel, the necessity of sacraments, and the sacrament of solidarity. Each topic is treated historically, based on sources such as the Scriptures, Tertullian, Augustine, Aquinas, and the contemporary magisterium—with special attention to Paul VI's *Evangelii Nuntiandi* and the texts from Medellín and Puebla. Gonzalez Dorado explains that he uses Tertullian, Augustine, and Aquinas because of parallels between their time and now. Tertullian is pertinent because of the similarity of the age of the martyrs and today's oppression in Latin America; Augustine because his task of explaining sacraments to the uneducated is similar to the contemporary challenge; Aquinas because his time resembled our own in its profound economic, political, and social change. He acknowledges his reliance on Schillebeeckx, Rahner, Yves Congar, Dionisio Borobio, Segundo, and Boff. Throughout, he treats the rites phenomenologically, is attentive to their liturgical structure and content, and tries to determine their theological meaning and their role in evangelization.

Among the more helpful methodological contributions is the way Gonzalez Dorado contextualizes familiar statements from theologians and the magisterium to determine precisely what was meant by what was said. He weaves issues from contemporary Latin American religious and sacramental practice with the traditional themes he treats. For example, the chapter on sacraments in history utilizes the theologians already cited as sources and then treats the evolution of sacramental practice in Latin America from colonial times to today.[62] In addition, he consistently and helpfully treats the interrelationship of theology and pastoral need, the relationship of anthropology and sacraments, sacraments as expressive of the wide reality of *mysterion* (understood as God's will for universal salvation and liberation), and the relation of contemporary theologians and the magisterium to pastoral issues of the day.

Gonzalez Dorado's sacramentology is christological, with an emphasis on soteriology and ecclesiology. This is complemented by treatment of the Spirit's role in sacramental celebration and in the life of the church.[63] Classical categories of sacramental theology receive fresh perspectives here: for example, symbolic causality as a way of discussing *ex opere operato*. When discussing the number seven, Gonzalez Dorado articulates his fundamental understanding of sacraments as festive encounters of the Christian community with Christ and the church. In Latin America today the "essential value" of sacraments is found in their being moments of "liberation,"[64] a phrase that recurs throughout the book.

Among the more challenging and creative sections are those concerning ministers as dispensers of the mysteries of God and the requirement that those who celebrate sacraments witness to the gospel. The term *minister* is relative, since Christ is the eternal High Priest who is the agent of all sacraments, acting through both a ministerial and common priesthood. Gonzalez Dorado prefers the terms *diakonia* and *oikonomos* to describe sacramental ministers of Christ, and the prime function in ministry is to integrate sacraments, life, and witness. The classical term for sacramental power, *potestas*, is best understood as the power to serve.[65] With regard to intentionality in sacraments, he argues that the category of effective intentionality respects human freedom and stresses that "intention" is a deliberate human act in relation to a specific object. He believes that the major issues in Latin America today are the divorce between faith and life and the incoherence between participation in sacraments and the absence of a vital faith life among participants.[66]

Discussing contemporary ecumenical issues, Gonzalez Dorado acknowledges the commonality of baptism and that many problems connected with Eucharist reflect deeper issues regarding ordination. He reiterates a main theme of the book by asserting that the crucial dialogue among churches deals not only with sacramental issues but also with working toward the liberation of the poor and the oppressed, for whom sacramental activity is a source of universal salvation and liberation.[67]

Many of the book's main themes are reprised in the final chapter on the necessity of sacraments. Sacraments are an essential part of the sharing in the good news and in the salvation God intends through Christ. They celebrate and effect the gospel here and now, and they are intrinsically related to the wider world and its salvation and sanctification in

God.[68] In the conclusion, Gonzalez Dorado offers a moving description of how sacraments, by their interior dynamism, transform and enliven faith that is weak or dead into a living faith that is vital and strong. Finally, he makes a plea for proper sacramental practice as exemplified in Mary's Magnificat, which he argues is the credo of believers and the canticle of liberating evangelization.

LOUIS-MARIE CHAUVET (B. 1942)

Louis-Marie Chauvet intends his work to be not only a theology of sacrament in the traditional sense but also a symbolic theology of the whole order of salvation, viewed from within sacramental practice.[69] To speak of the *symbolic* rather than simply of *symbol* avoids taking any symbol as adequate to the expression of the divine or fixing the gaze on symbols rather than on the one who approaches humanity through the symbolic.

Chauvet's major work, *Symbole et Sacrement*, is divided into four parts: from metaphysics to the symbolic, the sacraments viewed from within the symbolic web of ecclesial faith, symbolization of Christian identity and sacraments, and trinitarian Christology. The first and foundational part sets the method for the rest of the book. Following a Heideggerian critique, Chauvet criticizes the use of the notion of causality. It debases the gratuitous and personal character of divine grace celebrated in sacraments. The relation of mutual and reciprocal gift between lovers is a much better analogy for grace and sacrament than is that of the making or producing of things through instrumental causes. Language itself is instrumentalized when sacramental theory and practice is dominated by the notion of causality. Human communities must learn to see themselves as addressed and possessed by the language that they inherit, rather than as the users of language systems to meet their programmatic purposes.

As an alternative to metaphysical explanations, Chauvet appeals to studies of language and ritual to fill out the Heideggerian axiom. This he places within the framework of a church that acts as a community of grace and of interpretation, maintaining its institutionally expressed commitment to originating event and to biblical word within the ritual practice of paschal memorial. In a section on the ecclesial symbolic web, he attends especially to the use of Scripture within liturgy, to symbolic rites, and to the ethics that develop within this context. The Bible has a primary and dominant role, since Chauvet follows the trend in the study of language that gives some primacy to writing over speech. Meaning is not constituted in the presence of self to self nor of thought in speech; rather, to be established clearly and firmly it needs the distinction of writing. Ethical decision and sacramental celebration have in common the constant effort to retrieve into the present what has been set down in the Bible. Hence, ethical practice serves as a gauge of adequate sacramental practice.

In further discussing sacrament, Chauvet gives importance to the twofold basis of rituality and "institution." The latter is given a human and dynamic meaning rather than a juridical one. For Chauvet, there is a developed and sanctioned tradition of sacramental practice that cannot be treated in an arbitrary way, even though it is always open to critique and renewal. Further, it must be given diversified expression in different situations. Chauvet then distinguishes between semiotic entities and semantic entities. In a language system, the semiotic elements are finite and determined. Whoever wants to refer to something has to remain within this code. The semantic elements are the various possibilities of expressing reality that creative use of semiotic elements allows. Thus, it is within the code of sacramental rites that sacramental celebration and sacramental renewal take place, though in a creative way. Hence, through the notions of institution/church and instituting/instituted rite Chauvet deals with the given of the sacraments and with their constant creativity.

In the fourth part of the book, Chauvet gives his christological and trinitarian perspective on sacrament as gift.[70] The starting point, in keeping with language's priority, is the *lex orandi*, which gives primacy to the proclamation of the Pasch. According to this proclamation, God gives his love to humanity in the self-effacement of the divinity on the cross of Christ.[71] Through the power of the Spirit and in the memorial of the cross, God continues to reveal himself as "other" in human bodiliness, where he continues to efface himself. As sacramental celebration unfolds, it shows the presence of this self-giving and self-effacing God in the body of the church, which lives for others, and in the bodies of the suffering and despised of the earth, whom in Christ's name and Spirit it serves. This divine presence as "other" is manifest in the symbolic web of sacrament, as it is also in sacrament that the church is configured to the Christ of the Pasch.

In an earlier part of the book, Chauvet had treated the relation between word and rite in terms of "anti-ritual." The discussion of ritual is related to the word of the cross/Pasch, as well as to the *anamnesis* and *epiclesis* that flow from the word. This shows the nonidentity of God or of Christ with the ritual, introducing an element of the anti-ritual and breaking the pattern of the theophanic. Lest the idea of divine manifestation in visible symbol overshadow proclamation, there has to be the measure of anti-ritual in sacrament.

This postmodern sacramental theology then makes its own uses of language studies and ritual studies, inclusive of an appeal to the anti-ritual factor in ritual development. Chauvet thus explains both how ritual functions in sacramental theology from a socioanthropological perspective and how the appeal to the metaphoric word in sacrament is ever necessary in keeping memorial of Christ's Pasch. However, it would be wrong to think that Chauvet substitutes his explanation of the rite's functioning for causality. He knows the difference between phenomenology and ontology. The phenomenology opens up the ontological question but does not replace it. When we appreciate the inadequacy of symbol and rite to mystery, or even the split in consciousness that symbol induces, the relationship to mystery has to be explained by an ontology that avoids causality but keeps the reference to reality and the sense of gratuity alive.

Chauvet argues that God acts in human time but what is left is the trace of the divine action. On the basis of the traces found in the Scriptures, the church "writes itself" through its preaching, its theology, its ritual, and its ethics. This allows for the historicality of Christian expression and practice, as well as for the presence of the church as sacrament of Christ in divergent historical and cultural conditions. This historicality and presence are without recourse to a theory of divine or instrumental causality. The cross has a critical role in the life of the church, not only in its prophetic challenge but also in the way that it calls into question explanations offered in myth and in metaphysics.

Chauvet's work has been the subject of much discussion among theologians and has influenced sacramental practice, as well.[72]

CONCLUSION

This review has illustrated how contemporary Catholic sacramental theologians have moved the discussion from the parameters of the teachings of Trent to additional areas that serve differing contexts in the church's life. Edward Schillebeeckx and Karl Rahner argued the importance of Christ and the church as essential foundations for the enactment of sacraments, rather than seeing seven sacraments as discrete moments of grace. Rahner also influenced many others, such as Otto Semmelroth, by his understanding of the role of the liturgy of the sacraments.

Edward Kilmartin sought to probe the theological meaning of the liturgy of the sacraments, especially by emphasizing the work of the Trinity in sacraments in relation to a number of theologians in church history, especially German systematic theologians. Kenan Osborne offered both complete and helpful summaries of church teaching and several theologians from the Catholic tradition, in addition to engaging the postmodern world. Juan Segundo and Leonardo Boff offered insightful and incisive treatments of the power and value of sacraments from the perspective of liberation theology. Antonio Gonzalez Dorado articulated a sacramental theology based on the evolution of sources from the Catholic tradition, emphasizing at every turn the need for evangelization in Latin America.

Louis-Marie Chauvet sought to rethink and reimagine sacramental life, as opposed to seeking a systematic study of sacraments themselves. One contribution that Chauvet makes is his argument away from a metaphysical understanding of what sacraments do to articulating a theology of sacraments as "gifts" from God. While none of the theologians reviewed here ignored the principles of sacramentality and mediation, I would attest that Chauvet is the strongest among them for commenting and utilizing these principles. Once again allow me to assert that thus survey indicates that there has never been *one* or *the* sacramental theology and theology of liturgy for the whole church.

CHAPTER THREE

CONTEMPORARY ECUMENICAL TEACHINGS ON CREATION, ECOLOGY, ENVIRONMENT

The purpose of this chapter is to summarize the salient points and principles that authoritative church bodies have articulated about the environment. These include the World Council of Churches, the Ecumenical Patriarchate (Istanbul), and the Roman Catholic Church. Unlike many of the other issues in ecumenism that occupy the attention of church bodies to revisit issues where churches and denominations differ, ecology is an issue where churches can engage each other positively and collaboratively. This can and should be done by sharing insight from their respective churches, dialogue between and among churches, and invitations to action derived from all of these sources, some more authoritative than others.

1960–1990

World Council of Churches

James McPherson argues that the initial word on ecology under the auspices of the WCC from 1966 to 1987 was in the subunit called Church and Society, whose program was concerned with social ethics (rather than, e.g., systematic theology) and differentiated theological perspectives on the human relationship to the environment.[1] Ecology was a major concern of the Church and Society program from the 1966 Geneva Conference, *Christians in the Technical and Social Revolutions of our Time*, to the 1987 Amsterdam consultation, *Reintegrating God's Creation*. In the 1970s, the program The Just, Participatory and Sustainable Society (JPSS) emerged to consider environmental issues, among other justice concerns. The WCC Sixth Assembly (Vancouver, 1983) changed the program theme from JPSS to Justice, Peace and the Integrity of Creation (JPIC).[2] McPherson argues that the results of Amsterdam did not address several important questions, such as the precise meaning of "the integrity of creation," how humans positively or negatively affect the integrity of creation, and how the integrity of creation relates to God's actions and human efforts.[3]

The work of the 1990 *World Convocation on Justice, Peace and the Integrity of Creation* in Seoul, Korea relied upon the invitation by the WCC Sixth Assembly to respond to the growing awareness of the environmental crisis.[4] The members of the convocation sought "to engage...in a conciliar process of mutual commitment (covenant) to justice, peace and the integrity of creation" (1.1), and they affirmed the important work of the JPIC in the years since its formation from the Sixth Assembly. The *Final Document*, reflecting on the work at the convocation, applauded the diverse perspectives that formed the preparations and discussions, noting especially participation from numerous faith traditions (in addition to the WCC member churches) such as the Roman Catholic Church. The document drafters also anticipated that the work of the convocation would be influential for the upcoming WCC Seventh Assembly (Canberra, 1991; treated below). The *Final Document* includes ten affirmations on the theme "justice, peace and the integrity of creation." Of particular interest for ecology are affirmations 7 and 8: "creation as beloved by God" and "the earth is the Lord's" (2.2). In affirmation 7, the document provides explicitly trinitarian and biblical foundations. It recognizes the failures of humanity with regard to creation and the implications of these failures for future generations, and it describes the members' commitment to resist "the claim that anything in creation is merely a resource for human exploitation" (2.2, aff. 7). The document calls for urgent action in living as "co-workers with God" (2.2, aff. 7). In affirmation 8 ("the earth is the Lord's"), the document applies the above concerns to the specific issues of land and water rights. Following the affirmations, the *Final Document* lists and describes urgent and concrete actions that are be undertaken by churches and organizations (2.3).

Ecumenical Patriarchate

The Ecumenical Patriarchate's approach to ecology includes statements from the Ecumenical Patriarch, symposia, and prayer initiatives (some ecumenical). The Patriarchate has pioneered contemporary eco-political initiatives since (at least) 1981. John Chryssavgis marks the 1986 Pre-synodal Pan-Orthodox Conference in Chambésy as a particularly important moment in the Patriarchate's involvement in environmental issues.[5] The 1986 conference emphasized concern for the abuse of the environment by humans, the sacredness of the human person, and the importance of ecological issues for future generations. After the 1986 conference and inspired by the activities of the WCC following the 1983 Vancouver Assembly, several Inter-Orthodox consultations discussed environmental issues: 1987 in Sofia, Bulgaria; 1988 in Patmos, Greece; and 1989 in Minsk, Belarus (then part of the USSR). The 1988 consultation in Patmos included a recommendation for the ecumenical patriarch to set aside a day of prayer for creation.[6]

On September 1, 1989, Patriarch Dimitrios delivered the first message in what would become a custom of the ecumenical patriarch to address concerns about creation and Christian responsibilities toward creation.[7] Patriarch Dimitrios's 1989 message declared, for the Orthodox churches, September 1st to be a World Day of Prayer for the Protection of the Environment. This means that the liturgy of the day was adjusted to reflect and underscore praise, thanks, and intercession for creation and its protection. The service was commissioned to the famous hymnographer Fr. Gerasimos Mikrayiannanites, published in Greek in 1991 and translated into English by Ephrem Lash. This practice of liturgical prayer for creation highlights an important Orthodox contribution, namely, the way liturgy serves as an integrating element of belief and prayer. The following year, Dimitrios's 1990 message focused on acquiring an "ascetic ethos" regarding the use of natural environment.[8]

Around the same time, Metropolitan John Zizioulas of Pergamon delivered a series of lectures in London.[9] In the lectures he attributes the West's loss of cosmic awareness to the rise of Scholasticism, and he maintains that the Orthodox never lost their cosmic emphasis. Therefore, he suggests that the West's recent rediscovery of its cosmic awareness may be a key to reconciliation between East and West precisely at a time when the world needs a united Christian witness on environmental issues. Equally important is his analysis of the usefulness of "stewardship" as a useful way of dealing with humans' responsibility for creation, preferring instead the notion that we are all *priests* of creation who offer back to God (as priests) what we have gratefully received.[10]

Roman Catholic Church

Catholic papal teaching addressed ecology through encyclicals (the highest ranking document a pope can issue on his own) addresses and statements, starting with two documents of Pope Paul VI: his Encyclical Letter on the Development of Peoples, *Populorum Progressio*,[11] and his Apostolic Letter on the Occasion of the Eightieth Anniversary of the Encyclical "Rerum Novarum," *Octogesima Adveniens*.[12] Additionally, in a message to the United Nations *Conference on Ecology* (Stockholm, 1972), Paul VI speaks of the interdependence of all things on the earth, noting a corresponding solidarity among them. Next John Paul II, at the very beginning of his pontificate, issued his Encyclical Letter on the Redeemer of the Human Race, *Redemptor Hominis*, in which he notes that humans need to address the destruction of creation (8).[13] In his Encyclical Letter on Human Labor, *Laborem Exercens*, John Paul II asserts that humans have the responsibility to preserve and share resources of the whole earth and all that dwell in it (4).[14] In his Encyclical Letter on the Social Concerns of the Church, *Sollicitudo Rei Socialis*, he addresses contemporary ecological concerns and notes that justice means "a fair distribution of the results of true development" (26), that humans have "a certain affinity with other creatures" (26) that carries with it the "duty of cultivating and watching over the garden" (29), that this dominion "imposes limits upon the use and dominion over things" (29), and that when it comes to the natural world "we are subject to biological laws as well as moral laws" (34).[15]

John Paul II's most focused treatment of the environment is in his World Day of Peace Message, *Peace with God the Creator, Peace with All of Creation*.[16] He asserts that the earth's resources are for the common good, that "a new solidarity" should be exercised in their use (10) and that the environmental crisis is a moral crisis that requires simplicity, discipline, and self-sacrifice (13). He speaks of the interdependence of all creation (2, 8) and of the aesthetic value of creation (14).

In a real sense 1989 can be viewed historically as a watershed year for the depth and frequency with which these church bodies have addressed and continue to address ecology.

1990–2020

World Council of Churches

Since the 1990s members of the WCC, through its committees, consultations, and organizations, have formed practical initiatives, developed spiritual events and resources, and published numerous statements and messages on key elements of ecology, especially climate change (e.g., *Be Stewards of God's Creation!*[17]) and water issues (e.g., *Statement on the Right to Water and Sanitation*[18]). The statements and messages consistently root ecological concerns in theological (especially biblical) foundations, appeal to contemporary research in order to identify the foremost problems, and stress the urgent requirement to move beyond statements to their translation into practical action.

The ecological concerns addressed by various members of the WCC are connected with the WCC's overall mission to promote church unity. In the Faith and Order's *Canberra Statement* care for creation is integrated with communion.[19] The statement highlights God's plan to bring all of creation into communion with God, and it describes the church's role in uniting the human race and revealing the "fullness of communion with God, humanity, and the whole creation" (1.1).[20] The statement acknowledges that the unity of the church is expressed visibly in various ways, including the common mission in service of creation. In the consultation document *Costly Unity*, members working on the Unity and Renewal and JPIC programs explicate more fully the integration of church unity and the integrity of creation.[21] The document relies upon the *Final Document* from Seoul, 1990, and the *Canberra Statement*. It begins with the strong assertion that "the ecumenical movement suffers damage so long as it is unable to bring the justice, peace and integrity of creation process and the unity discussion into fruitful interaction" (1). In its consideration of the church as a moral community, it calls for a sacramental worldview. The document then affirms the work performed in the JPIC program to integrate worship and spirituality in its concerns for justice, peace, and care for creation, thereby uniting ecclesiology, ethics, worship, and spirituality. The document also links a biblical understanding of covenant to the Eucharist, the community of faith, and the transformation of the created order.

The statements of the WCC continually stress the urgent need to move beyond written documents into practical initiatives. One hallmark program that combines statements, action and advocacy is the Ecumenical Water Network (EWN). EWN's mission is to promote responsible water preservation and management and to advocate for equitable distribution. This is accomplished partly through messages, such as the *Statement on Water for Life* adopted by the WCC Ninth Assembly in Porto Alegre, 2006.[22] This statement reflects both theological and pragmatic concerns about water and its distribution, and it provides theological (especially biblical) foundations on the significance of water for human life, an overview of the threats to water and the implications of these threats, an appraisal of positive approaches already taken, and a call for better institutional structures and new lifestyles. At the same time, EWN's mission seeks to put these concerns and calls into actions through outreach, advocacy, and prayer (such as the "Seven Weeks for Water" Lenten prayer initiative).

Spiritual resources are also a key element of the WCC's approach to ecology. In response to the Third European Ecumenical Assembly (Sibiu, Romania, 2007), the WCC Central Committee, in 2008, initiated the *Time for Creation* prayer season. This "season of creation" extends from September 1st (in conjunction with the day of prayer for creation begun by Patriarch Dimitrios in 1989) until October 4th (the Feast of St. Francis of Assisi; more in chapter 7). Prayers and other resources are provided for this period of prayer for creation, as well as for other "weeks," "decades," and so on, dedicated to specific issues, such as prayers for the United Nation's Decade for Action *Water for Life* (2005–2015).

In more recent years, the members of the WCC have striven to situate specific ecological concerns (especially climate change and water issues) within the broader context of justice. Since 2005 the WCC has made a conscious effort to connect climate change with issues such as energy, biodiversity, desertification, and biotechnology.[23] In continuity with related concerns for how environmental destruction impacts the poor and marginalized (e.g., Second European Ecumenical Assembly 1997), one major concern in the recent statements on climate justice from diverse WCC bodies is advocacy for the victims of climate change. For example, the *Minute on Climate Justice* adopted at the WCC Tenth Assembly (Busan, 2013) describes victims of climate change as "the new face of the poor, widow, and stranger" (6).[24] This document identifies climate change as one of the most challenging global threats that impacts the most vulnerable, expresses regret that climate change has lost priority in the public sphere and not reached stated goals, and calls for advocacy beyond national interests to promote stewardship of creation and protection of basic human rights. These concerns are reiterated in statements from the WCC Executive Committee, such as the *Statement on UN Climate Change Conference (COP21) in Paris, December 2015*[25] and the *Statement on Climate Justice*.[26]

Ecumenical Patriarchate

The initiatives and activities of the Ecumenical Patriarchate from the 1990s onward draw from the foundations set in the preceding decade. Beginning in the early 1990s the Ecumenical Patriarchate has hosted regularly scheduled meetings on the environment with international and ecumenical participants.[27] These meeting have taken two forms. One is a series of seminars held at the seminary on the island of Halki. The topics include *Living in the Creation of the Lord* (1991), *Environment and Religious Education* (1994), *Environment and Ethics* (1995), *Environment and Communications* (1996), *Environment and Justice* (1997), and *Environment and Poverty* (1998). The second form is a series of international, interdisciplinary, and interreligious symposia hosted by the Religious and Scientific Committee of the Patriarchate. They study the fate of the rivers and seas (which cover two-thirds of the world's surface), gathering the participants at and on the bodies of water under discussion: *Revelation and the Environment* (Aegean Sea, 1995), *The Black Sea in Crisis* (1997), *River of Life* (Danube and Black Sea, 1999), *The Adriatic Sea: A Sea at Risk, a Unity of Purpose* (2002), *The Baltic Sea: A Common Heritage, a Shared Responsibility* (2003), *The Amazon: Source of Life* (2006), *The Arctic: Mirror of Life* (2007), and *Restoring Balance: The Great Mississippi River* (2009).

Patriarch Bartholomew has also continued the September 1st messages begun by Patriarch Dimitrios, and the Patriarchate has continued the day of prayer for the protection of the environment, also on September 1st. In the patriarchal encyclicals of Bartholomew, liturgy is closely linked to the reality of communion, especially as reflected in the interrelatedness of all creatures on the earth.[28] Bartholomew's repeated reminder that the human person is central to creation leads him to distinguish between *anthropomorphism* as the problem, not *anthropocentrism*.[29] Especially because icons hold a central place in Orthodox theology and practice, it is not surprising that Bartholomew argues that creation is linked to an icon in the same way as the human person, too, is created "in the image [or icon] and likeness of God" (cf. Gen 1:26).[30] He invites the Orthodox to contemplate the Creator God through the icon of the created world.[31] That we are all priests of creation offering back to God what God gave and gives to us in creation and redemption is a recurring and foundational theme in the patriarch's statements,[32] which (as noted above) is also strongly supported in the work of John Zizioulas. Not surprisingly, eschatology also figures prominently in Bartholomew's writings, especially as an eschatological vision requires action now for this generation and generations to come.[33]

Since the early 2000s the ecumenical patriarch and the pope have issued several joint statements on creation and ecology. At the Fourth Ecological Symposium (Adriatic Sea, 2002), Patriarch Bartholomew and Pope John Paul II issued their *Common Declaration on Environmental Ethics*.[34] In it both church leaders call Christians to repent by admitting humanity's faults and past actions and to convert by seeking new approaches in thought, action and prayer that addresses environmental issues and goals. In 2006 Bartholomew and Pope Benedict XVI issued a *Common Declaration* from the Phanar (Orthodox headquarters in Istanbul). The declaration addresses, among other concerns, violations against human dignity (especially the exploitation of the poor, migrants, women, and children) and the natural environment. Concerning the environment, the two bishops express "concern at the negative consequences for humanity and for the whole of creation which can result from economic and technological progress that does not know its limits" (6).[35] On May 25, 2014, in Jerusalem Bartholomew and Pope Francis issued a common declaration, among whose paragraphs is the following about creation and the environment:

> It is our profound conviction that the future of the human family depends also on how we safeguard—both prudently and compassionately, with justice and fairness—the gift of creation that our Creator has entrusted to us. Therefore,

we acknowledge in repentance the wrongful mistreatment of our planet, which is tantamount to sin before the eyes of God. We reaffirm our responsibility and obligation to foster a sense of humility and moderation so that all may feel the need to respect creation and to safeguard it with care. Together, we pledge our commitment to raising awareness about the stewardship of creation; we appeal to all people of goodwill to consider ways of living less wastefully and more frugally, manifesting less greed and more generosity for the protection of God's world and the benefit of His people. (6)[36]

In the Orthodox Church more broadly, a recent encyclical from the Holy and Great Council of the Orthodox Church, with membership from fourteen Orthodox churches (including Constantinople), provides important statements on ecology from a pan-Orthodox perspective. In the council's encyclical from the 2016 gathering in Crete, the council fathers address environmental concerns within the context of contemporary challenges faced by Christians. They identify the threats to and the destruction of the natural environment as among the dangers of not confronting the negative consequences of scientific and technological advancement (11).[37] They assert that "scientific knowledge does not motivate man's moral will," and they observe that "the answer to man's serious existential and moral problems and to the eternal meaning of his life and of the world cannot be given without a spiritual approach" (11). The bishops then develop their environmental concerns by identifying the roots of the ecological crisis as spiritual and ethical, calling for repentance, radical change, and asceticism (14). In the letter they also point to how the sacraments affirm creation and encourage humans to act as stewards, protectors, and priests of creation (14).

Roman Catholic Church

Pope John Paul II's teachings on ecological issues are christologically and anthropologically focused, though they also highlight the Trinity's work in creation and redemption. In response to human errors that contribute to environmental crises, the pope calls for a sacramental view and aesthetic appreciation of creation and for ecological conversion that understands stewardship as a moral obligation toward all creation. His writings note the interdependence of all creation, at the center of which is the human person.[38] John Paul II's anthropocentric axis is particularly strong in his understanding of "human ecology" as developed in his Encyclical Letter on the Hundredth Anniversary of "Rerum Novarum," *Centesimus Annus* (38),[39] and his Encyclical Letter on the Value and Inviolability of Human Life, *Evangelium Vitae* (42).[40] In these encyclicals John Paul II explains that ecology is not limited to "natural" preservation, which rightly deserves attention. It also includes a recognition of the human person as God's gift, and so it requires the safeguarding of human natural and moral structures, basic rights (e.g., water and food), and the dignity of human labor. Human ecology and natural ecology are necessary to prepare for future generations a world in conformity with God's plan. In John Paul II's Encyclical Letter on the Eucharist in Its Relationship to the Church, *Ecclesia de Eucharistia*, the pope speaks of the relationship between the Eucharist and the cosmos (8).[41]

Often called "the green pope," Pope Benedict XVI engaged the Vatican in preservation initiatives (e.g., by installing solar panels) and wrote frequently on the environment. His teachings highlight the bond between creation and redemption, the integration of nature and society/culture, and international and intergenerational solidarity. Benedict XVI develops the positive relationship of the Eucharist to the cosmos examined earlier by John Paul II. At the same time Benedict XVI notes that some gifts from creation, like water, have been misused, and such issues need to be addressed by the international community.[42] In his Encyclical Letter on Integral Human Development in Charity and Truth, *Caritas in Veritate*, he links natural ecology and human ecology by encouraging new lifestyles anchored in human ecology, which requires affirmation of the inviolability of human life, the family, and nature (51).[43] In his 2010 Message on Peace, Benedict explains nature and society/culture as integrated such that the decline and desertification of one leads to the impoverishment of the other.[44] Therefore, he calls for greater intergenerational solidarity, prudent use of natural resources as a common good, and a lessening of self-interest in policy and aid.

On March 19, 2013, Pope Francis preached to the world for the first time as pope on the Solemnity of St. Joseph. In that homily he referred to Joseph as the *custos* ("protector") of Jesus, Mary, and the church, and then he invited all to be "protectors" of creation. The die was cast, and Francis has made caring for creation a priority of his pontificate. As a priest, Jesuit superior, and finally archbishop in Argentina,

Francis experienced firsthand how the degradation of the environment caused suffering for many of his people. In 2007, he joined his brother bishops of the Consejo Episcopal Latinoamericano (CELAM; that is, the Bishops Conference of Latin America and the Caribbean) in Aparecida, Brazil. The meeting resulted in the *Aparecida Concluding Document*, whose final editor was Francis, then Jorge Bergoglio, the archbishop of Buenos Aires.[45] The document addresses "the evangelizing action of the Church" (1), calls for a "see, judge, act" method (19) and thoroughly combines evangelization with a number of related issues—catechesis, education, liturgy, sacraments—all in the context of decreased participation in church life and liturgy. It gives generous attention to care for the environment: stewardship (24), beauty of creation (27), natural resources and global warming (66), biodiversity and natural habitats (83–87), threats to nature (66, 113), human ecology and the dignity of the human person and human work (104–6, 126), the universal destiny of goods (125–26), and the role of science and technology (123–24). All of these environmental concerns are grounded in a rich theology and spirituality that includes attention to the liturgy (especially the Eucharist; 25, 250–51), Trinity (109, 126), ecclesiology, mission, and evangelization (1, 106, 181), and the saints (especially St. Francis of Assisi, 125). Since becoming pope, Francis has reiterated this call to care for the earth and decried a "throwaway culture."[46]

In May 2015 Pope Francis promulgated the Encyclical Letter on Care for Our Common Home, *Laudato Si'.*[47] Francis addresses every person on the planet, and he asserts the need for dialogue about the present ecological crisis, about the individual and communal initiatives that can be undertaken and continued and, in particular, about the contribution that Roman Catholicism can offer. In the encyclical he cites generously from Paul VI, John Paul II, and Benedict XVI, drawing upon their insights on faith and reason (62–64), interconnectedness (16, 48–56, 158), the bond of creation and redemption (73), trinitarian communion (5, 9, 65, 76, 89, 91–92, 216, 220, 228, 238–40), sacramentality (233–37), the dignity of the human person and human work (12–13, 19–30, 44, 67, 93, 103, 113, 120–29, 150, 156, 164), and international cooperation and intergenerational solidarity (chapter 5). Francis also speaks about the church as a universal church (66), and he looks to the wisdom of his brother bishops throughout the world, often citing documents from episcopal conferences worldwide. At the same time Francis makes a unique contribution by raising these teachings on the environment to the level of official Catholic social justice teaching. He develops the work of his predecessors in the papacy from concern for "stewardship" to "care" for creation (116, 236, as well as 10, 14, 28, 42, 58, 64, 70, 78–79, 144–46, 166, 167, 208–13, 220, 225, 228, 231), he moves from "natural" and "human" ecologies to an "integral ecology" (chapter 4, the heart of the letter), he argues strongly for the precautionary principle (109, 129, 162, 186) and he situates specific issues (e.g., climate change and water rights) within rich theological and spiritual contexts (chapter 5). He also invites an ecumenical conversation, generously citing the work of Patriarch Bartholomew and the Orthodox churches. In sum, what the pope calls for is conversion of mind and heart, a turning away from destructive habits in order to see God in all that lives. He develops these teachings from the basis of Scriptures, Catholic theological (and social justice) tradition, the wisdom of the mendicant traditions (personified by his patron, the *poverello* St. Francis of Assisi), and the church's whole spiritual tradition.

Later the same year in August 2015, Pope Francis declared a World Day of Prayer for the Care of Creation to be celebrated annually on September 1st, citing Orthodox custom.[48] Francis explains that the day of prayer will "offer individual believers and communities a fitting opportunity to reaffirm their personal vocation to be stewards of creation, to thank God for the wonderful handiwork which he has entrusted to our care, and to implore his help for the protection of creation as well as his pardon for the sins committed against the world in which we live." (Francis 2016). The following year, on September 1, 2016, Francis issued what he intends to be an annual message on the day of prayer for creation. The theme of the 2016 message, entitled *Show Mercy to Our Common Home*, corresponded with the Extraordinary Jubilee Year of Mercy (2015–2016) that was then underway. Francis begins the message by acknowledging the unity and support shared among Christians in praying for care for creation. He calls Catholics to implore God's mercy for the sins committed against the natural world (1–2), encouraging especially recourse to the sacrament of penance (3–5).[49] Importantly, the pope also offers a new work of mercy in the message: care for our common home (6).

In 2020 the pope began his message by stating that he was joining "the ecumenical family" who chose "Jubilee for the Earth" as the theme.[50] He then wrote of "remembrance" because our ultimate destiny "is to enter into God's eternal sabbath." It is a "time to return" in repentance over "the broken bonds with the Creator, our fellow human beings and the rest of creation." It is also "a time to rest" in accord with God's wisdom so that the land and its inhabitants could rest and be renewed." He addressed that ours is a "time to restore the harmony of creation and to heal strained human relationships." His concluding section concerned "a time to rejoice" because "a Jubilee was a joyous occasion," even as he reminds us that we need to be more responsive to the needs "of the poor" whose share of the world's resources is diminishing.

Pope Francis invited the bishops and other representatives from the Amazon region to the Vatican in October 2019 for a synod concerning that whole region. Environment and ecology were centrally important parts of their discussions and deliberations because of the diminishing resources in creation (including animals, the fruits of the earth, and the earth itself) while at the same time a host of other issues germane to this area were also discussed. The final document from the pope after a synod is called an "apostolic exhortation." It is from the pen of the pope based on the consultative documents preceding the synod, the immediate "work instrument" that almost always guided the deliberations[51] and the summary of the synod's work called the "Final Propositions."[52] The style of apostolic exhortations is usually straightforward theological summaries and papal additions to what occurred and concomitant suggestions for action.

In the case of *Querida Amazonia*, Pope Francis chose a different style, more akin to reflections and inspirations.[53] He says as much at the end of the introductory paragraphs (7):

> I dream of an Amazon region that fights for the rights of the poor, the original peoples and the least of our brothers and sisters, where their voices can be heard and their dignity advanced.
>
> I dream of an Amazon region that can preserve its distinctive cultural riches, where the beauty of our humanity shines forth in so many varied ways.
>
> I dream of an Amazon region that can jealously preserve its overwhelming natural beauty and the superabundant life teeming in its rivers and forests.
>
> I dream of Christian communities capable of generous commitment, incarnate in the Amazon region, and giving the Church new faces with Amazonian features.

At the same time, the pope is relentless when offering hard-hitting critiques of the ways that multinational corporations have raped this land, stolen recourses for their own profit, and abandoned the land raped and desolated. For example, at the beginning of the chapter, "An Ecological Dream," he says (42),

> The harm done to nature affects those peoples in a very direct and verifiable way, since, in their words, "we are water, air, earth and life of the environment created by God. For this reason, we demand an end to the mistreatment and destruction of Mother Earth. The land has blood, and it is bleeding; the multinationals have cut the veins of our mother Earth."[54]

A close reading of this chapter, 41–60, gives a rich summary and amplification on the combination of concern for the environment (especially water), continuing evangelization and respect for all the cultures in this land.

One of the key concepts that Pope Francis has brought back into the Catholic Church's theological vocabulary and experience is synodality. This term has its origins in the early church, where meetings of bishops were held in regions on any number of topics. The Second Vatican Council made the synod a staple in the church's life. Since 1971, these have been held regularly on a variety of topics. Clearly, Pope Francis wants to strengthen and deepen the church's experience of leadership, which includes local conferences of bishops.

On October 3, 2020, Pope Francis issued his second "social encyclical" addressed to all people of good will: *Fratelli Tutti*, on fraternity and social friendship.[55] Many commentators have asserted (rightly in my opinion) that this is a parallel to *Laudato Si'* on environment and creation and deals with its logical complement, the international human family in an increasingly nationalized and privatized world. At the end it contains "A Prayer to the Creator," which can be understood to be a fitting conclusion to both documents.

A PRAYER TO THE CREATOR

Lord, Father of our human family,
you created all human beings equal in dignity:
pour forth into our hearts a fraternal spirit

and inspire in us a dream of renewed encounter,
dialogue, justice and peace.
Move us to create healthier societies
and a more dignified world,
a world without hunger, poverty, violence and war.

May our hearts be open
to all the peoples and nations of the earth.
May we recognize the goodness and beauty
that you have sown in each of us,
and thus forge bonds of unity, common projects,
and shared dreams. Amen.

That issues of ecology and the environment have been in on the minds of authoritative church teachers and in authoritative church teachings is clear. This chapter has served as the third of the triad that fills out the ecclesial context for what follows in the balance of the book. Next, chapter 2 argues a method to be used for raising the inherent cosmic context and contents of the celebration of liturgy and sacraments and applies that method to baptism, Eucharist, and Hours. Chapter 3 concerns contemporary applications of the theology developed in chapter 2.

CHAPTER FOUR

METHOD

Much of my writing on liturgy and sacraments has concerned issues of method.[1] I acknowledge with deep gratitude my mentors at Sant'Anselmo (Rome): Burkhard Neunheuser, Salvatore Marsili, Cipriano Vagaggini, Gerhard Bekes, Magnus Lohrer, Adrien Nocent, and Basil Studer. They were steeped in liturgical and other theological sources and repeatedly invited my colleagues and me to think through issues of method at a time when determining a method for the study of liturgy was very much in flux in the post–Vatican II church.[2] In addition, when I was a doctoral student at Sant'Anselmo in the mid-1970s, several of the professors had contributed to the preparation and the drafting of Vatican II's Constitution *Sacrosanctum Concilium* on the Sacred Liturgy,[3] as well as the drafting of the revised rites.[4] My own doctoral dissertation concerned Roman Catholic–American Lutheran dialogue on the Eucharist, and in it I offered a proposal for ongoing dialogue based on the principle *lex orandi, lex credendi*.[5] I willingly admit now that this work was tied to the "texts" of the liturgies of both churches. In the intervening years, I have come to appreciate the intrinsic and inherent relationship between "texts" and "rites," which relationship will be a major part of the method issues presented here in this chapter and then applied in the subsequent chapters on baptism, Eucharist, and Hours.

This is to say that the texts and rites of the liturgy all reflect, sustain, and convey *theological meanings* and by extension implications for living the Christian life (e.g., moral and spiritual implications).[6] In addition, I will argue that more often than not the liturgy contains and sustains many meanings because the liturgy's texts and rites are inherently multivalent; that is, they contain a number of meanings.[7] While what follows comes from the Roman Catholic liturgy, it is meant to be a contribution to the ongoing ecumenical project of developing a proper method for liturgical studies in general and for liturgical theology very broadly conceived. The instructions from *Sacrosanctum Concilium* 16 deserve ecumenical attention: liturgy "is to be taught under its theological, historical, spiritual, pastoral, and juridical aspects." This will be presumed and expanded upon here.

What follows is intended to be a focused elaboration and expansion on my own work of relating "texts and contexts" in delineating a method for liturgical theology.[8] As suggested in the book's title, I intend to show the inherent relationship among ecology, liturgy, and sacraments beginning with laying out our central argument about method here. I intend to utilize a method that is both *comparative* and *contextual*. It will also engage what I will call *an ecological hermeneutic* to appreciate the inherent cosmic elements we raise up in worship,[9] namely the celebration of baptism, Eucharist, and Hours.

The method used here is *comparative*[10] in that it compares texts and rites for baptism, Eucharist, and Hours between the present revised liturgy with its immediate predecessors, that is, the Roman Ritual of 1614, the Roman Missal of 1570, and the Roman Breviary of 1568, and where necessary, any updates versions of these texts up through Vatican II. This approach to liturgical method is recent and builds on the years of dedicated research that was made possible by the publication of the number and variety of liturgical sources, especially in the past two centuries, which helped to guide and form the revisions in the liturgy of many Christian churches, the Roman Catholic included. In some of my writings I have used the phrase *the present reform of the liturgy*. I do this to reiterate that since the initial reform of the liturgy in Latin, several of the church's rites have had two or even three revisions, though they are admittedly few and largely do not change the structure of the rites. For example, the present English language Roman Missal is taken from the third amended edition of the *Missale Romanum.*

Hans Bernhard Meyer coined the important phrase "the critical function of liturgical theology."[11] The wealth of data available to us from largely historical sources can be used to interpret and even critique "the present reform of the liturgy." In addition to enabling us to assess the quality of the present reform of the liturgy, this critical function should be part of the process of inculturation of the liturgy. Admittedly and sadly, this has hardly begun, but it can be based on the best of liturgical scholarship that evaluates the strengths and weaknesses of the "present reformed liturgies." The kind of endorsement, not to say encouragement, that Pope Francis gives to inculturation for the liturgies of the Amazon region, for example, can be thus based on the best of liturgical scholarship.[12] Articles 37–40 of *Sacrosanctum Concilium* deserve to be reread and seen as more than an opening to the process of inculturation.[13] Much of what follows in this book is expository, based on the present reform of the Roman Rite. At the same time, on occasion I will indicate an avenue I judge worth looking as in the inculturation of the reformed liturgy.

The method is also *contextual* in that it raises up theological meanings that occur in rites surrounding the primal elements of earth, air, fire, and water, as well as manufactured symbols such as bread, wine, and oil. For example, the very fact that water is repeatedly raised up and revered in the liturgy shows reverence and respect for this "fellow creature" of our common home. In addition, the fact that water has been and is misused in our world today and is part of the ecological crisis that we face needs to be factored into any adequate liturgical-sacramental theology today.[14] The phrasing and terminology is important and deliberate. Verb forms like *we use* and nouns like *object* are deliberately avoided here in favor of the language of *Laudato Si'*.[15] That everything is interconnected and related and that all are "fellow creatures" is crucial to our argument emphasizing relatedness and relationship of all on this good earth. Therefore, we avoid any language that would objectify or reify fellow creatures.

The method is also contextual in that the various settings for liturgy raise up a variety of meanings because the "today" of the liturgy is not the same as yesterday or tomorrow. Similarly, a celebration in a monastery is not the same as in a mendicant setting, nor a cathedral the same as a parish church, a shrine as a hospital chapel, a diocesan convocation as a military outpost.

Finally, this method relies on *an ecological hermeneutic*, which is meant to express the combination of careful textual study with raising up theological meanings from the elements in worship independent of and yet also (obviously) related to the *lex orandi*, and in drawing them together to raise up ways of appreciating what the liturgy means by what it both says and does. This kind of hermeneutic also respects that the very engagement in liturgy and sacraments means that, by their very nature, many meanings can be and are expressed, not all of which can be articulated in texts. In my opinion, liturgical texts "tether the imagination" but do not determine how the liturgy is experienced and appreciated.[16] The parallel word *rites* will be emphasized so that their theological meanings can be drawn out in their intended variety. For example, water can give life, yet too much water can cause death.

In sum, this exercise is also meant to counter a certain "philoso-phization" reflected in some contemporary studies about liturgy. Using a phrase such as *the present Roman Rite* invites careful study of where the present texts and rites of the liturgy came from, to assess what the present rites say and do, and to look toward their further revision and inculturation. Liturgical studies is a relative newcomer to the theological scene. To align the method and results of the study of the liturgy too quickly or too tightly with systematics, for example, is as unwise as it is confounding for appreciating what the liturgy is and does when compared with other branches of theology.[17]

As we turn to examples of the way an "ecological hermeneutic" might function regarding the primal element of earth, air, fire and water, as well as manufactured symbols of bread and wine, we turn to the former and present Roman liturgy.[18] Among the issues that coalesce here are that all prayers contain a number of images and metaphors, that one prayer can never "say" all that might be said about what is occurring in the liturgy, and that interpreting liturgical texts always requires that the elements raised up in worship are always to be factored into and are part and parcel of the theological meanings they express the theological meaning of the rite.

METHOD, CLARIFICATIONS, AND THESES

The subtitle of my revised book *Context and Text* indicates that the book offers *A Method for Liturgical Theology*.[19] As I reflect on that book and on my recent writings about the liturgy, I would say that three themes are embedded in and suffuse those writings: history, theology, and sacramentality. I will emphasize the last theme—*sacramentality* under the broader category of *ecology*—because it is new to the customary uses of history and theology for the study of liturgy.

My *methodological* contribution here will be to offer six exemplary ways of researching the ecology of the liturgy. Among other things I intend to pay attention to the following in order to explore the intrinsic interrelationship of ecology, liturgy, and sacrament. The specifications of this method are baptism, Eucharist, and Hours.

1. We will explore the cosmic contexts for the liturgies under discussion to reveal what nature and the earth "say" about the liturgy we celebrate.

2. We will study representative parts of each of the revised rites of baptism, Eucharist, and Hours to uncover what these texts and rites say about the theology that is enacted when liturgy and sacraments occur. These always include aspects of a theology of creation, of the Trinity, of the paschal mystery, and of the church (among others).

3. We will distinguish between what I call "primal elements" (earth, air, fire, water) and the "elements manufactured" by "the work of human hands" (e.g., bread and wine for the Eucharist, "work of bees and your servants' hands" for the paschal candle). In studying each, we will emphasize how primal and manufactured elements reflect respect for our common home, for human nourishment, and for the proper distribution of primal and manufactured elements for the sake of all who share this "common home."

4. We will presume always to speak of the triad "ecology-liturgy-sacrament" as intrinsically interrelated and experienced together in the celebration of the sacred mysteries. I will adapt the term *perichoresis* referring to the three persons in God and use its more fundamental meaning of *a dance*. In the method offered here the interrelationship of ecology, liturgy, and sacrament is so intertwined that you cannot really appreciate one without the others.

5. As we seek for more ecologically attuned descriptions of what sacraments are and do, we will need always to recall that the texts and rites of the liturgy do not control or even necessarily dominate how those who make up the liturgical assembly experience them as intrinsically interconnected.

6. We also need to be respectful of the way what the liturgy enacts can never control how the act of sacramental liturgy is experienced. In that sense, the words and actions of sacramental liturgy are meant to be paradigmatic, but they cannot control the way sacramental liturgy can be experienced by communities of faith in this time and in this space. Our engagement in the elements of the liturgy "tether the imagination" where the liturgy is always experienced uniquely in a particular time and place, in communities that vary: monastic, mendicant, religious orders, parishes, campuses, hospitals, and the like. Familiarity with and reflection on the texts and rites of the liturgy can only enhance and deeper what we are meant to experience daily, weekly, and annually. Liturgical texts and rites are meant to be repeated. However, our engagement in them is always different.

Clarifications

Our Common Home

The first clarification concerns language and our use of language about our fellow creatures on this common home. From the very outset of *Laudato Si'* the pope engages in words of relationship, not words of objectification (1):

> "*Laudato Si'*, O mi' Signore"—"Praise be to you, my Lord."
> In the words of this beautiful canticle, Saint Francis of Assisi reminds us that our common home is like a sister with whom we share our life and a beautiful mother who opens her arms to embrace us. "Praise be to you, my Lord, through our Sister, Mother Earth, who sustains and governs us, and who produces various fruit with coloured flowers and herbs."

While some have criticized the female imagery here (and especially in 2), others counter that these pronouns reflect a deep Franciscan theology and spirituality of relatedness and relationship.[20] This paragraph exemplifies the ways in which Pope Francis always refers to "fellow creatures" on our "common home." He does not refer to others who inhabit this good earth as "things."

Further along in chapter 1 of *Laudato Si'*, Pope Francis offers a profound reflection on what he calls "the gospel of creation." In article 76, he summarizes the Catholic position[21] on creation and nature from a scriptural and theological perspective:

> In the Judeo-Christian tradition, the word "creation" has a broader meaning than "nature," for it has to do with God's loving plan in which every creature has its own value and significance. Nature is usually seen as a system which can be studied, understood and controlled, whereas creation can only be understood as a gift from the outstretched hand of the Father of all, and as a reality illuminated by the love which calls us together into universal communion.

This brief statement carries profound implications for the way Catholics view the world and how we are to revere all our fellow creatures.

Among the many and varied possible descriptions of "ecology" Pope Francis states (138),

> Ecology studies the relationship between living organisms and the environment in which they develop. This necessarily entails reflection and debate about the conditions required for the life and survival of society, and the honesty needed to question certain models of development, production and consumption. It cannot be emphasized enough how everything is interconnected. Time and space are not independent of one another, and not even atoms or subatomic particles can be considered in isolation. Just as the different aspects of the planet—physical, chemical and biological—are interrelated, so too living species are part of a network which we will never fully explore and understand.

The pope then describes both "environment" and "nature" (139):

> When we speak of the "environment," what we really mean is a relationship existing between nature and the society which lives in it. Nature cannot be regarded as something separate

from ourselves or as a mere setting in which we live. We are part of nature, included in it and thus in constant interaction with it. Recognizing the reasons why a given area is polluted requires a study of the workings of society, its economy, its behaviour patterns, and the ways it grasps reality.

The pope continues with what he calls "environmental," "economic," "social," and "cultural" ecology and "the ecology of daily life," ideas that support my method and its applications. In line with these, I add my own phrase *the ecology of the liturgy* (explained below).

Sign

Part of what I am concerned with here would have been captured by the notion of sacraments as sacred *signs*, employed as far back as St. Augustine and adopted by St. Thomas Aquinas and many others. In effect, God offers us these signs as ways to mediate the divine life to us. Sacraments are the premier "sign language of the church."

Notably, the revised Order of Mass contains a comparatively lengthy instruction on the "signs" for the Eucharist.

> 321. The meaning of the sign demands that the material for the Eucharistic celebration truly have the appearance of food. It is therefore expedient that the Eucharistic bread, even though unleavened and baked in the traditional shape, be made in such a way that the priest at Mass with a congregation is able in practice to break it into parts for distribution to at least some of the faithful. Small hosts are, however, in no way ruled out when the number of those receiving Holy Communion or other pastoral needs require it. The action of the fraction or breaking of bread, which gave its name to the Eucharist in apostolic times, will bring out more clearly the force and importance of the sign of unity of all in the one bread, and of the sign of charity by the fact that the one bread is distributed among the brothers and sisters.

This assertion puts to rest any thought and practice that there is "a priest's host" for himself and other hosts for everyone else. Another major "sign" in action at the Eucharist is the act that we all receive communion at the Eucharist that is being celebrated. The General Instruction of the Roman Missal (GIRM) states (13),

> Above all, the Second Vatican Council, which urged "that more perfect form of participation in the Mass by which the faithful, after the priest's Communion, receive the Lord's Body from the same Sacrifice," called for another desire of the Fathers of Trent to be realized, namely that for the sake of a fuller participation in the holy Eucharist "the faithful present at each Mass should communicate not only by spiritual desire but also by sacramental reception of the Eucharist."

This is specified in the GIRM when describing the Communion Rite (85):

> It is most desirable that the faithful, just as the priest himself is bound to do, receive the Lord's Body from hosts consecrated at the same Mass and that, in the instances when it is permitted, they partake of the chalice (cf. no. 283), so that even by means of the signs Communion will stand out more clearly as a participation in the sacrifice actually being celebrated.

Signs still matter a great deal, even though in customary English usage *sign* normally points to one thing rather than to a number of possible meanings to which liturgical signs refer. This led to the rediscovery of the importance of symbols and "symbolic language" when trying to describe liturgy and sacraments. One of the meanings of symbol for the patristic authors was "that which brings us together" in the reality of God (from the Greek verb *symballein*, meaning "to join together"). However, words evolve and their meanings change. Today, when we use the word *symbol* it has the meaning of "less than fully real," if not devoid of meaning. Liturgy and sacraments are the direct opposite!

If the word *symbol* cannot be used today to reflect the fullness of what the term meant in history, then we need to find other terms and words. I have chosen *ecology* based on my own research over the past twenty years into how Catholics understand and regard creation, the fruits of this "good earth," all who dwell on the land and the work of human hands. Again, I take my lead here from Pope Francis's encyclical *Laudato Si'* (235–36):

235. The Sacraments are a privileged way in which nature is taken up by God to become a means of mediating supernatural life. Through our worship of God, we are invited to embrace the world on a different plane. Water, oil, fire and colours are taken up in all their symbolic power and incorporated in our act of praise. The hand that blesses is an instrument of God's love and a reflection of the closeness of Jesus Christ, who came to accompany us on the journey of life. Water poured over the body of a child in Baptism is a sign of new life. Encountering God does not mean fleeing from this world or turning our back on nature. This is especially clear in the spirituality of the Christian East. "Beauty, which in the East is one of the best loved names expressing the divine harmony and the model of humanity transfigured, appears everywhere: in the shape of a church, in the sounds, in the colours, in the lights, in the scents." For Christians, all the creatures of the material universe find their true meaning in the incarnate Word, for the Son of God has incorporated in his person part of the material world, planting in it a seed of definitive transformation. "Christianity does not reject matter. Rather, bodiliness is considered in all its value in the liturgical act, whereby the human body is disclosed in its inner nature as a temple of the Holy Spirit and is united with the Lord Jesus, who himself took a body for the world's salvation."

236. It is in the Eucharist that all that has been created finds its greatest exaltation. Grace, which tends to manifest itself tangibly, found unsurpassable expression when God himself became man and gave himself as food for his creatures. The Lord, in the culmination of the mystery of the Incarnation, chose to reach our intimate depths through a fragment of matter. He comes not from above, but from within, he comes that we might find him in this world of ours. In the Eucharist, fullness is already achieved; it is the living centre of the universe, the overflowing core of love and of inexhaustible life. Joined to the incarnate Son, present in the Eucharist, the whole cosmos gives thanks to God. Indeed the Eucharist is itself an act of cosmic love: "Yes, cosmic! Because even when it is celebrated on the humble altar of

a country church, the Eucharist is always in some way celebrated on the altar of the world" (citing John Paul *Ecclesia
de Eucharistia* n. 8). The Eucharist joins heaven and earth; it
embraces and penetrates all creation. The world which came
forth from God's hands returns to him in blessed and undivided adoration: in the bread of the Eucharist, "creation is
projected towards divinization, towards the holy wedding
feast, towards unification with the Creator himself." Thus,
the Eucharist is also a source of light and motivation for our
concerns for the environment, directing us to be stewards of
all creation.

Care for the earth is essential if the world's resources are to be protected
and the world itself is to survive. In *Laudato Si'*, Pope Francis speaks
about our responsibility to "till and keep the earth" (66). We have every
right to reap the earth; we have no right to rape the earth.

Among the foundational principles for Catholic theology and a
Catholic worldview is the wider notion of *sacramentality*, which I argue is
to be understood here as a specification of *ecology*, as well as incarnation.

Another important example is Pope Francis himself in *Laudato
Si'*. One major contribution he makes—perhaps *the* major contribution he makes—is articulating the need for an "integral ecology," found
throughout the document and specifically addressed in chapter 4.[22]
Pope Francis moves beyond the phrase *human ecology* minted by John
Paul II. My inference here is that any discussion of ecology in light of
papal teaching is of diminished value unless it includes a treatment of
"integral ecology." Key phrases from the encyclical include "everything
is connected" (16), "all creatures are connected" (42) and variations on
this theme resonate with a theology of sacraments that combines attention to both ecology and liturgy.[23]

Sacrament

Pope Francis refers to "sacrament" in *Laudato Si'* (9) in a quotation
from the Greek Orthodox Patriarch Bartholomew about "the world as
a sacrament of communion." Quoting Bartholomew, Francis states (9),

As Christians, we are also called "to accept the world as a
sacrament of communion, as a way of sharing with God and

our neighbours on a global scale. It is our humble conviction that the divine and the human meet in the slightest detail in the seamless garment of God's creation, in the last speck of dust of our planet."[24]

Pope Francis's reference to this key insight from Orthodoxy at the very beginning of *Laudato Si'* reflects both his concern about the environment and his passion for ecumenical relations with the Orthodox.[25] With regard to reflection on sacraments, recourse to the Orthodox tradition offers rich insight and breadth from which Roman Catholics have learned and continue to learn. With regard to the method for our investigation, the use of "sacrament of communion" evidences that "sacrament" refers more than to seven sacraments. Our argument here is that sacraments are best understood as based on and evidence the foundational principle of sacramentality.

Sacramentality

Sacramentality is a worldview, a way of looking at life and living life fully on this good earth with each other and all creatures on the earth where even now we are immersed in God.[26] My study of and exposure to the initiatives of the Greek Patriarchate in this area was nothing less than mind changing and, literally, spiritually converting.[27] My interest in creation and sacramentality was fostered as early as 1993 at an interdisciplinary conference at Georgetown University and the subsequent publication of the book *Preserving the Creation: Environmental Theology and Ethics* (my own contribution is "The Sacramentality of Creation and the Role of Creation in Liturgy and Sacraments").[28] This interest is found in an initial way in the first edition of my book on method, *Context and Text* (1994) and as a substratum in the book's 2018 revision. I am guided here by Pope Francis's *Laudato Si'* and several of my recent publications.[29]

My own thought on the concept of sacramentality as it forms a basis for the theology of sacramental liturgy has evolved. The basis of Pope Francis's assertions in *Laudato Si'* about sacraments and the Eucharist is the principle of sacramentality in that God lives among us prior to, in a unique way within, and following upon the celebration of the liturgy (233–37). The function of sacramental liturgy is both to underscore how what we do in sacramental liturgy derives from the world and everyday life, as well as how we view daily life through the lens of the liturgy and bring to the world in which we live what we have experienced in the liturgy. From the perspective of sacramentality one can say that sacraments are less doors to the sacred than they are the experience of the sacred embedded and experienced in creation and all of human life. This experience is shaped in a unique and privileged way through the liturgical action of the sacraments in which we engage fellow creatures of "our common home."

"The Flesh Is the Instrument of Salvation"

As noted above, sacramentality is intimately related to incarnation. The rich phrase "the flesh is the instrument of salvation" from Tertullian (155–220) should be kept in mind throughout what follows so that all that the incarnation means is brought to bear on our articulating essential elements of creation in liturgy and sacrament.[30] This central Christian doctrine and reality is juxtaposed to any and every investigation into theologies of creation, especially the theologies of creation expressed through the liturgy. One of my concerns is the emphasis that has been placed on understanding what is going on in the liturgy, especially since the vernacular makes it more easily understood. At the same time, an allied concern is that the essential primalness of every act of liturgy can be severely mitigated, not to say lost. All sacramental liturgies involve our full humanity—body, mind, and heart.

The Liturgy Constitution (*Sacrosanctum Concilium*) speaks of Christ as "the Word made flesh" and states that "his humanity united with the person of the Word was the instrument of our salvation" (citing Tertullian, 5). Every act of liturgy is an act of "mediated immediacy."[31] This phrase is intended to mean that we experience God in the church's most privileged moments and manners through all that dwells in this world, through human beings and all who share our common home. One of the main values of the liturgy is that it invites us to a direct encounter and experience of God. It does so not by shunning the world, but by experiencing humanity and the elements of this earth as mediators of divine realities.[32]

Put differently, the liturgy presumes on and articulates the engagement of our bodies, including all our senses. The celebration of liturgy is meant to engage nonverbal as well as verbal messages, normally through actions and gestures. It is also true that gestures, movement, and song are intended to be a proper and essential part of the liturgy. The revised liturgical rites of the Catholic Church presume singing in the liturgy. The sense of smell is engaged especially when incense is used, as it is in the daily Maronite liturgy. These are simply examples of what can happen when we take seemingly innocent decisions that mitigate gesture, movement, and singing, possibly resulting in a one-dimensional teaching event with communion. There is precedent for various forms of the one Roman Mass celebrated as low with no music, high and solemn with music (to use the language of the Tridentine Missal). There are also distinctions to be made between, for example, monastic and cathedral structures of the Liturgy of the Hours. As another example, when little attention is paid to the gestures and postures of the assembly (as it was in the Tridentine Missal), liturgy is experienced as a set of texts spoken by the priest. Rather, Roman Catholic liturgy is meant to be fully incarnational, respecting and engaging the minds, hearts, and, yes, the bodies of *all* who participate in the celebration of the paschal mystery.

Liturgy respects and reverences our bodies and presumes the engagement of our own "flesh and blood." "The Word became flesh" results in the realities that he dwells among us still and we experience his glory in our very lives. These become premises for the act of worship. We do not (merely) think about God. We are drawn into a unique and privileged experience of the living God in the liturgy, which engages our senses in manifold ways. We engage the world and all who dwell on it, both persons and creatures, in words and actions that respect our humanity, our bodies, and our intelligence. It is through the engagement of our bodies that we experience the Triune God through Christ's paschal mystery made possible because of the incarnation. This same bodiliness should be borne in mind and in our actions when we celebrate all our liturgy. In the action of the Eucharist, bread and wine are transformed and become our spiritual food and drink. It is Christ, the true vine, who gives life to the branches (cf. John 15:1–6). As bread from heaven (cf. John 6:41), bread of angels, the chalice of salvation, and the medicine of immortality, the Eucharist is the promise of eternal life to all who eat and drink it (cf. John 6:50–51). The Eucharist is a sacred meal, "a sacrament of love, a sign of unity, a bond of charity," in which Christ calls us as his friends to share in the banquet of charity.

Ecology of the Liturgy

I turn now to a broader appreciation of the sacramental principle in order that it might reflect on an underlying principle for all liturgy, which I call "an ecology of the liturgy." As I begin, I want to offer two additional thoughts derived from *Laudato Si'* that help us to be as precise and nuanced as possible when arguing the value of sacramentality and the ecology of the liturgy.

In classical terminology, all creatures on our common home are bearers of the living God and thus reflect the principle of sacramentality. As noted above, sacramentality is a worldview, a way of looking at life and living life fully on this good earth with each other and all creatures on the earth where even now we are immersed in God. It means that through each other and all fellow creatures on our common home, God is revealed and discovered. At the same time, God is not yet revealed fully and totally. Like any understanding of the word *sacrament*, what happens in human life, and more specifically in the celebration of sacramental liturgy, is still not the fulfillment of our (eternal) life with and in God. Both the principle of sacramentality and the ecology of liturgy always lead us beyond the here and now to when this world passes away and when we will see God face-to-face. In the meantime, the fact that we experience God here and now through each other and on this good earth is the principle of sacramentality writ large that grounds all liturgy and sacraments.

To celebrate liturgy and sacraments does not mean that we shun the world and our fellow creatures. Rather it means that we *raise up* our fellow creatures in our common home in worship; we do not "use them." In raising them up, we engage the world at a deep level of reality through which we experience nothing less than the living God. After *Laudato Si'*, we should no longer use verbs such as *use* to describe how we regard fellow creatures in the liturgy: earth, air, fire, water, bread, wine. Nor should we refer to fellow creatures as "things." Rather we should use phrases such as *raise up*, *acknowledge*, and *reverence*, and *elements from our common home* (light, water, fire, oil, bread, wine, etc.). This terminology matters a great deal as it signals a major shift away from objectification and utilitarianism to profound respect and respectful engagement.

What follows in this book is a focused application of my major methodological mantra: *lex orandi, lex credendi, lex vivendi*.[33] The rites and prayers that I have researched here concern baptism, Eucharist, and Hours. In baptism we engage the primal element of water. In the Eucharist we engage both primal elements (earth and water) and "the work of human hands" (manufactured bread and wine, which are important combinations of primal elements and human productivity). The Liturgy of the Hours, by its nature as liturgical prayer throughout the day, relies on sun, moon, light, and darkness. For each example, I build on the *Sacrosanctum Concilium*'s phrase through rites and prayers. I do this to call attention to the theological meaning of the rites themselves (not simply rubrics as directions). Doing so also offers a counter to what I perceive to be the intense scrutiny we have given to liturgical texts since the reform, especially concerning vernacular translations.

Paradoxes/Opposites Held in Tension

Paradox

Our engagement with fellow creatures is always a paradox. Each of the primal elements I will describe contains, by nature, both rich positive characteristics and dangerous capabilities. We should not be overly optimistic or naïve when we reflect on these elements.

So many of the central tenets of our faith are paradoxes. The totally Other, almighty, and ever-living God became incarnate to restore us to a right relationship with him and the world. The fathers put it this way: God became human so that humans can become God. Why else do we bow during the Creed (or kneel on the solemnity of the assumption and of Christmas) at the words "and by the Holy Spirit was incarnate of the Virgin Mary and became man." How this happened is equally a paradox because Mary remained a virgin and gave birth to God's only Son. Virginity and giving birth do not usually belong in the same sentence. That is another paradox having to do with the incarnation.

The central "mystery of faith" is, of course, the paschal mystery: the betrayal, humiliation, suffering, death, resurrection, and ascension of Christ to the Father's right hand in glory. Once again, the notion of paradox looms large. We believe that what is apparently a complete defeat for the human Jesus becomes a victory for him and for our salvation. This can only be so because this is the paradox of our faith. What an astounding event in human history that continues among us here and now through the liturgy! Most explicitly this is to see the paradoxes of human life as ordered by the paradox of the Christian faith, where death give way to the only life worth living.

My application of paradox to primal elements as raised up in and through the liturgy is to argue that all of these elements carry both positive and negative meanings. Purely on the level of our human experience,

- We need the earth to plant and reap food so that we can eat to survive. The earth can "quake" and cause untold destruction.
- We thrive on sunny days with a gentle breeze. We fear and flee winds that damage and destroy. We await the birth of a child and are desperate to see that s/he takes a first breath.
- We welcome the warmth of a fire. We fear fires that are out of control and destroy.
- We relish a glass of pure, cool water to slake our thirst. Water also swells and floods simply crush and kill. The process of human birth involves life or death situations with water. Part of the world's landscape is comprised of approximately seventy percent water. From sea voyages across oceans for centuries, many successful but some not, to recreational boating on lakes and rivers, enjoyment turns to tragedy when people drown.

On the human, physical, scientific levels, these primal elements are not at all neutral. In fact, they represent extreme opposites—life and death—and more often than not we humans have to be prepared to both enjoy, and even relish them as well as be prepared to suffer and perhaps even die at their paradoxical characteristics.

Opposites

Engaging in the paradoxical elements of liturgy has us make deep, abiding, and penetrating expressions of our faith in the paschal mystery. The liturgy also invites, even requires, that when we celebrate the paradox, we deepen our conversion to living life according to this mystery. Suffering leads to healing, death leads to real life, humiliation leads to true victory in Christ, estrangement leads to reconciliation. This is to say that the positive and (eternal) life-giving effects of engaging these primal elements require that we face into the dark places in our lives where we hide from real conversion and engage in external rites only that do not impact us fully and deeply.

Our engaging in the primal elements in liturgy and sacraments makes the statement that we need the liturgy as a day in day out, week in week out, year in year out encouragement. We need these rituals to deepen our conversion and to admit the still unfinished business that our faith always is. On a deeper level, if we engage only in external rituals, the worship of the divine is a farce.[34]

At the same time, more often than not there is a fight between idealized expressions of these elements and the way we experience them in diminished ways because the elements are marred, have been overused, or the working conditions for manufacturing elements from human work warn us to leave aside any notions of a naïve optimism about the beauty of the earth or a presumed willing cooperation between workers and employees and owners. In that sense, we are like the colleagues of the Ecumenical Patriarch Bartholomew, whose meetings on the environment were most often held on ships in rivers, bringing to the forefront that the pollution of seas is a central "right to life" issue. It should be among the right to life issues of all faiths

PRIMAL ELEMENTS—EARTH, AIR, FIRE, WATER

What follows is an overview that is meant to indicate the range of issues involved in engaging especially primal elements in the liturgy and in all of life with richness and possibility as well as depletion and danger.

Earth

One of the most concise summaries for what *Laudato Si'* teaches is that we have to realize that a true ecological approach *always* becomes a social approach; it must integrate questions of justice in debates on the environment to hear *both the cry of the earth and the cry of the poor* (see 49).[35]

Ancient philosophers were not shy about reiterating that the earth was the first "primal element." It is to be respected and even revered. In biblical revelation one specific way of showing reverence for the earth is to let it lie fallow at regular intervals. The principle is to engage and respect the land. It is not to use and overuse the earth for our material gains.

However, we need to be realistic and honest in asserting that the earth has been pilloried and destroyed excessively for selfish purposes. The appeals of recent Catholic popes and Orthodox patriarchs, among others, reiterate the sin we humans have committed against the land. The immoral actions of multinational corporations in destroying land that is not their own needs to be recalled. Yes, God created all as "good." The world, "our common home," continues to be good. But is has been marred, destroyed, and polluted in scandalous ways by fellow brothers and sisters on this good earth. We have every right to "keep and till" the land (*Laudato Si'* 66, etc.). We have no right to rape the earth.

Closely allied with this in Catholic moral teaching is the issue of who "owns" the land. Recent religious leaders have emphasized that we have a "relative right to private property." The parallel teaching is the "universal destination of goods." While we may judge that "private property is personal to me" and "what is mine is mine only," Catholic moral teaching, not to mention an ecological approach to the liturgy, reminds us that all of creation is for "us" and for "the common good."

The inherent counterculturalism of biblical religion, specifically the gospel, is also expressed in and through the texts and rites of the liturgy into which we are drawn by God's gracious invitation. Selfishness, self-importance, and possessiveness have no place in the Judeo-Christian tradition. Among other things, the liturgy awakens and reminds us of the goodness of the earth and our responsibility for the earth hour to hour, day to day, season to season, year to year. Viewing the liturgy and experiencing the liturgy with an earth consciousness is inherent in what it is we celebrate through this good earth.

Air

Air and water are essential elements for life. It is as simple and as complex as that. People who suffer with congenital lung diseases literally gasp for air and rely on oxygen tanks. During the coronavirus pandemic, all of us had to wear masks so that we did not transmit or contract the disease through the air. During the pandemic, the number in hospitals who needed oxygen was simply astronomical. For some, even the oxygen did not help them pull through. The incidence of the second spike in coronavirus cases in India was notable for the numbers who were sick but more specifically by the lack of oxygen for their healing.

Some of the central issues that Pope Francis takes up in *Laudato Si'* is "the throwaway culture" (20ff) and his concerns about the fact of and causes of pollution. One particularly important text consolidates much of the assessment the pope puts forth about pollution:

51. Inequity affects not only individuals but entire countries; it compels us to consider an ethics of international relations. A true "ecological debt" exists, particularly between the global north and south, connected to commercial imbalances with effects on the environment, and the disproportionate use of natural resources by certain countries over long periods of time. The export of raw materials to satisfy markets in the industrialized north has caused harm locally, as for example in mercury pollution in gold mining or sulphur dioxide pollution in copper mining. There is a pressing need to calculate the use of environmental space throughout the world for depositing gas residues which have been accumulating for two centuries and have created a situation which currently affects all the countries of the world. The warming caused by huge consumption on the part of some rich countries has repercussions on the poorest areas of the world, especially Africa, where a rise in temperature, together with drought, has proved devastating for farming. There is also the damage caused by the export of solid waste and toxic liquids to developing countries, and by the pollution produced by companies which operate in less developed countries in ways they could never do at home, in the countries in which they raise their capital: "We note that often the businesses which operate this way are multinationals. They do here what they would never do in developed countries or the so-called first world. Generally, after ceasing their activity and withdrawing, they leave behind great human and environmental liabilities such as unemployment, abandoned towns, the depletion of natural reserves, deforestation, the impoverishment of agriculture and local stock breeding, open pits, riven hills, polluted rivers and a handful of social works which are no longer sustainable."[36]

One of my own experiences of severe pollution was when I visited the city of Bangkok, Thailand. I remember vividly how all the police wore white masks when on duty. The city's suffocating traffic and agricultural burning are among the causes of this situation. The beauty of the city and its network of the Chao Phrya River and canals is sadly diminished by the overwhelming pollution.

Paradoxically, it was during the utterly devastating coronavirus pandemic that the "blue Danube" became less gray and more blue; the Grand Canal in Venice became noticeably less polluted because of the absence of cruise ships; parts of the atmosphere became noticeably less polluted and toxic; the limitation of air travel enabled the air to be less toxic and polluted. While obviously we cannot "see" the air, sadly, we do see it when it is polluted.

Fire

The world and every being on it are imperceptible and unknowable without light. God created it first so that all the rest of creation could be appreciated and loved. For us who regularly (and usually unthinkingly) "turn on" lights, we deal with darkness regularly by casting it out by the flip of a switch. Not so before the invention of electricity. The "telling of time" had been so determined by the movement of the earth around the sun that the monastic witness the *Rule of St. Benedict* devotes chapters 8 to 19 to the distribution of the Psalms and the structure of the Office according to the rhythm of light and darkness.[37] Many of us go camping outdoors where we refine our skills at setting up the site and cooking meals over fire. This was simply the way it was for hunters and food gatherers. The fire that was needed for cooking was also needed for heating and sufficient warmth to live. Sitting by a fire at a campsite, in one's yard, or even in one's living room can be relaxing and a center for gathering and conversation. But minding the fire is crucial lest the light and heat get out of control and literally consume us.

Like the other primal elements, an unmanaged fire or too much fire causes damage, as well as the loss of human, plant, and animal life. Part of the destructive process is the result of smoke inhalation and smoke pollution of the atmosphere. Paradoxically when farmers start a fire on their land to clear it for a new planting season, those same fires can cause pollution (as in Bangkok). The regular damage from fires in places like California and Australia in recent years reflect an imbalance in the atmosphere, much of which is caused by climate change. Human behaviors can both cause and assist in the proper use of fire both for good and for destruction.

Water

As noted above, the only two elements without which we cannot live are air and water. The centrality of water in human life and the fact that we cannot live without it is the reason we engage water in baptism. The element needed for human life is the element needed to welcome us into eternal life at baptism. Patristic authors regularly call the baptismal font that gives life and a tomb in which we are buried in Christ and rise to new life.

Obviously, this life and death element needs to be protected and preserved as a "right to life" issue. The issue of who "controls" or "owns" water has consumed politicians as much as it controls human life itself. Commonly, the phrase in the Middle East is "water is the new oil." Among the most crucial issues between the Israelis and Palestinians is water. The expanding deserts of Africa attest to thousands of deaths by dehydration.

There is an enormous poignancy in *Laudato Si'* when Pope Francis contextualizes his comments on water (27–31) within chapter 1, which addresses pollution and climate change, loss of biodiversity, decline in the quality of human life, and the breakdown of society and global inequity. This is a typical of the pope, who often brings a global perspective and offers a challenge of enormous proportions to what we may not see as such a crisis. At the end of chapter 1 of *Laudato Si'* Pope Francis wisely calls upon the teaching of Patriarch Bartholomew:

8. Patriarch Bartholomew has spoken in particular of the need for each of us to repent of the ways we have harmed the planet, for "inasmuch as we all generate small ecological damage," we are called to acknowledge "our contribution, smaller or greater, to the disfigurement and destruction of creation." He has repeatedly stated this firmly and persuasively, challenging us to acknowledge our sins against creation: "For human beings…to destroy the biological diversity of God's creation; for human beings to degrade the integrity of the earth by causing changes in its climate, by stripping

67

the earth of its natural forests or destroying its wetlands; for human beings to contaminate the earth' s waters, its land, its air, and its life—these are sins." For "to commit a crime against the natural world is a sin against ourselves and a sin against God."

Is it any wonder that Pope Francis will subsequently leave us to wrestle what "ecological sin" looks like?

CHAPTER FIVE

BAPTISM

Here and in the next two chapters we will draw many ideas and intuitions for understanding the liturgy of sacraments and the Hours from the normative and normally used liturgies of the Roman Rite.[1] Our method presumes that these revised rites disclose many and multifaceted meanings from the elements of our common home and the work of human hands that we raise up in the liturgy, as well as the prayers and texts of the liturgy.

In addition, in light of the phrase "disciplinary complexity" for the study of sacraments, I will contextualize baptism and Eucharist within their celebration during the Paschal Triduum. The Triduum is called "the high point of the entire liturgical year" (*General Norms for the Liturgical Year* 18). It is the most sacred time when the church assembles for worship and so deserves pride of place. From our perspective the Triduum offers us what we might call *the paradigm for all liturgy*.[2]

For baptism in this chapter, we will engage the liturgy of the Easter Vigil as the premier source for our arguments about an ecologically inspired liturgical theology. It is a "premier source" because the Triduum contains the maximal ritual and symbolic expression of the realities of Christ's paschal mystery as this has, in the words of Leo the Great, "passed over into the sacraments." Where appropriate, the *Order for the Christian Initiation for Adults* and *Order of Baptism of Children*[3] will be cited and explored to draw out the deep and inherent ecological elements that contribute to a theology of baptism.

At the same time, lest this approach regarded as a liturgical fundamentalism—engaging *only* the liturgy for a theology of sacrament[4]—sacramental theology may be understood to be the systematic study of the sacraments based on reflection on the liturgical celebration of these rites throughout history and on the insights of theologians and other teachers in light of the magisterium. At given historical periods, certain theological points came to be emphasized, sometimes for polemical reasons. At other times, assertions of the magisterium clarified issues of conflict.[5] One purpose here is to restore cosmic elements of the theology of baptism and the Eucharist to the theological understandings of these sacraments. Doing so in light of the Triduum allows us to ruminate on baptism in its liturgical fullness. In effect, this means that we theologize from the fullest liturgical experience and expression of baptism as possible (rather than, e.g., an emergency baptism in danger of death).[6]

COSMIC PRACTICES AND ELEMENTS OF BAPTISM[7]

The heading's phrase *practices and elements* highlights from the outset that liturgy engages us precisely as human beings. Through the liturgy we engage in the cosmos at a deep level. We do not objectify the elements of our common home. At the Paschal Vigil we engage and are engaged by the primal elements of earth, air, fire, and water.[8] These elements are essential to appreciate the presumed but often neglected "ecological hermeneutic" of baptism in the Roman liturgy.[9] The present Paschal Vigil is the most "primal" of the revised liturgies of the Roman Rite. Because it expresses the Roman Rite in its ritual and cosmic fullness, it is the paradigm for all liturgies, in particular baptism and the Eucharist. Other liturgical practices should be measured against and informed by the liturgy of the Paschal Vigil.

The community is gathered "outside of the church," which is a reference to the custom of gathering in one place and processing (in)to the church. (A contemporary and very traditional example is when monks gather in the place called the *statio* and then process together into the choir for the particular Hour.) The gathering for the Easter Vigil occurs outdoors and on this night under the stars. The cosmic meaning is part of the first reading from Genesis 1:1—2:2, especially the light/darkness motif in its very first verses. In addition, the reading from Baruch 3:9–15, 32—4:4 refers to "the stars at their posts shine and rejoice; When he calls them, they answer: 'here we are shining for joy for their Maker.'"

There are important reminders of precedents for gathering outside the church, as well as processing from one place to another, such as on Palm Sunday of the Passion of the Lord. This is a reminder of the early medieval practice in Rome, especially during Lent, when the assembly would gather in one place and then process to another for the celebration of the liturgy. The prayer said before the procession and the prayer said once the assembly reaches the "station" church has been called the *ad collectam* prayer ("at the gathering"), or more fully *ad collectam populi* ("at the gathering of the people").[10] This connotes the physical assembling of persons to form a community for common worship beginning with the procession of everyone assembled, not simply clergy and ministers. The principle here is to see the theological import of actions in the present Roman liturgy that have rich meanings reflected and seen through the lens of the historical sources of the Roman liturgy. (The reference to inviting the priest here to "collect" prayer intentions silently before the collect prayer first occurs in Innocent III. Traditionally, the collect is about physical gathering, not a spiritualization to suit a pared-down liturgy.) *Ad collectam* prayed outdoors always presumes and carries with it the cosmic elements of earth and air.

The Vigil gathering occurs where "a blazing fire in prepared." This is a change from the pre–Vatican II Vigil, which required that the priest strike a flint to produce the fire: certainly a very primal experience, albeit a minimalist one. The accompanying prayer in that liturgy prayed, "Sanctify this new fire produced from a flint for our use."[11] The prayer for the blessing of fire in the revised liturgy states, "Sanctify this fire, we pray," without a reference to the flint. Several meanings can be adduced for the change including that the revised rite is drawn from the pre-Tridentine missals, whose roots go back to the pagan customs of engaging in rites and texts that signify the renewal of the cosmos in the spring. Among agrarian customs, this included cleansing fields and preparing them for seed time. The blazing fire means that a religious tradition believes in conquering the darkness of night with the hope of new light in the cosmos and new life on the earth. In addition to illumination, it also means "re-creation," as in the world being recreated through the liturgy.

The pagan festivals joined with Judaism's Passover festivals. The centrality of the rich liturgical meaning of engaging in a "memorial" (in Hebrew, *zikkaron*; in Greek, *anamnesis*) derives from such Judaic sources as the "Commentary" on the ceremonies of this night:

> In each and every generation a person is obligated to see himself as if he left Egypt (Exod 13:8). "For the sake of this, did the Lord do [this] for me in *my* going out of Egypt." Not only our ancestors did the Holy One, blessed be He, redeem, but rather also us [together] with them did he redeem, as is stated (Deut 6:23); "And he took us out from there, in order to bring us in, to give us the land which He swore unto our fathers."[12]

As our Easter Vigil begins outdoors, it orchestrates levels of meaning adopted and adapted from pagan and Jewish practices. The lighting of the paschal candle in the darkness of night dramatically sheds light as the priest or deacon enters a darkened church carrying the candle to sing, "Light of Christ." As he does, he articulates in this brief acclamation all that our forefathers and foremothers in both paganism and Judaism brought to bear on this same spring nighttime communal prayer.

The act of the assembly engaging their bodies in the procession from the fire to inside the church is but one example of the way that processions are an important part of the Vigil. Other processions include those engaged in by the elect and their godparents to and from the baptismal font. The bodiliness of liturgy could not be more fully expressed than at this Vigil.[13] With regard to baptism, it is notable that the Roman Missal states, "It is desirable that the bread and wine be brought forward by the newly baptized, or if they are children, by their parents or godparents." What are these gifts of "bread and wine" but the "work of human hands"? Another procession, particularly poignant for the newly initiated, is for communion.

The other part of the pagan and Jewish rites of spring concern the proclamation of stories about creation and the annual recreation of the earth. These texts are called "cosmogonic myths" of the renewal of creation in the spring.[14] Much of the commentary on such myths can be traced to now classic insights from Mircea Eliade.[15] These myths were proclaimed annually so that what they describe happens once more. These myths are not historical narratives describing any kind of historical telling of time. Rather they are like tales that begin "once upon a time" and contain a narrative about perennial truths about the cosmos. While these ceremonies form major parts of the annual Easter Vigil, they should be kept in mind as part of the essential cosmological context for the water baptism of adults and infants. The cosmic symbolism of darkness and light in paganism always contextualizes the way we acclaim Christ the Light. Also, it is by design that the first reading proclaimed at the Easter Vigil is the Judeo-Christian "cosmogonic myth" from Genesis 1:1—2:2 whose first words are "in the beginning." This is the Christian cosmic narrative; the Vigil is always cosmic, and baptism is equally cosmic.

In addition, Christianity adopted and adapted Jewish springtime Passover practices which take place after sunset. These include the foods of the Passover meal itself, one part of which is blessing fresh bread to signify passing over to a new year. This context helps illuminate the references to "yeast" in one option for the second reading of Easter Sunday (1 Cor. 5:6b–8):

> Brothers and sisters:
> Do you not know that a little yeast leavens all the dough?
> Clear out the old yeast,
>> so that you may become a fresh batch of dough,
>> inasmuch as you are unleavened.
> For our paschal lamb, Christ, has been sacrificed.
> Therefore, let us celebrate the feast,
>> not with the old yeast, the yeast of malice and wickedness,
>> but with the unleavened bread of sincerity and truth.

The new beginnings signified and accomplished in baptism are imaged here by referencing the new batch of dough. Out with the old, in with the new. Renounce Satan, affirm the Creed. Die with Christ, rise with Christ.

The singing of the Exsultet immediately follows the entrance procession of the entire assembly, once everyone is in place. It contains a kind of "Judeo-Christian cosmogonic myth" with references to creation, the call of Israel, Christ's cross overcoming Adam's sin, continual references to this candlelight scattering the darkness of night, and Christ overcoming the darkness of sin. Some of its more poignant references to creation are the following:

Be glad, let the earth be glad, as glory floods her...
Let all corners of the earth be glad...

Four poignant references to "this is the night" (*haec nox est*) follow, including:

This is the night
    that a pillar of fire banished the darkness of sin...
This the night
    of which it is written:
    the night shall be as bright as day,
    dazzling is the night for me,
    and full of gladness.

The Exsultet continues:

May this flame be found still burning
    by the Morning Star:
    the one morning star that never sets,
    Christ your Son...
It ends with a poignant cosmic reference:
May this flame be found still burning
by the Morning Star:
the one Morning Star who never sets,
Christ your Son,
who, coming back from death's domain,
has shed his peaceful light on humanity,
And lives and reigns for ever and ever.
    Amen.

Interestingly, two very significant references to bees are embedded within the Exsultet as evidence of the cosmic elements of candle making and candle burning:

On this, your night of grace, O holy Father,
accept this candle, a solemn offering,
the work of bees and of your servants' hands,
an evening sacrifice of praise
the gift from your most holy Church.

> ...a fire into many flames divided,
> yet never dimmed by sharing of its light,
> for it is fed by melting wax,
> drawn out by mother bees
> to build a torch so precious.

The reference to "melting wax drawn out by mother bees" is a reminder of the crafting of the candle from the work of bees, noted for their industry and hard work. Beeswax was used in ancient Persia to encase a dead body; it was used in ancient Rome for facemasks of the dead. Beeswax was and still is used for beauty products and fragrant soaps. The combination of "the work of bees and your servants' hands" evokes how, in addition to primal elements, the liturgy engages and reveres "the work of human hands." Consider, for example, baking bread and making wine for the Eucharist.[16]

These understandings should be brought to bear on our experience of every liturgy of baptism as celebrated according to the *Order of Christian Initiation of Adults* and *Order of Baptism of Children*. Each of these liturgies presumes this theology even though they do not reproduce what can be spoken and engaged in at the Vigil. For example, every time we celebrate the rite for the baptism of children, we should recall the movements of our bodies even as we celebrate the rite for infants in a series of processions. We begin at the church door (34), process into the assembly to listen to the word (42), process to the font for baptism (53), and then process to the altar (67), where we pray the Lord's Prayer with the following introduction (68):

> Dear brothers and sisters:
> these children, reborn through Baptism,
> are now called children of God, for so indeed they are.
> Through Confirmation they will receive the fullness of
>   the Holy Spirit
> and, approaching the altar and table of the Lord,
> they will share at the table of his Sacrifice,
> and will call upon God as Father in the midst of the Church.

This is to argue that the rite for the baptism of children should be celebrated as laid out in the ritual for several reasons, among which is the theology conveyed by movement and assigned places in the church, for these mimic the movement and actions of the Easter Vigil. Diminishing the bodily processions that have rich theological meanings also diminishes the experienced act of baptism.

Another example is that each time we celebrate baptism, we share the flame from the paschal candle to light individual candles for the newly baptized. The meanings argued above are conveyed simply through our sharing "the light of Christ" by holding a candle respecting "the work of bees and your servants' hands."

Again, liturgy is always a multilayered phenomenon and a multivalent reality. One of the values of liturgy as ritual is that the rites and texts come back again and again so that one's experience of a liturgy or sacrament on one occasion might well be different on another occasion despite the fact that the same texts and rites are used. As noted in the previous chapter, there is no such thing as a repeated liturgy, even though by their very nature the same texts and rites are used.

LITURGY OF THE WORD AT THE PASCHAL VIGIL

One major change from the celebration of sacraments before Vatican II to their celebration now is that every liturgy of a sacrament now contains a Liturgy of the Word (with exceptions for cases of emergency).

For the Paschal Vigil, nine readings are proposed: seven from the Old Testament and two from the New. The directions state, "The number of readings from the Old Testament may be reduced, always bearing in mind that the reading of the word of God is a fundamental element of the Easter Vigil." The stories of faith read this night recall the works of saving history in the Old Testament, their completion in the New and our appropriation of them precisely through hearing and receiving them in the liturgy. The dynamic of hearing the texts, responding in psalms, and praying collect prayers is meant to foster abiding gratitude and awareness of how salvation is effected among us, especially through Word and Sacrament, particularly baptism and Eucharist. The use of collect prayers (almost all of which date from the old Gelasian sacramentary) draws out the paradigmatic character of the readings and allows them to impact on us in new and different ways.

The spoken introduction to this part of the liturgy brings out the importance attached to the reading of these texts:

> Let us now listen with quiet hearts to the Word of God.
> Let us meditate on how God in times past saved his people
> and in these, the last days, has sent his Son as our Redeemer.
> sent his own Son to be our Redeemer.
> Let us pray that our God may complete this paschal work
> of salvation
> by the fullness of redemption.

Underlying this statement is an appreciation for the word of God as fundamentally anamnetic and sacramental—it accomplishes what it proclaims. God's active presence in creation and salvation history, as recorded and recounted in the scriptures, is presently active and effective in the community that hears the word in faith. This Liturgy of the Word is another occasion when the words of the classic invitatory psalm at the Hours, Psalm 95, take on deeper meaning and offer us a significant challenge:

> Today, listen to the voice of the Lord:
> Do not grow stubborn, as your fathers did
> in the wilderness,
> when at Meribah and Massah
> they challenged me and provoked me,
> Although they had seen all of my works.

The first reading of the Easter Vigil, Genesis 1:1—2:2, is about the creation of the world. It fits into the annual recreation of the world associated with spring festivals found in the rites of many primitive religions. This premise was taken over by Israel, whose annual commemoration of becoming a people chosen by God coincided with the spring renewal of the earth. This first reading places our Christian celebration within the same framework. We recall origins and beginnings; in recounting them, we are remade and renewed. The evocative and sacramental power of the word is at work. In listening to God putting chaos into order, we ourselves are remade and refashioned as his creatures, as were Adam and Eve. Similarly, we are reminded of the stewardship required of us as we live from and on this good earth.

The darkness and light motif appears clearly at the beginning of the text, along with the subtle but important notion that "days" begin with the evening: "thus evening came, and morning followed: the first day" (Gen 1:3). This way of counting time and marking the passage of a day continues in Jewish and Christian liturgy. The celebration of Evening Prayer I of solemnities on the evening before the solemnity itself is based on this numbering. Hence, it is most appropriate that this reading about the days of creation should be the first proclaimed this evening, which is the beginning of the great day of rejoicing, the day of resurrection.

The motif of seven days is also significant liturgically. After describing the separation of light from darkness, the creation of plants, animals and then human persons, the reading ends by referring to the completion of creation on the seventh day: "Since on the seventh day God was finished with the work he had been doing, he rested on the seventh day from all the work he had undertaken" (Gen 2:2). Thus, the Sabbath rest was established. This notion of a Sabbath day of rest is changed in Christianity in favor of Sunday, the day of the Lord, the day of the perfecting of all creation since it was on this day that Christ rose from the dead to inaugurate the new creation. Our share in that absolutely new relationship with God through Christ is sustained and renewed weekly in the Eucharist. It is therefore most appropriate that at the Easter Vigil we begin this Great Sunday by recalling all that preceded it in terms of God's acts creation in the world and recreation in Jesus.

The use of Psalm 104 or Psalm 33 as responses to the first reading reflects well the creation motif so central to this reading. We now ask the all-powerful Spirit of God that created all things to renew and recreate us: "Lord, send out your Spirit, and renew the face of the earth" (Ps 104:30). It is also the mystery of God's divine action at work in the world that causes us to acclaim: "The earth is full of the goodness of the Lord" (Ps 33:5).

In the two prayers that follow, the goodness of creation is coupled with our being recreated by God and the gift of redemption:

Almighty ever-living God,
who are wonderful in the ordering of your works,
may those you have redeemed understand
that there exists nothing more marvelous
than the world's creation in the beginning

except that, at the end of the ages,
Christ our Passover has been sacrificed.

Such concluding prayers function as particularly important summaries of how a reading or some aspect of the life of Christ is operative here and now in the liturgical gathering and in the lives of those who celebrate. The prayers demonstrate how the main import of the reading concerns the continuing providence of God at work in our lives. The first prayer deals with creation in general and its fulfillment in Christ. The second deals specifically with the creation of humankind, but again looks to this fulfillment in the "still more wonderful work" of redemption.

The second reading, Genesis 22:1–18, deals with the sacrifice of Isaac. Already proclaimed in the Lenten liturgy on the second Sunday in the B cycle, this text is a favorite of patristic authors and liturgical commentators as a way of relating the attitude of Jesus as he went to death for us. Isaac's trust in his father Abraham is the model of Jesus's trust in his Father and of our trust in God. As Isaac obeyed and Jesus obeyed, so are we invited to obey our Father's will, even though this could mean separation from family and friends or even death Jesus. The Responsorial Psalm brings out this attitude of confidence and trust when it states:

O Lord, my allotted portion and cup,
   you it is who hold fast my lot. (Ps 16:5)
you will not abandon my soul to the nether world,
   nor will you suffer your faithful one to undergo corruption.
      (Ps 16:10)

Once again, the collect that follows helps to apply this text to our lives:

O God, supreme Father of the faithful,
who increase the children of your promise
by pouring out the grace of adoption
throughout the whole world
and who through the Paschal Mystery
make your servant Abraham father of nations,
as once you swore,
grant, we pray,
that your peoples may enter worthily
into the grace to which you call them.

The condition required here is acceptance of God's grace, the price we must pay is obedience to his will. The typology of Isaac and Jesus is completed when we ourselves become examples of those who have committed their lives to the Lord as our "portion and cup." (The phrase "death and resurrection of Christ" is from the Latin *paschale sacramentum*, which refers to the liturgical appropriation of the whole paschal mystery, especially this evening.)

The third reading is particularly significant because of its obvious liturgical reference to water, the key primal element we raise up at baptism, and to the act of freeing Israel from its bondage through water. This text, Exodus 14:15—15:1, is frequently used as an Old Testament ground and support for theological and spiritual expositions on Christian baptism. Hence, it is important as a key reading to direct us toward the baptismal emphasis of this liturgy.

The response is taken from the text in Exodus 15:1–6, 17–18 that follows. It is the song of Miriam used at morning prayer on Saturday of week one in the Psalter: "I will sing to the Lord, for he is gloriously triumphant; horse and rider he has cast into the sea" (Exod 15:1). Israel used this song to refer to the Lord's present action on their behalf as based on this significant intervention in their history. It is used in Christian worship to remind us that the same Lord who brought Israel through the Red Sea leads us through the waters of baptism to union with him. The baptismal reference inherent in the use of this reading on Easter is brought out in the prayers that follow (the second of which was assigned to the vigil of Pentecost in liturgical tradition):

> O God, who by the light of the New Testament
> have unlocked the meaning
> of wonders worked in former times,
> so that the Red Sea prefigures the sacred font
> and the nation delivered from slavery
> foreshadows the Christian people,
> grant, we pray, that all nations
> obtaining the privilege of Israel by merit of faith,
> may be reborn by partaking of your Spirit.

The fourth reading, Isaiah 54:5–14, applies even more directly to our situation as we celebrate the annual liturgy of Easter, for it recounts a later intervention by God for Israel, long after Israel's victory at the

Red Sea. In this section of Isaiah the Lord calls to his people and brings them back to him. The covenant is thus reestablished, never to be broken again. There is a clear parallel here between God's act of calling a people to himself in baptism and in the renewal of the covenant in our annual celebration of Easter. The psalm response is a poignant reminder of our individual and personal relationship with God and our trust in him: "I will praise you, Lord, for you have rescued me" (Ps 30:2). In a particularly moving verse, the Psalmist states, "At nightfall weeping enters in, but with the dawn rejoicing" (Ps 30:6). For our Christian celebration this could be a reference to the death of Jesus and his burial at night leading to our night celebration of his resurrection, which celebration itself leads to rejoicing in the brightness of Easter day. The relationship of Israel to the Christian church is emphasized in the collect that follows in which we ask that we may "see in the Church the fulfillment of your promise." This underscores God's initiative and sustaining grace as that which calls us more and more deeply into the divine life. In this context, "adoption" signifies God's unfailing call to us to the life of grace.

The fifth reading, Isaiah 55:1–11, speaks of the everlasting covenant we share with God and God's offer of salvation to all nations, through the mediating power of God's word. The efficacy of the word of God has caused this text to be stressed in reflections on the importance of the revealed word:

> It shall not return to me void,
> but shall do my will,
> achieving the end for which I sent it. (Isa 55:11)

For those who have pondered the word of God in Lent and who have celebrated the liturgies of Lent as enactments of this announcement of salvation, this text functions as a fitting reminder of the importance of this liturgy as the fulfillment and completion of Lent. Lent leads to Easter as the catechumenate leads to baptism, and both are accomplished at this night vigil of the resurrection.

The response to this text also comes from Isaiah (12:2–6) with the implicit reference to initiation: "You will draw water joyfully from the springs of salvation" (Isa 12:3). The continuity of the testaments Old and New and the place of the proclamation of the word in revealed religion is stressed in the collect:

who the preaching of your prophets
unveiled the mysteries of this present age,
graciously increase the longing of your people
for only at the prompting of your grace
do the faithful progress in any kind of virtue.

The sixth reading, Baruch 3:9–15, 32—4:4, proclaims the Lord as the fountain of wisdom and his revealed word as its clearest manifestation. In praise of the wisdom in the law of Moses the prophet proclaims, "Hear, O Israel, the commandments of life: listen and know prudence" (Bar 3:9). The central place of the word for Israel is thus reiterated, yet the history of Israel shows that fidelity was not always the response of those who heard this word. The God who addresses us through Baruch is the God of creation whom all are to obey. He is the Almighty One who has given life to Jacob and to Israel and to all his chosen ones. Hence, for us to hear the precepts of the Lord and to follow them in our lives is the way to salvation. It is this pattern which marked the catechumenate in its various stages, always relying on the proclamation of the word and acting upon it in life as the criteria and means for conversion.

The importance of the word is seen in the response to the psalm that follows this text: "Lord, you have the words of everlasting life" (John 6:69; a similar response is used with Ps 19 on the Third Sunday for Lent, B cycle). The psalm itself deals with the familiar terms of covenant religion: laws, decrees, and precepts of the Lord, all of which we understand only from the perspective of the graciousness of the Lord's invitation to his people. It is on this basis that the invited can respond in faith and deed. This same psalm is used on Monday of the first week of Lent, a fitting way to begin this season of initiation preparation and renewal. The prayer that follows applies all of this to baptism by stating that the church calls all people to salvation. We pray that God will

graciously grant
to those you wash clean in the waters of Baptism
the assurance of your unfailing protection.

The seventh (and last) Old Testament reading is Ezekiel 36:16–17a, 18–28 about the scattered people of Israel being brought again to one land by the Lord. Relying on Exodus terminology and imagery, the author assures the people that the Lord "will sprinkle clean water upon you to cleanse you from all your impurities" (Ezek 36:25), just as in Exodus blood was sprinkled on the door posts of those to be saved. The Lord will continue to sustain this chosen people by giving them a new heart (Ezek 36:26) and by putting his spirit within them enabling them to live by his statutes and decrees (Ezek 36:27). "You shall live in the land I gave your fathers; you shall be my people, and I will be your God" (Ezek 36:28). This last statement is most important, for it reiterates the foundation of the election of Israel and assures them of God's sustaining presence always. This abiding presence of God with Israel is fulfilled in and through Jesus. Again, this text has clear baptismal overtones that reflect the dynamic of the catechumenal process of responding to God's invitation and relying on his continued presence with us as we live according to his word.

The Responsorial Psalm can be either from Psalm 42, "Like a deer that longs for running streams, my soul longs for you, my God" (Ps 42:2), or Psalm 51, "Create a clean heart in me, O God" (Ps 51:12; used frequently in Lent from Ash Wednesday onward). The prayer completes the proclamation of this reading by relating the text to our situation:

> O God of unchanging power and eternal light,
> look with favor on the wondrous mystery of the whole Church
> and serenely accomplish the work of human salvation,
> which you planned from all eternity;
> may the whole world know and see
> that what was cast down is raised up,
> what had become old is made new,
> and all things restored to integrity through Christ,
> just as by him they came into being.

These significant images invite us to reflect on God's continual call for us to turn to him in true conversion and to rely on his presence and grace to sustain and complete this conversion.

With the readings from the Old Testament concluded, the congregation joins in the Glory to God hymn. On this Easter night we are invited to pay close attention to and experience fully the meaning of the familiar text:

> Lord Jesus Christ, Only Begotten Son,
> Lord God, Lamb of God, Son of the Father

you take away the sins of the world,
    have mercy on us;
you take away the sins of the world,
    receive our prayer.

The reference to being freed from the "sin of the world" is an important way in which the liturgy relates the paschal mystery of Jesus to our present situation. We who experience both intimacy with God in prayer and estrangement from him by our sins are once more brought near to this source of eternal life through the liturgy. It is here, especially in the sacraments of baptism and penance, that we experience most personally this salvation from God because our sins are forgiven, and our hearts are washed clean in the blood of the Lamb of God. In the Easter Vigil, these ideas are most important to underscore because baptism will soon take place and the Eucharist will follow: baptism for the remission of our sins and Eucharist as a continuation of our share in the paschal mystery "so that sins may be forgiven."

The association of baptism with the darkness and light motif already established in this liturgy is underscored in the prayer (from the former Roman Missal) that follows: "who make this most sacred night radiant with the glory of the Lord's Resurrection." The sense of petition in the Latin original of the prayer is that the spirit of adoption among the members of the church be deepened so that our whole lives may be dedicated to "whole-hearted service."

In the Epistle reading, Romans 6:3–11, St. Paul speaks eloquently of the resurrection of Christ. Here, Paul uses the dynamic of Christ's dying and rising as a way of interpreting the rites of initiation. The symbolism of being immersed in baptismal waters and emerging as a new creation is used to remind Christians that this symbolic cleansing is a real participation in Jesus's own death and resurrection. The baptismal font is truly a tomb, like the tomb in which Christ lay for three days. In emerging from the font, the new Christian puts on Christ and shares intimately in his resurrection. Just as the death of Jesus led to his being raised to life with the Father, so our dying to self and to sin symbolized by baptism leads to our being raised to the fullness of real life with God on earth as we look for its completion and perfection in the kingdom forever. The eschatological reference here is strong and should not be missed. Baptism is a pledge of union with God we will one day share completely. We who are baptized have forsaken sin and selfishness; in

Christ we emerge from the baptismal font to live fully alive in Christ Jesus forever (Rom 6:11).

Next follows the singing of the Easter alleluia and Psalm 118, a psalm frequently used during the Easter season. As an introduction to the Gospel and as a response to the reading from Romans, this text is pivotal. It marks the community's acknowledgment and ratification of all that is inherent in the rites celebrated this night. We proclaim that "the right hand of the Lord is exalted" (Ps 118:16) and that "the stone which the builders rejected has become the cornerstone" (Ps 118:22). Christ is our cornerstone and key stone in the structure of his body, the church.

The proclamation of the Easter Gospel now follows from one of the Synoptics. From all that has preceded in the Liturgy of the Word we can say that this proclamation is a synthesis and the fulfillment of salvation history. Creation is made new in Christ's resurrection. The exodus is fulfilled in the paschal mystery; passing through the Red Sea gives way to our leaving behind our old selves and putting on new life in the resurrection. The free offering of Isaac by Abraham fades now in comparison with the Father's offer of Jesus his Son, whose dying and rising makes us free to live his risen life here and now on earth. He who was forsaken and condemned in the passion accounts how gloriously rises to life so that we who know well our weakness and sin may come to ever new experiences of union with God through the grace and love of his Son. Christ's resurrection is the way we come to new life through sacraments and symbols. His resurrected life enlivens and empowers the rituals we celebrate so that even in this passing world we might bear the beams of God's life and love. All this is possible for us and accomplished in Christ's resurrection.

BAPTISMAL LITURGY AT THE PASCHAL VIGIL

We now move to the theological meanings associated with the rites of baptism and confirmation at the Paschal Vigil.

This begins with the direction that "the priest goes with the ministers to the baptismal font. If this can be seen by the faithful. Otherwise, a vessel with water in placed in the sanctuary" (37). The issue here is visibility. In designing and renovating churches the font deserves a prominent place. In particular, it should be a place that the whole assembly can see. A further point concerns how we prepare the celebrations of other sacraments in terms of visibility of those involved. For example, lining up confirmands two by two with their backs to the gathered assembly does not facilitate visibility for the assembly.

The procession of those to be baptized to the font "takes place led by the paschal candle" carried by a minister (41; see also 39). This rehearses the procession into the church with the paschal candle at the beginning of this liturgy. After water baptism the "Priest or Deacon receives the paschal candle from the hand of the minister, and the candles of the newly baptized are lighted" (52). This indicates the importance attached to the paschal candle itself when lighting candles at the Vigil. A related issue is that all of the candles to be used at the Vigil are all presumed to be made of (mostly) beeswax. The same is true for the candles at daily liturgy. The concession here is that in many countries it is difficult to shape and form candles because of the lack of beeswax.[17]

The renunciation of Satan and the profession of faith follow. In these dialogues with the presider in the presence of the assembled community the elect do what Jesus did when he renounced Satan's temptation (First Sunday of Lent) and they fulfill what was done at the scrutinies in the period of purification and enlightenment in Lent (Third, Fourth, and Fifth Sundays). The symbolism of water and light is now brought to completion in the immersion of the elect in the blessed water and by giving them candles lighted from the Easter candle. These symbols achieve their most important power and effect when they are thus used liturgically. The water, light, and life symbols of the Johannine Gospels in Lent are brought into clear relief here in the act of sacramental initiation.

We need the primal elements of air and water to live. Without air and water we die. Staying hydrated when we are ill (as well as during exercise) is simply a life and death issue. So too, baptism is a life and death issue. Water can be a frightening element because of the possibility of drowning and flooding. People who fear the water may envision their possible deaths too vividly by floods or by an undertow that can cause us to lose our footing, submerge, and die. In effect, the cosmic element water manifests a cosmic struggle between life and death. Water is indeed a paschal element from our common home.

In the mid-second century, Justin Martyr wrote about a place of baptism that seems to be distant from the place where the Eucharist was celebrated immediately afterward: "We lead them to a place, where there is water" (*First Apology*, 61; see also 65). At this early time in Christianity, "a place, where there is water" can hardly indicate a building built as a Christian baptistery. The earliest sources indicate that rivers were used. The Acts of the Apostles mentions the celebration of baptism in rivers; the Didache (first/second century) emphasizes how important it is to have running water, and states that a river is preferable; Tertullian (second century) still mentions rivers.

One of the ancient practices in the Roman Rite that was native to the celebration of the Eucharist during Lent was the daily celebration at different churches. The phrase "Station Masses" is associated with this practice because the Latin word *statio* means a "place" or "location." The station Mass ritual consists of gathering in one place then processing with a relic of the true cross to the place where the Mass will be celebrated. The next day the assembly gathers at the place where the Mass was celebrated the previous day. From that location the assembly walks in procession to the place where the Eucharist will be celebrated. Sometimes the location of the Lenten Mass would influence the choice of the Scripture readings of the day. In particular, these would be references to water leading up to engaging in the "creature water" at the Easter Vigil.

For example, in the former Roman Missal, most of the Mass formulas (antiphons, prayers, and readings) for a given day indicated the church in Rome that was the "station" for that day. On the Friday of the First Week of Lent, the Mass was celebrated in downtown Rome at the Church of the Twelve Apostles containing the tombs of Sts. Philip and James. It is located near the Trevi Fountain, whose waters flowed to Rome by aqueducts. The Gospel assigned for this day was John 5:1–15, the healing of the man who was paralyzed for thirty-eight years and lay near the pool of Bethesda. Jesus cured him and advised him to take up his mat and walk. Engagement in water at the Easter Vigil is presaged here. Some patristic authors comment that an angel would occasionally stir the waters of the pool and the first person to dip in the water was cured. Immersion in water in baptism similarly cures and heals us.

PRAYER TO BLESS WATER AT THE PASCHAL VIGIL

One of the most significant adjustments in the reformed Catholic liturgy has been the revision and, in some cases, adoption of prayers to bless elements raised up for worship (e.g., the prayer to bless water, the eucharistic prayer, and the prayer to consecrate chrism). This is decidedly true for the adoption of the prayer for the descent into the font for baptism, its accompanying litany and the "blessing of the font" (*Benedictio fontis*), which we now use from the eighth-century *Gelasianum Vetus*.[18] Among the more obvious and important adjustments in this revised rite, compared with the missal of 1570, is the elimination of adding the oil of catechumens and sacred chrism to the water as it was being blessed.[19] In the previous Roman ritual, the water blessed at Easter was kept in the sacristy and used for the entire next liturgical year, which often meant that the blessed water did not reflect freshness or life giving properties, during the duration having become rancid and sour smelling.

The prayer from the present Easter Vigil begins by asserting that God has "prepared water, your creation, to show forth the grace of Baptism" (*et creaturam aquae*, which would have been better translated "creature water").[20] The *anamnesis* of saving history in this central text spans from creation in Genesis 1 to Matthew 28. Among others, this includes references to water in saving history: "O God whose Spirit in the first moments of the world's creation hovered over the waters," from Genesis 1 (*Deus, cuius Spiritus super aquas inter ipsa mundi primordia ferebatur*); "God who by the outpouring of the flood foreshadowed regeneration" (*Deus, qui regenerationis speciem*) "so that from the mystery of the one and the same element of water" (*ut unius eiusdemque elementi mysterio*) and "would come an end to vice and a beginning of virtue" (*et finis esset vitiis et origo virtutum*), from Genesis 9. These references are notable because the "Noahic" covenant in Genesis has been enormously influential on many interreligious dialogues about the environment.[21]

The prayer continues that the crucified "gave forth water from his side along with blood" (*una cum sanguine aquam de latere suo produxit*), from 1 John 5:8, which text gives rise to St. Augustine's profound reflections that the sacraments come forth from the side of Christ; that those who are found worthy may be "found worthy to rise to the new life of newborn children through water and the Holy Spirit" (*in novam infantiam ex aqua et Spiritu Sancto resurgere mereatur*)[22] from Romans 6.[23] Other references to "water" in this prayer include the petition, "May this water receive by the Holy Spirit the grace of your Only Begotten Son" (*Sumat haec aqua Unigeniti tui gratiam de Spiritu Sancto*) for those "who are washed clean through the sacrament of Baptism from all the squalor of the life of old" (*sacramento baptismalis a cunctis squaloribus vetustatis ablutus*). Another reference to water concerns "the very substance of water" (*aquam natura conciperet*).[24] The prayer concludes with important rites incorporating the paschal candle:

> *And if appropriate, lowering the paschal candle into the water either once or three times, he continues:*

> May the power of the Holy Spirit,
> O Lord, we pray,
> come down through your Son
> into the fullness of this font (*in hanc plenitudinem fontis*),

> *and, holding the candle in the water, he continues*

> so that all who have been buried with Christ
> by Baptism into death
> may rise again to life with him.
> Who lives and reigns with you in the unity of the Holy Spirit,
> one God, for ever and ever.
> R. Amen.

> *Then the candle is lifted out of the water, as the people acclaim:*

> Springs of water, bless the Lord;
> praise and exalt him above all for ever.

Notably, the lowering of the paschal candle is no longer required as it was in the previous Easter Vigil. Critics of its inclusion reject its obvious phallic and vaginal symbolism as presuming male initiative on female passivity. At the same time, the inclusion of this ritual expresses in a nonverbal way the fecundity and new life that comes from the water in the font.

In the former prayer used to bless water at the Easter Vigil, the first section speaks generously about what it will effect by using phrases such as "the spirit of adoption to regenerate the new people from the font of baptism" (*recreandos novos populous...fons baptismatis...spiritum adoptionis*).[25] This section does not mention water but rather speaks about the "font" that contains it. The structure of the prayer then imitates the structure of prefaces at Mass (and the Exsultet) and acclaims how the Spirit hovered over the waters at creation (*Deus, cuius Spiritus super aquas*), as well as the flood (*per aquas abulens*), again Genesis 1 and 9. It cites the "nature of water" (*aquarum natura*), as well as "this water of regeneration" (*qui hanc aquam regenerationis*). To such positive images are added phrases, such as "may all unclean spirits depart" (*omnis spiritus immundus abscedat*) and "may the whole malice of devilish deceit be entirely banished" (*procul tota nequitia diabolicae fraudis absistat*), which phrases are followed by an explicit exorcism of the water. Toward the end of the prayer the singular is used: "I bless you creature water" (*creatura aquae*) and "I bless you also by our Lord Jesus Christ" (*benedico te et per Iesum Christum Filium eius unicum, Dominum nostrum*). The presider says, three times, "May the power of the Holy Spirit descend into the water of this font" (*Descendat in hanc plenitudinem fontis virtus Spiritus Sancti*). He then prays, "Make the whole substance of this water fruitful for rebirth" (*huius aquae substantiam, regnerandi fecundet effectu*). The oil of catechumens is added to the water to the words, "May this font be made fruitful by the oil of salvation" (*et fecundetur fons iste Oleo salutis*), and chrism is added, calling it "the Chrism of holiness [and] the oil of anointing and the Water of Baptism" (*Commixio chrismatis sanctificationis et Olei unctionis, et aquae baptismatis*).[26]

In between the reference to "fruitful for rebirth" and the pouring of the oil of catechumens and chrism into the water is the following very different rite: "Make the whole substance of this water fruitful for rebirth," with the accompanying rubric: "He lowers the candle three times in the water." The prayer continues:

> Here may the stains of all sins be washed out. Here may human nature, created in your own image, and reformed to the glory of its Maker, be cleansed from all filth of the old man. May all who receive this sacrament of regeneration be

born again new children of true innocence through our Lord
Jesus Christ your Son, who shall come to judge the living and
the dead and the world by fire. Amen.

There are clear advantages in the revised prayer, among which are its
emphasis on the span of saving history not seen in the former prayer, the
use of "we" throughout rather than the singular "I," and a worldview that
emphasizes the positive and life-giving qualities of water as opposed to
the former prayer, which exorcizes this primal element.

Some commentators regret that the present prayer for blessing at
the Vigil places more (and unprecedented) emphasis on a paschal theology of baptism rather than a theology of "rebirth." But when initiates are
immersed in the "creature water," is not the theology of rebirth always
operative precisely because of the element water?

The relationship of initiation to Eucharist is made clear in the fact
that the celebration of the paschal Eucharist follows the renewal of baptismal promises by the gathered assembly and the sprinkling of holy
water on the already baptized. Once again, lighted candles are used for
all to renew their baptismal promises and the symbol of water is used as
a ratification and symbolization of what they acclaim with their voices.
The central symbols of light and water are used once more to confirm
in the community the power and grace of God operating at this Easter
Vigil. Confirmation for adults follows next in a relatively simple form
because it is part of the whole Paschal Vigil. This brief rite includes an
introduction, a prayer and chrismation through which the initiated are
sealed with the Spirit, the gift of the Father. The inclusion of confirmation with baptism at the Easter Vigil shows the unity of these as sacraments of initiation, which sacraments rely on the powerful presence of
the Holy Spirit in the community.

RITE FOR THE BLESSING AND SPRINKLING OF WATER ON SUNDAYS

We now move to a review of the newly added prayer for blessing water on Sundays, a practice loosely connected to a similar rite that
could take place before one Mass on a Sunday in the previous Roman
Missal (i.e., sprinkling with *Asperges me* and *Vidi aquam*, a text is still in

the revised Vigil to be sung after the renewal of baptismal promises).[27] The logic follows what the *Universal Norms on the Liturgical Year and the Calendar* (4) state about the nature of Sunday:

> On the first day of the week, which is known as the Day of the Lord, or the Lord's Day, the Church, by an apostolic tradition that draws its origin from the very day of the Resurrection of Christ celebrates the Paschal Mystery. Hence, Sunday must be considered "the primordial feast day."

Hence, we move to a consideration of what this prayer reveals about ecology, liturgy, and sacrament.

The rite of the blessing and sprinkling of water for use "from time to time" on Sundays as a renewal of baptism is included in the appendix of the revised missal. References to water abound in the present prayers, but most notable is the invitation. It asks God "to bless this water he has created," which Latin phrase, *ut hanc creaturam aquae benedicere*, explicitly refers to "the creature water" (which would be a better translation both literally and theologically).[28] The first prayer then speaks of water as "the fountain of life and source of purification" (*fontem vitae ac purificationis principium*) through which "souls should be cleansed and receive the gift of eternal life." The priest then asks that God "bless this water by which we seek protection on this your day," then "renew the living spirit within us" and that "by this water we may be defended from all ills of spirit and body" (*omni malo spiritus et corporis*).

A second prayer asks that God "bless this water" (*hanc aquam*) "to implore forgiveness for our sins," "to obtain the protection of your grace," that the "living waters [*aquae vivae*] may always spring up for our salvation," "so may we approach you with a pure heart and avoid all danger to body and soul." A third prayer (for the Easter season) asks God to bless the water (*hanc aquam benedicere tu dignare*) and contains images from saving history (specifically the desert, the Prophets, and Christ in the Jordan). These are accompanied by references to water, which God "created...to make the fields fruitful, and to refresh and cleanse our bodies" (*et levamen corporibus donaret et lavem corporibus nostris*). Toward the end, the prayer speaks of baptism as "the bath of regeneration."

While not an exact parallel, the former *Ritual Romanum* contains a prayer for blessing water outside of the Easter Vigil.[29] Its first section is called the "exorcism," containing the then-customary references to what the priest does by stating twice that "I exorcise you" "in the name of Christ" "from every power of the enemy," that this "creature water" (*creatura aquae*) may be a "fountain of water springing up unto life everlasting." The second section is entitled "Prayer," naming God as "sanctifier of spiritual waters," who is asked to send "the angel of holiness upon these waters" (*et super has aquas*) so that those who are baptized in it may have "the sins of their past life washed away, their guilt wiped out, that they may be reborn as a pure dwelling place for the Holy Spirit." Then the priest pours both the oil of catechumens and chrism into the water, speaking about their union with "the water of baptism" (*aquae Baptismatis*). The rite concludes with a reference both to the font (the translation says "water" where the Latin reads *fons*) and "those who will be reborn in it."

One distinct advantage of this rite for baptismal renewal on Sundays is that it places a ritual in the Roman Rite that draws out the meaning that every Eucharist is a covenant renewal first forged sacramentally in baptism and renewed at the altar—as stated at every Eucharist: "the blood of the new and eternal covenant." Among the issues that coalesce here are that all prayers contain a number of images and metaphors, that one prayer can never "say" all that might be said about what is occurring in the liturgy and that interpreting liturgical texts always requires that the elements raised adverted to and raised up always to be factored into the theological meaning of the rite.

BAPTISMAL MOTIFS IN OTHER RITES

It is significant that in three places in the *Rite for the Pastoral Care of the Sick, Rites of Anointing and Viaticum* the sprinkling with holy water is suggested as a part of the opening of these celebrations (82, 116, 198). This mirrors the optional blessing and sprinkling with holy water on Sundays and the signing of oneself with water from the baptismal font to celebrate the Eucharist as the renewal of the covenant of baptism.

The Order for Christian Funerals begins by blessing the body with holy water at the door of the church as a reminder of baptism (at whatever age) through which the deceased entered the church for the first time. The Mass is celebrated with the paschal candle lighted. In fact, this is the only time outside of the Easter season when the paschal candle is prescribed to be lighted. A dramatic part of the entrance rites involves the placing of the funeral pall on the casket. This recalls the custom of placing a full-length white garment on the body of those who emerged from water baptism at the Easter Vigil.

CONCLUSION

In sum we have laid out what the liturgical rites say and enact with regard to baptism and to the primal element of water. We will treat the implications of this study in chapter 9.

CHAPTER SIX

EUCHARIST

In line with the methodological premises in chapter 4, this chapter will be divided into four parts. The first concerns a liturgical theology of the Eucharist based on the texts and rites of the Evening Mass of the Lord's Supper on Holy Thursday. The second concerns a comparative study of texts in the Roman Missal that deal specifically with creation and ecology. The third indicates when and where words related to creation are found copiously in the Roman Missal. The fourth summarizes the significance of the Eucharist for theologies of creation and ecology.

A LITURGICAL THEOLOGY OF THE EUCHARIST FROM THE EUCHARIST

In order to delineate the church's primary theology *of* the Eucharist *from* the liturgy of the Eucharist itself we will discuss the cosmic and liturgical contexts, as well as the texts and rites, of the Evening Mass of the Lord's Supper on Holy Thursday. This evening liturgy functions as a juncture between the liturgy of Lent and the solemn commemoration of the Paschal Triduum. The Liturgy of the Hours on this day (up to evening prayer) and the Chrism Mass still form part of Lent. At the Evening Mass of the Lord's Supper, the "forty days" of Lent come to an end and the "three days" of the Paschal Triduum begin.[1]

As is so often the case in Christian liturgical usage, these three days mark the Christian adoption and creative adaptation of a Jewish feast, specifically the central Feast of Passover. The Passover of Israel from Egypt—from slavery to freedom, from sin to forgiveness, from estrangement from God to union with him—is the theological and liturgical foundation for what is often popularly called our Passover in Christ. Through, with, and in Christ we pass from alienation to relationship with God, from estrangement to reconciliation, from infidelity to more faithful service, from the darkness of sin to the light of God's grace.

The liturgy we celebrate this evening both adopts and adapts the Jewish Passover seder meal celebrated "in the evening." This reflects and respects the way Jews "tell time": at sunset one day gives way to the next day, recalling the recounting of the days of creation in Genesis. The liturgy we celebrate these days is not a dramatic recollection of the events of first-century Palestine, or even a prayerful recollection by means of which we understand and appreciate more fully what God has done for us. Despite the dramatic impact of these liturgies, we do not dramatize what happened once in the history of salvation. Through these liturgies we are *inserted into* and are *made sharers* in the same saving deeds Christ accomplished once and for all for our salvation, redemption, reconciliation, and sanctification. We do not observe again what Jesus accomplished; we *participate in* them through his saving paschal mystery.

Liturgical tradition reveals that the liturgical and theological realities of the earlier part of the day on Holy Thursday were associated with the reconciliation of penitents and with the blessing of oils to be used in the sacraments of initiation and the anointing of the sick, ending with the celebration of the Eucharist. The themes of reconciliation reflected in the liturgy of Lent derive from the theology and practice of the church when structures of public reconciliation paralleled those of adult initiation. On Holy Thursday morning, the bishop celebrated a communal act of reconciling public penitents. The public acknowledgment of sinfulness and alienation from Christ that the church performed on Ash Wednesday, followed by forty days (or at times a much longer period), find its complement and conclusion at this public reconciliation. The sign of peace enacted by an embrace by the bishop on Holy Thursday was a definitive sign that those who were literally "excommunicated" (forbidden from sacramental communion) were now welcomed back into the Body of Christ, the church, to partake of the body of Christ, the Eucharist.

The blessing and consecration of oils also has important liturgical associations with Holy Thursday, although not always at a separate morning Mass or one performed by the bishop. It was papal custom at the Lateran Basilica to celebrate one midday Mass *in coena Domini* ("at the Lord's supper") to bless oil, consecrate chrism, and commemorate the Lord's Supper in a special way. In addition, other evidence points to blessing oils and consecrating chrism at another Mass in Lent close to the Triduum. With the Tridentine reform, the consecration of chrism and blessing of oils were assigned to take place at a morning Mass on Holy Thursday, and the Mass was celebrated by the bishop at the cathedral. The 1955 revision of holy week prescribed a morning Chrism Mass and an evening Mass of the Lord's Supper, the latter with the optional action of washing of the feet. The present Chrism Mass is assigned to Holy Thursday morning, but it may be transferred to an earlier day should this be pastorally desirable.[2]

In the medieval period and then again after Trent, initiation for adults and public reconciliation structures had collapsed and more emphasis had been placed on an individual priest's power to consecrate bread and wine at Mass. As a result, the emphasis at the Holy Thursday liturgy shifted to the association between the Eucharist and the ordained priesthood. In addition, as popular participation in the liturgy also collapsed and popular piety stressed looking at the elevated host and chalice ("ocular communion"), greater attention was given to the procession of the Eucharist to the repository at the end of this Mass and to private devotions that stressed visiting a number of repositories for adoration, rather than emphasizing participating in the liturgy and receiving communion.

Reform of the Liturgy

In the present reform of the liturgy the reconciliation of penitents is seen more as an element in the liturgy and theology of Lent (especially in the Gospels for the Third, Fourth, and Fifth Sundays of Lent during the C cycle). Emphasis is also given when communal celebrations of the sacrament of penance take place, especially toward the end of Lent. The appendix to the revised rite of penance offers examples of communal forms of penance, which are intended to be part of a community's normal experience of this sacrament. Hence, the notion of being reconciled for participation in the paschal communion can be said to be operative still, albeit in a less obvious way than earlier in the church's tradition.

Also, in the present reform there is a morning Mass on Holy Thursday entitled "Chrism Mass" that continues the tradition of blessing oils for use in the coming year. While this liturgy contains a renewal of commitment to priestly service for ordained presbyters, this renewal has no precedent in liturgical history and was first inserted into this Mass in the late 1970s by Pope Paul VI at the urging of John Cardinal Wright. (Cardinal Wright was serving in the Vatican as prefect for the Congregation of the Clergy, and he was deeply concerned about the number of ordained priests who were leaving the active ministry.) This is all the more reason this liturgy should be seen through the lens of liturgical history and theology, understanding it as an important ecclesial event of the whole church. The presence and participation of representatives of the whole diocese with varied talents and gifts should also be encouraged, lest the overindividualization of priestly ministry associated with some medieval understandings of this day be allowed to dominate.

For the Evening Mass of the Lord's Supper, the title is to be noted precisely and carefully because it avoids the term *Last Supper*. One can argue from this title that the focus of the liturgy is on ritualizing the central events of the paschal mystery during the triduum in such a way that the whole mystery (obedient life, betrayal, suffering, death resurrection, ascension) is commemorated each day in the liturgy—not individual aspects on individual days. The paschal mystery cannot be divided into separable parts nor can its commemoration in the liturgy be separated (e.g., suffering only on Good Friday). Should this have been the intention, this liturgy could well have been called the liturgy of the "Last Supper." In fact, this liturgy (and every celebration of Eucharist) is not a commemoration of the Last Supper. It is a commemoration of the passion, death, and resurrection of Jesus in the setting of a sacrificial meal. We do not imitate what Jesus did at the Last Supper.

The importance of our appropriation of and in the paschal mystery is presumed in the texts of the Roman Mass. Notably, these texts never speak about Christ's paschal mystery without speaking about how the church in always incorporated into that mystery in and through the liturgy.[3] This begins in baptism and deepens whenever we celebrate the sacraments and all acts of liturgy. Dining on the eucharistic bread and cup is one of the ways that we participate in the paschal mystery and the saving sacrifice of Christ in the Eucharist.

That the reform intends to emphasize the coming together of the whole community for this liturgy (rather than several scheduled Masses for convenience) is seen in the directions for the liturgy, which state, "All Masses without a congregation are prohibited," and that there is to be one evening Mass in which all participate. Another Mass is tolerated "for those who are in no way able to take part in the evening Mass." A subtle but nonetheless important way of associating this evening liturgy with that of Good Friday also appears in the directions that the Eucharist consecrated today is to be of sufficient quantity for distribution both Thursday and Friday. In fact, the Roman Pontifical states that when a bishop visits a "station" or parish in the (arch) diocese to celebrate the Eucharist, the tabernacle is to be empty. This rubric reflects the liturgical integrity of the one act of worship as the act of worship unfolds. It does not rely on or focus on hosts reserved in the tabernacle. This allows for and in fact requires the ritual integrity of consuming at one liturgy the bread and wine consecrated at that celebration as is stated in the General Instruction of the Roman Missal (85).

In the present reform of the liturgy of Holy Thursday, the action of the washing of the feet has been restored as an option following the Gospel reading from John 13 about Christ's example of washing the feet of his disciples and his command to love each other. The distribution of the Eucharist under the form of both bread and wine emphasizes the symbolic value of these central elements in Eucharist, which are the work of human hands.

"The Work of Human Hands"— Manufacture of Bread and Wine

In line with our previous discussions about the manufacture of oils and candles for the liturgy, we begin with the cosmological and anthropological context for the celebration of the Eucharist as revering and raising up "the work of human hands." The manufacture of the eucharistic elements falls at the intersection of physical and spiritual hunger, the ingenuity and productivity of human beings and the contribution that engagement in bread blessed and wine outpoured at the Eucharist reflect deep meanings associated with eucharistic sacrifice. All of this signals our engagement in the central mystery of faith: the paschal mystery.

The gifts of bread and wine are from the earth but are also the result of human "work." *Work* means human ingenuity, productivity, and "manufacture" (*manu-factus* means "made by hand"). That some central elements used in the liturgy are the "work of human hands"— such as oil, bread and wine—respects humans' ingenuity to produce works that literally reproduce in themselves the paschal process of dying and rising. As the pope reminds us in *Laudato Si'*, humans are to "have dominion" over the earth (cf. Gen 1:28), to "till it and keep it" (Gen 2:15). He deepens these assertions in article 67:

> We are not God. The earth was here before us, and it has been given to us. This allows us to respond to the charge that Judeo-Christian thinking, on the basis of the Genesis account which grants man "dominion" over the earth (cf. Gen 1:28), has encouraged the unbridled exploitation of nature by painting him as domineering and destructive by nature. This is not a correct interpretation of the Bible as understood by the Church.

He then asserts that "tilling" refers to cultivating, ploughing, or working, while "keeping" means caring, protecting, overseeing, and preserving. This implies a relationship of mutual responsibility between human beings and nature. Each community can take from the bounty of the earth whatever it needs for subsistence, but it also has the duty to protect the earth and to ensure its fruitfulness for coming generations. This is part of the theology that underlies our working with fellow creatures to manufacture bread and wine for the Eucharist. There is a rich theology of creation in reflecting on the "bread-ness" of the bread and the "wine-ness" of the wine that we consume in the Eucharist.

Among the things we offer in the Eucharist as the work of human hands is the sweat of the human brow. Part of the theology of this eucharistic "sacrificial sacrament" is the human work that makes all the things we will use for the Eucharist.[4] So, the worship and honor we *offer* to God in the Eucharist starts long before the liturgy in church begins. It commences in the liturgy of human life as blessed by God, with humans planting, harvesting, baking, winemaking, and delivering these gifts to the church for the Eucharist. The talents we humans have for thought and work fashion what we need to celebrate the Eucharist. What we are and use outside of the liturgy is brought into the act of liturgy to be transformed. Simply put, what lies behind the manufacture of the bread and wine for the Eucharist is that they are *paschal processes*. There is a dying and rising in planting, harvesting, baking, and fermenting, all of which make up the foundation for the celebration of the paschal mystery in the Eucharist and for our participation in the dying and rising of Christ in and through the Eucharist. There is an important link between the paschal process involved in manufacturing bread and wine and the fact that dining on consecrated bread and wine is the uniquely eucharistic means we have to participate in Christ's paschal dying and rising. In addition to the manufacture of bread and wine, there is the important notion that humans participate in the Eucharist by presenting gifts.[5]

Clearly in the revision of the *Missale Romanum* after Vatican II one of the most obvious revisions was the elimination of the five (or six, on certain days) "offertory prayers." The fathers of Vatican II had called for a simplification of the rites in the Constitution *Sacrosanctum Concilium* on the Sacred Liturgy (see 50); Pope Paul VI himself noted this in his apostolic constitution *Missale Romanum*, and gave special attention to the rites of offering the bread and wine, those of the breaking of the bread and those of communion.[6] Members of *coetus* group ten, tasked with the reform of the Mass, sought to simplify these rites and prayers. The question that was seriously debated concerned whether and what "formulas" should replace the "offertory prayers" and accompany to the act of "presenting" the bread and wine at the "preparation of the altar" (note that the word *offertory* is not used here).

One reason for eliminating the "offertory prayers" was that they resembled the words of the Roman Canon and thus were regarded by some as a "mini-canon." Among the proposals was a citation from the Didache, chapter 9, about the ecclesiological meaning of bread manufactured from many grains to form one bread.[7] Another was from Proverbs 9:1–2: wisdom has "built herself a building…and prepared wine on its altars."[8] The third, which was eventually adopted, contains the phrases "blessed are you," "work of human hands" and "blessed be God forever." Choosing an acclamation to insert at this part of the *Ordo Missae* took time and informed debate. A chief aspect of all eucharistic participation is to allow the paschal dying and rising enacted through what occurs at the altar table to be the true measure of anything that is of real value in life. The challenge is twofold. First, it is to allow what we enact in the Eucharist to be the measure of our lives. In effect, we are to view life through the lens of the paschal mystery, which mystery helps us evaluate what is important in life. It is this lens that allows us to look at apparent defeats—sickness, suffering, and setbacks in life, even death itself—and to evaluate them against the paschal mystery. Second, a requisite consequence of eucharistic enactment is to share the goods of this earth with the poor and the needy.

Returning to the Evening Mass of the Lord's Supper, important ritual gestures and movement occur during the presentation of the gifts. The directions of the missal note that at the time of the presentation of the gifts, there may be "a procession of the faithful in which gifts for the poor may be presented with the bread and wine." This simple statement reflects the intrinsic connection between the celebration of liturgy and the implications of ritual worship in caring for each other. The fact that this follows soon after the washing of the feet makes it a kind of communal extension of this gesture. The same community that was involved in the procession with palm branches on the previous Sunday is now invited to join in procession with gifts (food, clothing, etc.) in imitation of the Savior they acclaimed as Messiah and who this evening, as Lord and servant, washes his disciples' feet. At the end of the liturgy, the movement of the community is envisioned in the transfer of the Eucharist to the repository.

With regard to the Scripture texts chosen for proclamation, the *Introduction* of the *Lectionary for Mass* states, "On Holy Thursday at the evening Mass the remembrance of the supper preceding Christ's departure casts its own special light because of the Lord's example in washing the feel of his disciples and Paul's account of the institution of the Christian Passover in the Eucharist" (99). In addition to the Scriptures, the liturgical texts themselves (prayers, antiphons, preface, etc.) bring out the significance of what is taking place in the language of symbolic and gestural expression. An attentive review of texts helps underscore what is intended in the liturgy this evening, especially as this helps set this celebration within the context of all that is implied in the celebration of the Paschal Triduum.

Texts and Rites of the Liturgy

The entrance antiphon assigned to this liturgy points to the whole Triduum since it focuses our attention on the cross of Christ: "We should glory in the Cross of our Lord Jesus Christ, in whom is our salvation, life and resurrection, through whom we are saved and delivered" (see Gal 6:14). The cross is the symbol of the fullness of salvation; the Eucharist is the setting for our present participation in that same redemption.

The opening prayer this evening has been newly composed; it links the whole liturgy with the entrance and with the second reading from 1 Corinthians 11. We gather to share in the "Supper" that Jesus left us when he was "about to hand himself over to death," and it was precisely this death that inaugurated his paschal mystery. The reference to the Eucharist as the meal Jesus "entrusted to the Church...the banquet of his love" is taken from the beginning of this evening's Gospel: "[Jesus] had loved his own in the world, and would love them to the end" (John 13:1). This same reference is the source for the text of the institution narrative in the fourth Eucharistic Prayer: "he always loved his own in the world." The prayer goes on to situate Jesus's institution of the Eucharist "when about to hand himself over to death." This reference recalls the entrance antiphon and looks to the second reading from 1 Corinthians 11:23–26, particularly the introductory formula in verse 26: "I received from the Lord what I handed on to you, namely, that the Lord Jesus on the night in which he was betrayed took bread...."

The specification that the Eucharist is "a sacrifice new for all eternity" points to the Passover prescriptions contained in the first reading (Exod 12:1–8, 11–14), which have been transcended in favor of the "newer rites prevailing" (*novo cedat ritui*) from the hymn *Pange Lingua* that accompanies the transfer of the Eucharist to the repository at the end of the liturgy this evening. The concluding reference in the prayer to finding "the fullness of charity and of life" from this great mystery.

The first reading, Exodus 12:1–8, 11–14, describes the Passover ritual that Israel would use to commemorate their "passing over" from slavery into freedom. This same Passover notion grounds our annual spring festival of liberation from sin to forgiveness in and through Christ, our Passover and priest. Interestingly, some other Christian churches (e.g., *Lutheran Book of Worship*) use Jeremiah 31:31–34 about the new covenant on this night, that is, rather than Exodus 12. The text of Jeremiah, when read in this liturgical context, indicates from the start that we commemorate a new kind of liberation in and through Christ.

The significance of the Exodus reading is that it recalls important theological and liturgical notions that undergird Roman Catholic eucharistic theology and practice. For an appreciation of many images and symbols that we still use in the eucharistic liturgy, a text like this is most instructive. What we enter into each and every time we celebrate the Eucharist is "a memorial feast" (Exod 12:14), which like the Passover incorporates us into the very act of redemption that Christ accomplished through his passion, death, and resurrection. Yet this night is especially significant, for it shares the overtones of renewal and rebirth in nature associated with the "first month of the year" (Exod 12:2). This annual festival in religious ritual is grounded in the agricultural cycle of new life from the earth, renewal, and rebirth. Most appropriately, this cycle of nature was chosen to mark Israel's Passover; this same nature cycle (albeit overlaid with the Exodus interpolation) grounds the Christian observance of the paschal mystery.

As has already been noted the use of the lamb and the blood, while most significant for the Exodus, is taken over by the liturgy and Gospel writers to express important insights about the passion. Specifically, the mention of slaughtering the lambs on the fourteenth of the month during the evening twilight (Exod 12:6) is important for John's Gospel (to be read on Good Friday) where the hour for sacrificing lambs is the very hour when Jesus is condemned to death. Hence, obvious and significant parallels between Exodus and our Paschal Triduum liturgies should not be overlooked.

The Responsorial Psalm links the Exodus reading with the new covenant by using the statement from St. Paul (1 Cor 10:16) as the response: "our blessing-cup is a communion with the blood of Christ." The "cup of blessing" is a most significant part of the Passover rite, and the prayers and toasts offered as it is raised have been interpolated and adapted for Christian usage in the Eucharistic Prayer. Once again, a simple reference when understood in biblical and liturgical usage reveals a wealth of meaning. Psalm 116, when used this evening, offers much insight about the liturgy we celebrate. The clear statement about the "cup of salvation I will take up, and I will call upon the name of the Lord" (Ps 116:13) has been used in the Roman liturgy to refer to the priest's drinking from the chalice in the private prayers formerly required between the priest's receiving the host and drinking from the chalice. Further, while exegetes discuss the exact meaning of "precious in the eyes of the Lord is the death of his faithful ones" (Ps 116:15), this text has nevertheless been used in our liturgy to refer to the death of Christ, the chosen one of God. The "servant" reference in the next verse has been used in a similar way.

The second reading, 1 Corinthians 11:23–26, is the Pauline account of the institution of the Lord's Supper. The context of this passage within the letter as a whole is significant because the Corinthians' behavior is far from exemplary, especially as they gather for the supper.

The divisions that exist in their body give a lie to the supposed and fostered unity of the supper of the Lord (1 Cor 11:17–22). That the paschal mystery is the presupposed and emphasized context for the Eucharist is demonstrated even in these short verses by the introductory words that Jesus took bread "on the night in which he was betrayed" (1 Cor 11:23).

This would obviously mean that at his last Passover with his disciples, Jesus "took bread" and performed the customary ritual. But then, in the midst of this tradition-bound ritual, he inserted meanings that would forever change the meaning of this liturgy for his followers. When Jesus had given thanks and broke the bread (Passover ritual), he then declared, "This is my body, which is for you. Do this in remembrance of me" (1 Cor 11:24). By this action Jesus determines that from now on this blessed and broken bread would no longer commemorate the Passover. Now, it commemorates his death and resurrection and the community's share in this mystery. The "memorial feast" of Exodus has become the act of remembrance for Christians.

This is reiterated when the last cup of wine is raised with the statement, "This cup is the new covenant in my blood. Do this…in remembrance of me" (1 Cor 11:25). The tradition adopted by St. Paul here clearly reflects the important place of the Eucharist as a real sharing in the new covenant. The uniqueness of the covenant relationship with Israel is now transcended by a new, unique relationship through Jesus's blood. The repetition of the Eucharist is noted here as the central means we have to participate in Jesus's paschal mystery. "Every time, then, you eat this bread and drink this cup, you proclaim the death of the Lord until he comes" (1 Cor 11:26). This memorial meal is our way of being drawn into Christ's active offer of salvation and sanctification.

Taken together these first two readings offer us more than ceremonial details. They offer us a way of seeing beyond rites and ceremonies to their true depth and meaning, especially as these meanings involve us in the redemption won for us in Christ. For both the writer of Exodus and St. Paul, those who participate in these rites must already possess a level of conversion and commitment to God. For St. Paul these same people are to live out the full meaning of what they receive in the Lord's Supper by living lives of unity and peace. This important notion of living lives congruent with the celebration of liturgy is at the heart of the Gospel proclaimed this evening.

The Gospel, John 13:1–15, recalls many significant Johannine motifs already seen in the latter part of Lent. These themes are used or referred to throughout what has come to be called the high priestly prayer of Jesus in John 13—17. The command of love is introduced here with the clear statement that Jesus "had loved his own in the world and would show his love for them to the end" (John 13:1). This sentiment finds clear expression in the fourth Eucharistic Prayer, which states in Johannine language, "He always loved those who were his own in the world. When the time came for him to be glorified by you, his heavenly Father, he showed the depth of his love." Both this opening verse of the Gospel and this section of the Eucharistic Prayer reflect the Johannine notions of self-sacrificing love, which required that Jesus die for our salvation. The Johannine Gospel continues by referring to the betrayal of Jesus by Judas (John 13:2), a scene already recounted in the liturgy on Tuesday of Holy Week (see John 13:21–33, 36–38). Interestingly, John notes that the "devil had already induced Judas" to betray Jesus. The fight between light and darkness, good and evil, God and Satan is played out here once again in a simple but theologically significant reference to the "devil." It is this same combat against evil, darkness, and Satan that characterizes believers of every generation. This combat is especially clear in the scrutinies of Lent and the celebration of initiation at the Easter Vigil.

That Jesus adopts the posture of servant is clear from the action of pouring water into a basin and washing his disciples' feet (John 13:5). The humility of the servant demonstrated here in graphic detail illustrates carefully what has been proclaimed in the first reading on the first three days of this week from the Servant Songs from Isaiah. The clear and unmistakable act of humility shows once again the initiative taken by Jesus for our salvation. He takes the initiative to wash the disciples' feet and soon will initiate the unfolding of the paschal mystery by openly welcoming Judas his betrayer. Jesus's command to love one another takes on greater significance when he draws out the implication of this humble act by inviting his followers to do the same. "But if I washed your feet—I who am Teacher and Lord—then you must wash each other's feet" (John 13:15). The usage of "Teacher" and "Lord" is most significant here, for these terms of respect and status are turned inside out and made meaningless in comparison with Jesus's new role as servant and slave. This role is to be adopted by his disciples. As Jesus has done, so they must also do.

What is most significant here liturgically is the clear association between celebrating the Lord's Supper and the act of humiliation in service. Jesus's followers are to take up the towel of humble service as quickly as they take up the cup of blessing in praise and thanksgiving. To celebrate the memorial meal of Jesus with his disciples would mean an implicit act of commitment to the meaning he gives to the Passover meal: mutual forgiveness and love. Significantly, the first two readings provide the context and necessary underpinning for the Gospel whose meaning is drawn from the Passover ritual. That Christ's command to love one another is a central focus this evening is also noted in the directions in the missal that state that this is one of the themes to be explored in the homily.

The gesture of washing feet follows the homily. It is not simply a literal or a dramatic repetition of what Jesus did. Rather, it is a significant gesture that reflects the example and command of Jesus. It is especially important to keep this symbolic understanding in mind so that this action is not misunderstood. The point of our enacting this rite is to reiterate Jesus's command and to recommit ourselves to serving the needs of each other as an essential complement to what engaging in the act of Eucharist means. The antiphons offered as accompaniment to this gesture are drawn from John 13 and from 1 Corinthians 13:13, for example:

Let faith, hope and charity, these three, remain among you,
but the greatest of these is charity.

The prayer over the gifts (taken from a different day in the former missal) contains the particularly significant theological statement that "whenever the memorial of this sacrifice is celebrated the work of our redemption is accomplished." Most appropriately the use of "memorial" here reflects the statement from the first reading about Passover as "a memorial feast for you, which all your generations shall celebrate with pilgrimage to the Lord, as a perpetual institution" (Exod 12:14). In addition, the reference to "the work of our redemption" picks up on a theme seen very often in prayers over the gifts. Such a reference is proleptic in the sense that what it refers to is accomplished only through the eucharistic prayer and communion to follow.

The first Preface of the Holy Eucharist (taken from two sections of the *Bergamo Sacramentary*) reflects the centrality of the Eucharist as a unique means of joining our self-offering with that of Christ the high priest "who instituted the pattern of an everlasting sacrifice." This is a central theme from the section of Hebrews 4:14—5:10 proclaimed at the Office of Readings this morning. This act is renewed at every Eucharist but most especially this evening, which sacrifice is appropriately described as the offering Jesus taught his followers to make "as his memorial." The second section of the Preface contains two significant sacrificial references, the "flesh that sacrificed for us" and his blood "poured out for us." These references parallel what we derive from the Eucharist: "we are made strong" and "we are washed clean." The eucharistic meal is thus most appropriately imaged as Christ's true and eternal sacrifice in which we directly participate and from which we gain strength for the journey of life and cleansing from our sins.

On Holy Thursday evening the tradition of using variable prayers within the Roman Canon is revived where two proper parts may be proclaimed. The first refers to Christ's betrayal

> celebrating the most sacred day
> on which Our Lord Jesus Christ
> was handed over for our sake,

which is repeated at the institution narrative in the third Eucharistic Prayer ("on the night he was betrayed"). The second variable text in the Roman Canon states,

> Graciously accept this oblation of our service,
> that of your whole family,
> which we make to you
> as we observe the day
> on which our Lord Jesus Christ
> handed on the mysteries of his Body and Blood
> for his disciples to celebrate.

The communion antiphon is fittingly taken from the second reading (1 Cor 11:24, 25), thereby linking Word and Sacrament in a subtle way. The more important references are to the "body...given for you," underscoring a sacrificial understanding of the meal celebrated, and to our receiving the eucharistic gifts "in remembrance of me," which is a final reference in this Mass formula to this eucharistic "memorial" of our salvation.

The direction of the missal that follows states that the "ciborium with hosts for Communion on the following day is left on the altar" for the transfer procession following the prayer after communion. Once again, the ritual direction reiterates the close association of this liturgy with tomorrow's.

The prayer after communion (from the *Missale Gothicum*) contains a helpful eschatological reference, reflective of the passage from the second reading about proclaiming the death of the Lord until he comes. This prayer links our present celebration of Eucharist with our hope that "we may enjoy his banquet for all eternity." Our present liturgy is a unique merging of the past and future coming of Christ at the supper of the Lamb in the kingdom forever (see Rev 19:9).

The conclusion of the liturgy this evening calls for a procession and the transfer of the Eucharist. In comparison with the procession to the repository in the former Holy Thursday liturgy, the reforms of 1955 and our present liturgy are very simple and direct. The procession is led by a cross bearer, two ministers carrying candles, and a thurifer. Significantly, the procession with the Eucharist to be distributed on Good Friday is headed by the image of the cross, which was emphasized in the liturgy on Palm Sunday of the Passion of the Lord, which was referred to in this evening's entrance antiphon and which will be emphasized even more on Good Friday. The symbolism of this nonverbal link to the whole of the Paschal Triduum should not be overlooked. The priest carries the ciborium in procession covered only with a humeral veil. No prayers are said after the prayer after communion. The movement of the community in procession is accompanied with the *Pange Lingua* (or another eucharistic hymn) and when all have reached the place of repose the *Tantum Ergo* is sung. After the hymn the assembly prays in silent adoration for a suitable period after which the ministers leave. The powerful force of gesture and procession should be understood as a primary liturgical means of communication, and in this case, of showing reverence. All are encouraged to continue private adoration after the liturgy until midnight.

COMPARISON OF TEXTS ON CREATION AND ECOLOGY

By way of comparison, it is notable (not to say regrettable) that some "traditional" Catholic practices associated with the earth found in the *Missale Romanum*[9] promulgated after the Council of Trent (sometimes called the Tridentine Missal) were not retained as required in the *Missale Romanum* promulgated after the Second Vatican council: namely, Rogation Days and Ember Days. On the other hand, the present *Missale Romanum* contains a wealth of additional prayers related to creation and the earth.

Rogation Days

The interrelationship of liturgy and (medieval) Catholic life is neatly expressed in Nathan Ristuccia's assertion:

> Rogationtide—the three-day processional feast before Ascension Thursday—embodied the social imaginary. At the Rogation procession, Christians acted out their relationship to God, their fellow believers, the realm, creation and the cosmos of physical and spiritual hierarchies that enmeshed them.[10]

In the medieval church these days were the second most prominent holiday of the year (after Easter).[11] They involved grueling tasks, often included exorcisms, and were very serious, even pessimistic expressions of how "sin had rendered a good creation dangerous and spread strife within human communities."[12] These processions were originally an antidote to a pagan procession that took place in Rome on April 25 each year, with the Christian procession ending at St. Peter's. When held outside of Rome, these processions often marked out a parish's geographical territory and asked God to drive away evil spirits. The phrase the "beating of the bounds" is often associated with these processions.

By the time these days were codified in the Tridentine Missal, they consisted in a procession accompanied by a litany of the saints and then several petitions for protection from sin, from wrath, from an unprovided death, from the scourge of earthquake, from plague, famine, war, and more. Toward the end, the petitions also prayed that God might "give and preserve the fruits of the earth."[13] While this was not a major motif of the litany, processing on a special day to mark out a special place carried with it obvious creation motifs. Rogation Days were retained in the 1966 "interim" *Sacramentary for Mass* with the rubrics in Latin and the texts in English.[14]

Many have critiqued the revised Missal for deleting Rogation Days from the liturgies around April 25. Chapter 9 of the GIRM, "Adaptations within the Competence of Bishops and Bishops Conferences," states, "In the drawing up of the calendar of a nation, the Rogation and Ember Days should be indicated, as well as the forms and texts for their celebration, and other special measures should also be taken into consideration" (394). In a trenchant critique of the lack of imagination on this issue exercised by the American bishops, Ristuccia asserts,

> In 2003 the Committee on Divine Worship of the United States Conference of Catholic Bishops allowed dioceses to treat civic holidays like Independence Day, Labor Day, and Thanksgiving as "equivalents to Rogation Days." Ironically, a once vibrant medieval Christian feast is now [to be] observed on days established by the secular American government—none of them in the springtime.[15]

In the face of these post–Vatican II missteps, it is important to recall our present cultural context. Michael Foley states, "We live in an age marked by unprecedented disconnect from the land and by a growing anxiety over it."[16] Or in the words of Vincent Miller, "We nourish ourselves on food from nowhere and dress in clothes made by no one."[17]

Ember Days

The historical evolution of Ember Days and delineating their theological meanings involves complex issues that are not easily summarized.[18] While they were celebrated four times a year in the Roman liturgy and can be understood to mark the four seasons, there are other themes and liturgical actions connected with them in liturgical history (e.g., ordinations). For our purposes, it is notable that they were observed on Wednesday, Friday, and Saturday four times a year during December (Advent), Lent, after Pentecost, and in September. The Liturgy of the Word for these days contained three readings and a "prayer of the assembly" introduced by "Let us pray, let us kneel" (as on Good Friday). What made Ember Days memorable for the majority of the faithful was the strict fasting and abstinence regulations in effect on these days. While requirements and observances were varied in many dioceses in the United States before Vatican II, the norm was that the amount of food taken at two smaller meals should not equal the amount taken at the main meal of the day. On these days the consumption of meat was prohibited.[19] That these were also dropped after Vatican II is notable, recalling again the citation above from the GIRM about Rogation and Ember Days.

Various Prayers

MISSALE ROMANUM 2010/2011	MISSALE ROMANUM AFTER TRENT
Pro circumstantibus publicis For Various Needs and Occasions	Orationes Diversae Various Prayers
26. For the Sanctification of Human Labor A and B	not found
27. At Seedtime A and B	not found
28. After the Harvest	not found
33. Famine / Those Suffering Hunger A and B	Oration (OR), Prayer over the Offerings (POO) Prayer after Communion (PAC)
34. In Time of Earthquake Collect Only	OR, POO, PAC
35. For Rain Collect Only	OR, POO, PAC
36. For Fine Weather Collect Only	OR, POO, PAC
37. For an End to Storms Collect Only	To avert storms
	OR, POO, PAC
	In Time of Animal Plague
	OR, POO, PAC

The schema above indicates the addition of Mass formulas in the present *Missale Romanum* for the sanctification of human labor, at seedtime, and after harvest. The others parallel the Tridentine Missal (although some new formulas have a collect only). Given destruction due to climate change and global warming, the prayers about cosmic disasters might be options presiders might choose more regularly. Given the demise of the "family farm," the first three sets of prayers might be prayer more than occasionally in such circumstances. A brief review of these Mass formulas reveals important concepts and nuances about creation.[20]

For the Sanctification of Human Labor

The first entrance antiphon cites the creation story in Genesis 1:1, 27, 31, reiterating its important place at the Easter Vigil and in Vesper hymns. The second from Psalm 90:17 begs God to "give success to the work of our hands." The first collect names "O God, Creator of all things" and asserts that God has "commanded the human race to bear the burden of labor." We then ask that

> the work we are beginning
> may bring [both] progress in this life and
> ...advance the spread of the Kingdom of Christ.

The second collect addresses God, "who through human labor never cease to perfect and govern the vast work of creation." We then ask,

> Grant that all men and women
> may find work that befits their dignity
> joins them more closely to one another
> and enables them to serve their neighbor....

The prayer over the offerings calls on God and makes the parallel between food for humans here on earth and the Eucharist that is celebrated:

> Who in the offerings presented here
> nourish the human race with food
> and renew it with your Sacrament
> grant, we pray,
> that the sustenance they provide
> may not fail us in body or in spirit.

The assignment of Sunday Preface VI of Ordinary Time continues these themes from the creation story in Genesis (the world and humans) and our responsibility:

For you laid the foundations of the world
and have arranged the changing of times and seasons;
you formed man in your own image
and set humanity over the whole world in all its wonder,
to rule in your name over all you have made
and for ever praise you in your mighty works.

The communion antiphon is from Colossians 3:17: "Whatever you do in word or deed, do everything in the name of the Lord Jesus Christ, giving thanks to the Father through him." The prayer after communion combines several important ecological and eucharistic themes:

Partakers of this table of unity and charity
we beseech your mercy, Lord,
that through the work you have given us to do
we may sustain our life on earth
and trustingly build up your kingdom.

Other important phrases found in the second Mass formula are "God who willed to subject the forces of nature to human labor," in practicing sincere charity and in advancing the fulfillment of "your divine work of creation," and "Grant that, through the human labor we offer you, we have a part in the work of Christ the Redeemer."

At Seedtime

The optional entrance antiphon for the Mass for the Sanctification of Human Labor is used here: "May your favor, O Lord, be upon us, and may you give success to the work of our hands (Ps 90:17). The collect subtly warns against any Pelagianism as it addresses God:

By whose help we sow seeds in the earth
that will grow by the effect of your power,
grant that what we know to be lacking in our labors
may be supplied abundantly by you
for you alone give the increase.

A similar theological strain is found in the prayer over the offerings:

O God, you are the true Creator of the earth's produce
and nurture carefully the fruits of the spirit,
give success to our labors…
so that we may gather the fruits of the earth in abundance
and that all things, owing to their origin in a single providence,
may always work as one for your glory.

Reliance on the Lord is found in the Communion Antiphon: "The Lord will bestow his bounty, and our earth shall yield its increase" (Ps 85:13). The tightly compact prayer after communion combines several things that are a fitting conclusion to the Eucharist:

O Lord, who renew us with your Sacraments,
assist, we pray, the work of our hands,
so that we, who live and move and have our being in you
may, through your blessing of the seeds of the earth,
be fed by abundant crops.

In the second Mass formula the opening prayer relies on God's blessing:

Pour out your gracious blessing on your people, Lord God,
so that through your generosity
our land may yield its fruits
for us to enjoy with ever-grateful hearts
to the honor of your holy name.

The prayer over the offerings uses the rich and familiar imagery from the Didache and applies it both to the Eucharist and to the fruits of the earth when it asks,

Look with favor on our offerings, O Lord,
so that we who bring you grains of wheat made into bread
to be changed into the Body of your Son,
may find joy in the blessing you bestow
on the seed to be sown on the earth.

The prayer after communion parallels nourishment on earth with the important notion that it is a *pledge* of what we will receive in eternity:

Grant to your faithful, almighty God,
abundance of the earth's fruits,
that, nourished by these in the present age,
they may also grow in spiritual things
and so obtain the good things of eternity,
of which they have received a pledge in this Sacrament.

After the Harvest

The "after harvest" context for this liturgy is acclaimed in the entrance antiphon: "The earth has yielded its fruit; may God, our God bless us" (Ps 67:7). Humanity's obligations are the focus of the collect, which uses the adjective *good* to address the Father:

Lord, good Father, who in your providence
have entrusted the earth to the human race,
grant, we pray, that with the fruits harvested from it
we may be able to sustain life
and, with your help, always use them
to promote your praise and the well-being of all.

This same obligation is seen in the second collect, which also names God's providence and applies agrarian terms to the Christian life:

We give you thanks, O Lord,
for the fruits that earth has given to benefit the human family...
as the working of your supreme providence has produced them,
so you may cause the seed of justice and the fruits of charity
to spring up in our hearts.

The parallel of the earth's produce and heavenly fruitfulness to seen in the prayer over the gifts:

We ring to you with thanksgiving from the fertile earth
and, as you give us a rich harvest of the earth's produce,
so make our hearts abound with heavenly fruitfulness.

The communion antiphon from Psalm 104:13–15 acclaims, "The earth is replete with the fruits of your work, O Lord; you bring forth bread from the earth, and wine to cheer the heart." The parallel between the earthly gifts and "greater blessings" is found in the prayer after communion:

> As we give you thanks, in this saving mystery
> for the crops harvested from the earth,
> we may, through the same mystery working within us,
> be worthy to receive still greater blessings.

"CREATION" AND "CREATOR" IN THE ROMAN MISSAL

This section reviews specifically how the words *creator, creo, creatio, creatura, condo,* and *conditor,* as well as additional terms referring to creation (namely, *auctor, dispono, facio, fundo,* and *opera*), are used in the *Missale Romanum* of Paul VI. This study is aimed at determining how the liturgy articulates a theology of creation and what contribution this study grounded in the church's *lex orandi* can have for the church's *lex credendi* and (what are now commonly termed) creation theology and creation spirituality. Clearly, this exercise is indicative of what could be found by a similar search into the other reformed liturgies.

Creator

The term *creator* is found seven times in the Missal of Paul VI: in three prayers and once each in an introit, a prayer over the offerings, the renewal of baptismal promises at the paschal vigil and the fourth Eucharistic Prayer. The last two examples are of import because they come from the particularly significant liturgical texts, a profession of faith and an anaphora, and both refer specifically to God the Father as Creator. In the first question at the renewal of baptismal promises the term *creatorem* follows the specification *Deum Patrem omnipotentem:* "do you believe in God the Father almighty, creator of heaven and earth?" Found in the postsanctus of the fourth anaphora, this term refers to man and woman made in God's image and likeness who are to serve God as creator and to exercise dominion over the rest of creation (see Gen 1:26, 28): *ut, tibi soli Creatori serviens, creaturis omnibus imperaret.* This section of the Eucharistic Prayer is introduced by addressing God as *Pater sancte.*

In two of the prayers (*orationes*[21]) *creator* is used with other terms to address God (*Deus*). On the twenty-fourth Sunday of the year the text reads *Respice nos, rerum omnium Deus creator et rector*, which acknowledges God as one who creates and governs, guides, or rules all things or who is master or proprietor of all he has made. At the Mass celebrating the anniversary of marriage, the prayer (*oratio*) opens with *Deus, creator omnium, qui virum et feminam in principio condidisti*. Notable here is the juxtaposition of *creator* with the verb *condidisti*, insuring a double emphasis on God's creative hand. In the third prayer (*oratio*) of the Mass for reconciliation, *creatorem* is used not to name God (the phrase *Deus clementiae et reconciliationis* is used) but rather is found in what is asked as a result of the prayer, namely, that all may come to know God as Creator and Father of all things (*creatorem et patrem agnoscendum*).

In the prayer over the offerings on Tuesday of the First Week of Lent, *creator* is again juxtaposed with *Deus* and *omnipotens* to address God: *Suscipe, creator omnipotens Deus*. In the introit of one of the commons for the Blessed Virgin Mary *creatorem* refers to Jesus, whom Mary was privileged to bear: *Beata es, Virgo Maria, quae omnium portasti creatorem; genuisti qui te fecit*.

In sum, the term *creator* is used four times as an attribute of God (*Deus*), once as an attribute of God the Father (*Deum Patrem*), once as a complement to how we know God as Father of all (*creatorem et patrem*), and once in reference to Christ (*portasti creatorem*). What is significant in the fourth Eucharistic Prayer is that *Creatori* denotes a relationship both to God as Creator and to the rest of creation (*creaturis omnibus imperaret*).

Creo

The verb *creare* is used twenty times in the missal. Five times it refers specifically and exclusively to God's act of creating a spiritual gift or virtue within us. Of the fifteen references that are germane, nine refer to God's act of creating humanity in Genesis 1:26–28. Reference to the creation of humanity (Gen 1:27) is found in three places: the prayer after the Genesis reading at the Easter Vigil (*creasti hominem*, with the immediate accompaniment of redemption, *et mirabilius redemisti*), in a proper Preface for marriage (*qui hominem pietatis tuae dono creatum*, followed later by a reference to God's creating out of love, *quem enim ex caritate creasti*) and as part of the solemn blessing for the dead (*qui hominem ineffabili bonitate creavit*). Specific reference to the creation of man and woman is found in one prayer (*oratio*) for a wedding: *Deus, qui in humano genere creando, unitatem inter virum et mulierem esse voluisti.* In five places the creation of man and woman is specified as being in God's image/likeness (Gen 1:26). These are in two nuptial blessings (*qui hominem ad imaginem* and *qui virum atque mulierem ad imaginem tuam*), in the introit for a Mass to bless human labor (*et creavit Deus hominem ad imaginem suam*), in the prayer (*oratio*) of the Mass for a happy death (*Deus, qui nos ad imaginem tuam creasti*), and in a prayer (*oratio*) for a deceased person (*ut, quem ad imaginem tuam creare dignatus es*).

Reference to creating the cosmos is found in three places. The first is in the hymn to Christ the King on Passion Sunday referring to the praise offered by the angels, mere mortals, and all created things: *coetus in excelsis te laudat caelicus omnis, et mortalis homo, et cuncta creata simul.* The second is from part of a prayer over the people addressing God as Creator and ruler (*auctore et gubernatore*) and asking him to renew what he has made and to preserve what he has renewed (*et creata restaures, et restaurata conserves*). The third is the text of Genesis 1:1, found in the introit for the blessing of human labor: *et creavit Deus caelum et terram.*

Two most significant references to this verb remain. The first is from the Roman Canon before the *per ipsum*, which section may well be regarded as a classical *locus theologicus* that underscores the relationship of the blessing of the heavenly gifts of bread and wine at the Eucharist with the blessing of other foodstuffs (or other elements) at the end of the Canon. The text is *per quem haec omnia, Domine, sanctificas, vivificas, benedicis, et praestas nobis.* The second reference is found in the fifth Sunday Preface subtitled *De creatione*, newly added to the Roman Rite. The specific use of *creare* is most significant because it refers to humanity's stewardship of all that God has created since God placed all he made under humankind's care: *et rerum ei subiecsti universa miracula, ut vicario munere dominaretur omnibus quae creasti.*

In sum, the *lex orandi* underscores the goodness and worth of what God has created. In using *creare*, the missal emphasizes human beings, created in the divine image and likeness, more frequently as evidence of God's creative work. At the same time, the fact that the Roman Canon and a Sunday Preface speak clearly of other created things indicates more than an openness to the cosmos, as is evidenced in the other three cosmic references already noted. While almost all references to *creare* are to God's creative work, the fact that a Sunday Preface directly stresses humanity's stewardship of creation is most significant, both as a liturgical validation of the Genesis text (Gen 1:26–28) and because the notion of stewardship is a focal argument for many contemporary theologians who speak of humanity's responsibility for creation.

Creatio

Some of the same theological conclusions drawn above for the verb *creare* are at issue in the missal's use of the (abstract) noun *creatio*. This term is found in a prayer for blessing holy water during Easter, in two prayers (*orationes*), and in one prayer over the offerings. The text used for blessing water at the Easter Vigil when no baptisms occur is also used throughout the Easter season for the rite of water blessing and sprinkling. In this instance God's wonderful work of creating humanity is underscored in relation to the more wonderful work of redemption: *et nobis, mirabile nostrae creationis, sed et redemptionis nostrae mirabilius, memorantibus.* God's work of creating good gifts from the earth is noted in the prayer over the gifts on the fourth Tuesday of Lent. In speaking of the gifts used at the Eucharist we acknowledge that they are given to us by God both as signs from creation to help us in our mortal lives and as evidence of the divine promise of eternal life: *munera quae dedisti, ut et creationis tuae circa mortalitatem nostram testificentur auxilium, et remedium nobis immortalitatis operentur.* Interestingly both prayers (*orationes*) are taken from Masses for the blessing of human labor and speak to humanity's cooperation in the divine work of creation. The first acknowledges God's using our human labors to complete and direct the great work of your creation: *Deus, qui humano labore immensum creationis opus iugiter perficis atque gubernas.* The second use of *creatio* speaks of humanity's collaboration in the divine plan of creation: *et creationi divinae perficiendae sociam operam praestare mereamur.*

Thus, the term *creatio* refers to the good things of this earth that become the eucharistic gifts, of the creation of humanity, and of humanity's cooperation with God in the work of creation.

Creatura

In all, the term *creatura* is found twenty-seven times in the missal. In four instances it is used to refer to the new creation established in Christ, three times in relation to the incarnation and once in relation to Easter. More to the point of our investigation, however, are the references to the cosmos, to the world (more specific than cosmos), as well as to angels, humans, and gifts from God's creation.

The introduction of the fourth Eucharistic Prayer to Catholic euchology in the missal of Paul VI has been hailed for a variety of reasons, not the least of which is its extended *magnalia Dei* as motivation to praise God for creation and redemption. This is most significant for our investigation because in four places this prayer uses *creatura*, twice to refer to the whole cosmos and twice to creation in general. The cosmic references are in the Preface leading to the Sanctus, where humanity is imaged as giving voice to the praise of all creation: *cum omnibus et nos et, per nostram vocem, omnis quae sub caelo est creatura nomen tuum in exsultatione confitemur, cantantes.* It is used in the last section, before the *per ipsum*, speaking of Mary, the saints, and the whole creation: *Maria, cum Apostolis et Sanctis tuis in regno tuo, ubi cum universa creatura.* The other two references in this prayer are to God's filling all creatures with his blessing (in the preface: *ut creaturas tuas benedictionibus adimpleres multasque laetificares*) and to humanity's exercising dominion over all created things (in the postsanctus: *eique commisisti mundi curam universi, ut, tibi soli Creatori serviens, creaturis omnibus imperaret*).

Two additional references to creation are found in the formulary for Christ the King. The prayer (*oratio*) speaks of all creatures, freed from slavery and sin, serving and praising God forever: *omnia instaurare voluisti, concede propitius, ut tota creatura, a servitute liberata, tuae maiestati deserviat ac te sine fine collaudet.* The preface refers to all creation under Christ's rule: *suo subiectis imperio omnibus creaturis, aeternum et universale regnum immensae tuae traderet maiestati.*

Two other parts of Eucharistic Prayers also refer to creation, in general, praising God. The first is in the third common Preface: *unde merito tibi cunctae serviunt creaturae.* The second is in the postsanctus of the third Eucharistic Prayer: *vere Sanctus es, Domine, et merito te laudat omnis a te condita creatura.*

In five other places the missal refers to creation in general. The first is the prayer (*oratio*) from the Feast of St. Polycarp, where God is named as the God of all creatures: *Deus universae creaturae.* The second is in the prayer (*oratio*) for the blessing of the civil year, referring to God as source of all created things: *Deus, qui, sine initio et sine fine, totius es principium creaturae.* The third is from the prayer (*oratio*) for Masses in time of famine, referring to God providing for all creatures: *Deus, qui bonus et omnipotens omnibus provides creaturis.* The fourth is from the prayer (*oratio*) for the dying, which acknowledges God's unfailing love for all his creatures: *omnipotens et misericors Deus, qui amorem tuum creaturis.* Of particular interest is the fifth instance because it is one of two examples of a negative reference to *creatura* in the missal. Taken from Romans 8:38–39, the antiphon for Masses commemorating several martyrs states that nothing can separate us from the love of Christ: *neque mors, neque vita, neque creatura.* The only other negative reference was already noted in the fourth Eucharistic Prayer about all creation being freed from sin and death through Christ's redemption.

All four references to humans that use *creatura* are found in Masses connected with the spread of the gospel. In two places the text of Mark 16:15 about going into the whole world and preaching the gospel to all creatures is used as a communion antiphon, once on the Feast of St. Mark and once in a Mass for evangelization. This same phrase (to the whole world) inspires two prayers (*orationes*) for Masses of evangelization: *et operarios in eam mitte dignanter, ut omni creaturae Evangelium praedicetur et ad omnem creaturam salvandam urgentius vocari se sentiant.*

The last four references to *creatura* are less likely to be translated in vernacular texts simply because the term sets up references in blessing prayers to water and salt. The first reference is in the text of the blessing of water at the Easter Vigil introducing the elaborate recounting of how water was used in salvation history: *et creaturam aquae multis modis praeparasti.* The next two references are in the introduction to the blessing of water at the Easter Vigil when baptisms do not take place and at the Sunday rite of blessing and sprinkling holy water: *ut hanc creaturam aquae benedicere dignetur.* The last reference is also to the Sunday rite of water blessing; the phrase *ut hanc creaturam benedicere* is used in the prayer for blessing salt if this is mixed with the blessed water on Sundays.

Of the terms studied thus far, *creatura* yields rich insight about the value of the God's presence and work in the cosmos, in the universe, on this earth, and among human beings. A positive appreciation of all these things is reflected in the Roman Missal, which underscores the goodness of God's creation and a theology bespeaking this goodness in terms of the world's sacramentality. The fact that bread and wine, water and salt are also referred to as specific aspects of God's creation and are used in the celebration of baptism and Eucharist underscores the relationship of sacramentality in general to the celebration of sacraments.

The cosmos does indeed provide an arena and forum for humanity's sharing in God's good gifts.

Condo

The verb *condere* is found twelve times in the Roman Missal. Each use refers to God's action, past or present. Five of these have already been noted above: once when naming God as Creator, twice when speaking of the creatures God has created, both persons and things (bread and wine), and twice when speaking of the creation of human beings. One addresses God as *Pater sancte*, having created humanity in his image, and another addresses God as *Creator omnium*, having created male and female in the beginning.

One use of *condere* is found in the hymn text for adoration of the cross on Good Friday and refers to Christ as a child having been placed in the manger: *vagit infans inter arta conditus praesaepia*. Another use of *condere* refers to God's having used water to set his people free and to slake their thirst in the desert (*aquam etiam tuae ministram misericordiae condidisti*) in the blessing prayer at the Easter Vigil. All the remaining uses of *condere* juxtapose God's having created human beings with humanity's fulfillment in God or redemption in Christ. The reference to God creating humans and their finding true peace in him is in the prayer for those who do not believe in God used on Good Friday: *qui cunctos homines condidisti, ut te semper desiderando quaererent et inveniendo quiescerent*. The first explicit christological reference to creation is the classic prayer (*oratio*) for Christmas day about human dignity and its restoration in Christ: *Deus, qui humanae substantiae dignitatem et mirabiliter condidisti, et mirabilius reformasti*. The second speaks about humankind made in God's image and being freed from the state of the fallen to new life through baptism: *ut homo, ad imaginem tuam conditus, sacramento baptismalis a cunctis squaloribus vetustatis ablutus*. The final christological reference is in the second common Preface, which speaks of humanity created, condemned, and redeemed: *qui bonitate hominem condidisti, ac iustitia damnatum misericordia redemisti: per Christum Dominum nostrum*.

When assessing the references to *condere* apart from the five already treated above in relation to other creation terms, it can be said that all usages relate to salvation history (humankind's creation in Genesis or water in Genesis and Exodus), to God as the source of true peace for humanity or to Christ's redemption that restores humanity to its lost innocence or redeems him with one specific reference to the sacrament of baptism. Thus, there is not a theology of creation per se here, but a theology of creation leading to the already established recreation in Christ.

Conditor

In all, *conditor* is found eleven times in the missal, one of which was already discussed above in relation to the word *creare* found in the nuptial blessing (acknowledging God as holy Father, Creator of the universe: *Pater sancte, mundi conditor universi*). In the hymn for the veneration of the cross on Good Friday, Christ is acclaimed as coming from God the Father, the Creator of the world: *Missus est ab arce Patris Natus, orbis conditor*. In two places God is named as *Rerum conditor, Deus*, and on both occasions this title leads to a reference to human work. The first is from the prayer (*oratio*) of St. Joseph the Worker: *qui legem laboris humano generi statuisti*. The second is from the prayer (*oratio*) for the blessing of human labor: *qui hominem iussisti laboris officia sustinere*. In one of the prayers (*oratio*) for Masses for peace, God is named simply *conditor mundi*.

In four places God is addressed as *conditor et redemptor*, three of which are from prayers for commemorations of the faithful departed. In first prayer (*oratio*) commemorating all the faithful departed the petition is that the departed come to see their Creator and Redeemer: *concede famulis tuis de functis*. In the second prayer (*oratio*), the petition is that the named persons may contemplate God forever: *concede famulis tuis (N. et N.)...possint perpetuo contemplari*. In the third, God the Creator and Redeemer is asked to forgive them their sins: *famulis tuis remissionem cunctorum tribue peccatorum*. The fourth prayer (*oratio*) is used in Advent on December 17th and refers to the Creator and Redeemer of human nature: *humanae conditor et redemptor naturae*.

In the third common Preface, God the Father is addressed as both the Creator and merciful Redeemer of mankind: *qui per Filium dilectionis tuae, sicut conditor generis es humani*. The final reference to *conditor* also occurs in a christological context. In the proper preface for Mary Mother of the Church it states that the Virgin gave birth to the Creator, *pariens Conditorem*.

This review discloses that there are about an equal number of references to *conditor* alone as there are to *conditor et redemptor*. More often than not the references are to humans as products of God's creative work for whom God is asked for a variety of things, including remission of sins.

Additional Terms

Albert Blaise offers a series of terms dealing with creation as found in the liturgy. Of this list, the following usages bear on our investigation.

Auctor

Of the thirty-three uses of *auctor* in the missal, six refer to the creation in terms of God's act of creating and two refer to symbols used at particular liturgies—light and baptism. Regarding creation, God is named *auctorem et gubernatorem*, Creator and guide of creation, in the prayer (*oratio*) for the eighteenth Sunday and the eighth prayer over the people. God is named Creator of all that is good (*bonorum omnium... auctori*) in the prayer (*oratio*) for the thirty-third Sunday. He is acknowledged author/source of (all) life (*auctorem vitae*) in the solemn blessing of the Virgin Mary and in the prayer (*oratio*) for the common of Mary in Christmastime. God is acknowledged as source/Creator of the fruits of the earth and of the spirit (*auctor fructum et spiritalium*) in the prayer over the offerings in the Mass for blessing of the fields (sowing time).

Of note are the references to God in relation to light and baptism. The reference to true light and source of eternal light—*Deus, lumen verum, aeternae lucis propagator et auctor*—is in the prayer for the blessing of candles on the presentation. The reference to Christ as the author of baptism occurs in the Preface for the solemnity of the birth of John the Baptist, which is repeated on the feast of his beheading: *suae regenerationis congoscat auctorem*.

While normally we have been reticent to include references to recreation and redemption in Christ, the fact that these two uses occur in relation to the symbols of light and water are most significant in themselves and methodologically.

Dispono

The first reference to *dispono* is in the fifth Sunday Preface (already reviewed) about creating all things that are, which is in a section that includes the creation (*facere*) of humanity in God's image: *qui omnia mundi elementa fecisti, et vices disposuisti temporum variari; hominem vero formasti ad imaginem tuam.* These same sentiments are found in the nuptial blessing that speaks of God creating the universe and creating humanity in the divine image: *qui, dispositis universitatis exordiis et homine ad imaginem tuam.* God's involvement in ruling all creation in divine providence (*Deus qui mirabili consilio universa disponis*) is cited in the prayer (*oratio*) for Masses for one's country or state. God's arranging and directing all creation is similarly noted in the prayer (*oratio*) for international meetings.

Facio

Of the hundreds of times this term is used in the missal, ten are germane for our task here. In two introit antiphons God is praised for having done marvelous deeds: *faciens mirabilia* and *quia mirabilia fecit Dominus.* In another introit he is praised for creating all things in heaven and on earth: *tu enim fecisti omnia, caelum et terra.* Finally, in two other antiphons God is praised for having created us (*qui fecit nos*) and for having created all things for us in true justice (*omnia, quae fecisti nobis, Domine, in vero iudicio fecisti*).

In the five properly euchological references that remain, two uses of *facio* are in the fourth Eucharistic Prayer: God as source of life (preface: *fons vitae cuncta fecisti*) and as having made all things in wisdom and love (postsanctus: *quia magnus es et omnia opera tua in sapientia et caritate fecisti*). The term is used in reference to God having created all things on the earth, which leads to the reference to creating humankind: *qui omnia mundi elementa fecisti.* It is used in the prayer for blessing water during Easter in reference to water's life-giving properties: *ipsam enim tu fecisti, ut et arva fecunditate donaret.* In one prayer (*oratio*) for the faithful departed, *facio* is used to draw out that God has created us and granted us to share in the status of adoption: *quem ad imaginem tuam creare dignatus es et adoptionis participem fecisti.*

If one asserts that a Preface and Eucharistic Prayer are among the most important euchological texts in the missal, then the uses of *facio* referring to creation (world and human beings) are most significant since they comprise four of the five texts reviewed.

Fundo

Of the ten uses of *fundo* in the missal, only one is germane here. It is somewhat paradoxical because it is found in the prayer (*oratio*) from Masses in time of earthquakes. This prayer refers to God having founded the earth on its firm foundations: *Deus, qui terram super stabilitatem suam.*

Opera

Of the two uses of *opera* the more important for us is the reference in the prayer (*oratio*) and for blessing human labor that refers to our cooperating with God's creative power: *et creationi divinae perficiendae sociam operam praestare mereamur.*

ECOLOGICAL SIGNIFICANCE OF THE CELEBRATION OF THE EUCHARIST

To this point, we have seen that the work of gathering and making by humans for the Eucharist are linked to the sacramentality of all of life. We see how the Eucharist continues Christ's paschal victory via death and resurrection. This combination of life and death, positive and negative, puts the world into proper perspective as both graced filled and flawed and in need of complete redemption. Our eucharistic liturgy prevents us from becoming too optimistic about the world.

Yet the celebration of liturgy also combats pessimism about the world and world events. By its very shape and structure, liturgy is a ritual experience that reflects an optimistic approach to human life. In the end, "all will be well." In the meantime, we need sacramental liturgy to put the world into focus and perspective. Opportunities for experiences of hope abound in the celebration of sacraments—hope in the act of liturgy and hope derived from the act of liturgy which enables us to deal with life.

A second important point is that the celebration of the liturgy reflects the contemporary emphasis on the theology of creation and places it on a truly theological ground by emphasizing that God's goodness is the source of the things of this earth raised up in liturgy. For example, water is a natural symbol from God's providence; bread and wine result from human manufacture of what the earth has produced.

Third, liturgy enacts our belief that we worship God by using the elements of this world. This means that liturgy is always both anthropological and cosmic; it articulates what we believe about the human person and the cosmos. Better yet, through sacramental liturgy human persons put their lives and the world itself into proper perspective. We use "daily and domestic things" in liturgy, specifically in eucharistic food and dining, and they remind us of the goodness, generosity, and largesse of the God we worship.

The three steps of manufacture, proclamation, and sharing of food apply to the eucharistic liturgy because this dynamic happens in daily life. Liturgy thus provides the lens we need to view all of reality, which reality is always integrative of the sacred and secular and of what is both fully divine and fully human. Having a wide-angle lens on as much of life as possible is true to what I now call the principle of the *ecology of the liturgy*. Part of the challenge that celebrating sacramental liturgy can offer is to help us reflect on the world in which we live and to ponder our care for it as well as our concern for those who dwell on it. This means taking seriously our obligation of being in communion with and caring for our common home. We are never to presume that we are masters or lords of our common home. We are fellow companions, responsible to succeeding generations for our care of it.

Elements from Human Manufacture

In addition to engaging us in rituals that articulate multifaceted theological meanings of the primal elements when expressed through the texts and rites of the liturgy, the sacraments in particular engage us in "the work of human hands." The human capacity for thinking and working (*homo faber*) are always presumed in the experience of liturgy. The acclamation at the presentation of the bread and wine at Mass states it succinctly: "Through your goodness we have received the bread/wine we offer you, fruit of the earth and the work of human hands."

We engage our bodies in the primal elements—earth, air, fire, and water—and in the work of human hands, which respects all that goes into the preparation for and execution of the liturgy. Among other things, "the work of our redemption" promised and accomplished by the will and act of God the Father is brought about by the incarnation:

> For whenever the memorial of this sacrifice is celebrated
> the work of our redemption is accomplished.
> (Prayer over the Offerings, Second Sunday in Ordinary Time and
>   Prayer over the Offerings, Evening Mass of the Lord's Supper)

A more subtle and yet important assertion about the value of the human manufacture of some elements of the liturgy is toward the end of the Exsultet during the Easter Vigil when the deacon/priest praises "the work of bees and of your servant's hands." The very act of acclaiming saving history through the Exsultet, which is sung praise in the light of the paschal candle, is to acknowledge that the candle itself is the product of "the work of human hands."

In the book *Sacred Oils*—a careful commentary on *The Order of Blessing the Oil of Catechumens and of the Sick*—Paul Turner observes,

> Trees produced the olives, and the olives produced the oil so abundant throughout the Old Testament Mediterranean world. Its production required considerable skill and intense labor. Even the trees grew well in the local climate, farmer had to care for them, and workers had to harvest the olives. Someone had [sic] carry heavy stones to an accessible site. Someone had to fashion them into a mill. Someone had to operate the mill, pressing the olives to release their treasure. Someone had to create flasks and arrange storage space. Someone had to collect the oil and carry it home. Though it often gives pleasure, oil results from hard work.[22]

This same process should be borne in mind as we address how the Eucharist is also "the work of human hands."

Some prayers of the Roman Missal speak of "a holy exchange" and "a holy exchange of gifts." The word *exchange* is the key here, but it is also multivalent. In some contexts, it refers to the incarnation, humanity, and divinity joined. In other places, it refers to the gifts of bread and wine (to) become the body and blood of Christ. Examples include the third Christmas Preface: "For through him the holy exchange that restores our life has shone forth today in splendor." The prayer over the offerings at Christmas is also an important example:

> That through this most holy exchange
> we may be found in the likeness of Christ
> in whom our nature is united to you.
>
> (Mass during the Night)

> ...that, just as Christ was born a man and also yet
> shone forth as God,
> so these earthly gifts may confer on us what is divine.
>
> (Mass at Dawn)

Liturgical Theology—Multivalence, Not Ambiguity

We have presumed here that each of us is engaged in the act of doing liturgical theology as we are engaged in the sacred liturgy. In addition, the engagement of our senses and our intellect in the liturgy combine to foster an experience of the most profound mysteries of our faith, not "merely our understanding of them. Didacticism and engaging in the liturgy only for education misfire and do not allow the liturgy to be acts of incorporation into the living God. It cannot be stressed enough that words like action, event, dynamism, and engagement should always mark our appreciation of what the liturgy is. The information we glean from liturgical theology should lead to a deeper incorporation into the mystery of God. The understanding we glean of the sacred sites and what they mean always should lead us to a deeper experience of the mystery that is God.

Precision in appreciating the spoken words of the liturgy of the sacraments should lead us to engage in what St. Augustine called the "visible words" of the sacraments. Liturgical theology shies away from definitions and leads to a "free fall" of our individual and collective imaginations. Liturgical theology is more often than not engaging us in poetry and metaphor than in theological definitions. One of the challenges of translating the liturgy into the vernacular is that even as we continually seek for the least inadequate terminology for the liturgy. No words can ever really be adequate and perhaps even some finely minted words and phrases can get in the way of mediating the immediate encounter with the mystery of God even through the liturgy.

We do not give voice to creation in the liturgy. Rather, we revere the voice creation gives by being its very self to its Creator and the maker of heaven and earth. We humans made in God's image and likeness reflect the mystery of the incarnation as we live and abide in the Triune God "in whom we live and move and have our being" (Sunday Preface VI). The liturgy respects the still imperfect pilgrim church as the already deified Body of Christ, with all our talents and gifts, including creativity and human work.

CONCLUSION

Our studies of creation and of the work of human hands in the present missal indicate that reference to God as both Creator at the beginning and sustainer of all he has created is prevalent. A doxological cast is given to some references as motives to praise God as found in blessing prayers especially. The teaching of Genesis on God's having created human beings in the divine image and likeness, male and female, is underscored repeatedly and human labor is sanctified when it cooperates with God's creative plan. This liturgical theology is not insignificant. The reliance on Genesis in terms of creating man and woman in God's image and likeness and acknowledging that humans are endowed with creativity and responsibility for creation is itself a worthy insight into a systematic theology of creation and an ethical response to how creation is to be treated. The stewardship motif from the Scriptures and the liturgy is a key insight and can be a focus for a substantial theology of creation.

The combination of references to creation with the use of liturgical symbols is also of import. When they refer to *water, salt, light,* and *bread and wine*, these terms articulate what is inherent in every liturgy, namely, engagement in symbols taken from creation (earth, air, fire, and water) and symbols manufactured by humans that are the result of ingenuity and labor. In all of this, the *lex orandi* challenges and focuses the *lex credendi*.

Given the classical status of referring to creation in liturgy and the environmental crises today, are additional references to creation required for the eucharistic liturgy? While some would ask for such inclusion, it should be recalled that liturgy as event is central and euchology accompanies that event. Texts set up and enhance, but should not define or discourse about, what takes place. Actions are primary; texts support. Thus, one could argue that what is done nonverbally, but very truly, should be respected as conveyors of levels of meaning that cannot be disclosed sufficiently with words on any account. The inherent multivalence of all liturgy makes one cautions about adding too many words because in the end words serve an encounter with the divine on many levels. They are not to dominate over it.

Gratefully, one aspect of the current liturgical reform is greater engagement by the assembly in the symbolic actions of the sacraments. Thus, words are no longer needed to make up for what is not experienced by the faithful in the liturgy (e.g., infrequent communion), and what is experienced liturgically today ought not be accompanied by too many words and explanations. In fact, the wordiness of the contemporary liturgy as sometimes pastorally implemented is a defect. Paucity of words and maximal use of symbols allow sacraments to be bearers of many levels and kinds of meaning. From what we have seen here we can state that the theology of creation in the Roman Missal is both endorsed by its euchology and demonstrated regularly in the eucharistic action itself. Some references reviewed here are pithy. But they are powerful accompaniments to a rich complex of liturgical actions.

There are several contexts within which to consider the symbolic reality of sacrament: cosmic, anthropological, ecclesial, christological, pneumatological, trinitarian, and eschatological. Our investigation of the *lex orandi* substantiates the cosmic and anthropological aspects of this theology in that creation and the work of human beings in creation are two strata in the interpretation of the eucharistic liturgy in the *Missale Romanum* of Paul VI. Our investigation also relates directly to the remaining sacramental contexts in that every act of liturgy is an expression through human means of the properly theological categories: ecclesial, christological, pneumatological, trinitarian, and eschatological. Each of these contexts is articulated in the missal's euchology. Yet, throughout this review of sacramental contexts, it is the genius of the liturgy that these themes are expressed and experienced, not just thought about, in relation to each other, and they are experienced by humans precisely through symbolic encounter, particularly the use of creation and the work of human hands.

It can be argued that there is a danger in the current emphasis on creation and anthropology in theology because these themes can become detached from true Christian theology and become pantheistic and Pelagian. We would argue that it is their very contextualization in the act of liturgy and in association with the other sacramental contexts just articulated that make them intrinsic factors in developing a true and proper Christian theology. Here, *lex orandi* as expressed in the liturgy grounds and nuances *lex credendi* so that theology is neither too worldly nor too ethereal. A cosmic and anthropological anchor preserves the incarnational foundation of sacramental liturgy and theology. Sacramental theology is diminished, especially its symbolic appreciation, if the christological, trinitarian, ecclesial, and eschatological contexts are not viewed in relation to what we might call the foundational contexts of the cosmic and the anthropological. When all these contexts are taken together and creation given its due import, then a balanced and theologically substantial sacramental theology can result.

The enormity of what is contained in the liturgy is unfathomable. Our active participation in the liturgy should include, presume, and involve our experiencing the God beyond all understanding, the God beyond all categories of thinking, the God beyond all imagining—indeed the God beyond all praising.

CHAPTER SEVEN

LITURGY OF THE HOURS

In light of our method and explorations into the sacraments of baptism and Eucharist, we turn now to the Liturgy of the Hours. The reclamation of the celebration of Hours for all members of the church was a specific intention of the Council fathers (see *Sacrosanctum Concilium* 99) and was subsequently taken up by Pope Paul VI in 1970 through his apostolic constitution *Laudis Canticum*, introducing the four-volume revision of the former *Breviarium Romanum*.[1] In fact, the simple phrase *four-volume revision* introduces several issues to be dealt with in terms of the shape and content of this chapter.

Because of the breadth of the revision of the Hours, this chapter will first address the cosmic contexts in setting the times and seasons for the celebration of the Hours. Then it will review the contents of the hymns that have been traditionally sung at Evening Prayer on weekdays in Ordinary Time and address the contents of names for God as Creator. Finally, it will provide a summary of the contents and importance of the Liturgy of the Hours in the celebration of the Paschal Triduum. This chapter cannot address all issues given the breadth of the revised Hours, and the rationale for these choices will be noted as each part of the chapter unfolds.

COSMIC CONTEXT—TIMES FOR CELEBRATION

Daily

The determination of times for celebration of the daily Liturgy of the Hours, the seasons of the church year, and some feast days derive from the rhythm of the cosmos.[2] Dawn for morning prayer and dusk for evening prayer is underscored in the General Instruction on the Liturgy of the Hours (GILH), which states that morning prayer is "celebrated... as the light of a new day is dawning" (38). It is appropriate that Zechariah's canticle is always used at this hour:

> The dawn from on high shall break upon us,
> to shine on those who dwell in darkness
> and the shadow of death. (Luke 1:79)

It is not a coincidence that this same text is used as the communion antiphon for the Solemnity of the Nativity of John the Baptist, since the date of this feast, June 24th, was deliberately chosen in accord with the length of the sun's rays as experienced in the Northern Hemisphere. When the daylight begins to diminish after June 21st (often called the longest day of the year), the church commemorates the birth of the Baptist, whose saying, "He [Jesus] must increase, but I must decrease" (John 3:30) determined the date for this commemoration. The sign of diminishing daylight in the cosmos has determined the feast of the one whose self-effacement ("decrease") led to people's putting their faith in Christ ("the dawn from on high"). That this feast has a rich tradition of liturgical importance is attested by the fact that the only other births commemorated in the calendar are those of Jesus and the Blessed Virgin Mary. Its significance is further emphasized by the number of Mass formulas honoring the Baptist in the early Verona collection of euchology.[3]

GILH states that when evening approaches and the day is already far spent, Evening Prayer is celebrated, "[when] we join the Churches of the East in calling upon the 'joy-giving light of holy glory'...[and we sing in praise] now that we have come to the setting of the sun and seen the evening star" (39). The Jewish tradition of the *lucernarium*, the lighting of the lamps in the temple at prayer in the evening, is also part of the liturgical ritual traditionally attached to this hour.[4]

Seasons

The phases of the moon and its location determine the date for our celebration of Easter. The interplay of light and darkness is also reflected in the theory of the origins of Christmas that adapts the pagan light festival of the *Dies Natalis Solis Invicti*.[5] The diminishing intensity of the sun in the Northern Hemisphere is reflected in subtle ways in the lections and euchology of Advent and Christmas, texts that become more compelling when this natural phenomenon is experienced. References to the cosmos in the liturgy's assigned Scripture readings and prayers through Advent-Christmas-Epiphany are few, but the fact that there is diminished light (in the Northern Hemisphere) affords a useful cosmic and liturgical context for these weeks in the calendar. Such contexts point to sacred realities that are also transtemporal and metahistorical—within but not bound to historical time and place. It also relays many meanings inherent in the cosmos as this affects how the liturgy is experienced.[6]

Liturgists from the Southern Hemisphere have appropriately critiqued this facile presumption that the cosmic phenomena of light and darkness in the Northern Hemisphere is an essential part of these celebrations. While these arguments should not be jettisoned, the fact that the debate is over cosmic phenomena underscores our point about the cosmic nature of the dating of both Christmas and Easter. At the same time, in praying the liturgy for Advent-Christmas-Epiphany and Lent-Easter-Pentecost, one should be very careful not to presume that the light and darkness phenomenon in the cosmos is universal.[7] The cosmic experience of diminished light at Easter in the Southern Hemisphere could, for example, provide the basis for emphasizing the eschatology of all liturgical feasts and seasons. In other words, cosmic phenomena help us to appreciate that the liturgy is not only a commemoration of historical events of our redemption but also an experience of our experience of these saving mysteries in the cosmos here and now, as well as their hoped-for fulfillment in the kingdom of heaven.

The fact that the dates for Passover and Easter are variable depending on the way different churches interpret the cosmic phenomenon of springtime is itself an important ecumenical phenomenon and challenge. As early as 1963, the fathers at the Second Vatican Council offered that the Christian churches determine a "fixed date for Easter."[8] At the same time, there are calendar issues about the length of Lent and those churches that introduce Lenten disciplines in the weeks prior to Lent itself (e.g., Orthodox Churches and Eastern Catholic Churches). Determining the date for Easter each year has obvious repercussions about the seasons before and after Easter. The shape of thirteen and a half weeks of the liturgical year are determined by the way churches "tell time" at Easter.

Liturgical seasons also have wider influence in the life of the church. For example, the date when an encyclical letter is signed by the pope is important, introduced by the time-honored phrase "given at Rome." For example, John Paul II dated his encyclical on the Eucharist on Holy Thursday 2003, the day when we commemorate the institution of the Eucharist. Pope Francis signed *Laudato Si'* in 2015 on the solemnity of Pentecost, a day commemorating the coming of the Holy Spirit. The refrain for the Responsorial Psalm on Pentecost Sunday is "Lord, send out your Spirit, and renew the face of the earth," with verses from Psalm 104, often called a psalm of "Praise of God the Creator." This same refrain and psalm are used as the response to the first reading at the Easter Vigil from Genesis 1:1—2:2, which recounts the creation story. In both liturgical contexts, these texts reflect a re-creation and renewal of the earth. In addition, the traditional and present entrance antiphon for Pentecost is from the Book of Wisdom (a book frequently quoted in the encyclical) connecting the "Spirit of the Lord" with all of creation: "The Spirit of the Lord has filled the whole world and that which contains all things understands what is said, alleluia" (Wis 1:7).

Pentecost is also a creation feast in that it derives from the Jewish feast of Shavuoth (the Feast of Weeks), a festival that comes at the conclusion of the seven-week period of the grain harvest in early spring. The actual beginning of the grain harvest was marked by the sacrifice at the sanctuary of the *omer* (the first sheaf of the newly cut barley)—the Passover. Then, fifty days later, at the close of the harvest period, two loaves of bread baked from the wheat of the new crop were offered as a sacrifice to God. This offering was made as a token of thanksgiving to God for making the land fertile enough to produce food.

According to Deuteronomy 26:1–11 and 16:9–12, Shavuoth is also a time to commemorate the exodus from Egypt, the giving of the Torah, and God's self-revelation ("theophany") on Mt. Sinai. Shavuoth is a time to thank God for providing land "flowing with milk and honey" (Exod 33:3). It is customary during Shavuoth to eat leavened bread baked from the new wheat because leavened bread symbolizes freedom. The leavened bread is a product of one's own land, as opposed to unleavened bread eaten in haste during the exodus. Traditionally, dairy products and honey are also eaten as a reminder of God's promise to the children of Israel that he would give them land flowing with milk and honey. It is a time to remember that God freed a people once in bondage, a commemoration conducted through sharing the fruit of the earth. Our continued call for God to remember his promise of freedom, lived out through our offering of the fruits of the earth, is echoed in the first words of the hymn assigned for First Vespers on the solemnity of Pentecost, a ninth-century text attributed to Rabanus Maurus: *Veni Creator Spiritus*, "Come Creator Spirit."

ECOLOGICAL CONTENTS— *LEX ORANDI*

The following two sections concern examples of what is found in the revised *Liturgia Horarum*.[9] The first is chosen because translations of these important hymns did not find their way into the American English translation of the Hours. The second is because of the importance of appreciating the variety of names we use to call on God as Creator and the various nuances these names can offer about insights about the "maker of heaven and earth."

Hymns for the Days of Creation

The ecological and cosmic contents of some of the seasons of the liturgical year are clear and often used as a measuring point for the cosmic dimensions of all liturgy, the premier example of which is the Easter Vigil.[10] It is not a coincidence that the first reading at the Vigil is the creation story Genesis 1:1—2:2.[11]

The singing of hymns is a traditional component of Hours in the Roman Rite. They are often referred to as "sung theology"—quite rightly. However, many of the hymns in the revision of the Liturgy of the Hours in English are from contemporary sources. A sad lacuna has been the lack of the hymns acclaiming the six days of creation. These will be restored in the (still forthcoming) English retranslation of the Hours. Fruitful discussions continue about who the author of these hymns (or some of the hymns) might be, and in any case, our argument concerns their contents.[12] These hymns were included in the breviary of 1568; the reform preceding this breviary revised the Latin texts to reflect a more "classical" style (to appeal to Renaissance humanists). These texts remained in the official books of the Roman Rite up to Vatican II. They were also included in the Hours for the Franciscans, while the Benedictines, Cistercians, Dominicans, and some other orders retained their own traditional texts.[13] Peter Jeffery summarizes the hymns in this way:[14]

HYMN	VESPERS	SOURCE	CREATION
Lucis creator optime	Sunday	Gen 1:1–5	light
Inmense caeli conditor	Monday	Gen 1:6–10	heaven separated from earth
Telluris ingens conditor	Tuesday	Gen 1:11–13	plants
Caeli deus sanctissime	Wednesday	Gen 1:14–19	sun, moon, planets
Magnae deus potentiae	Thursday	Gen 1:20–23	fish, animals
Plasmator hominis deus	Friday	Gen 1:24–31	mammals, human beings

Jeffery continues by indicating references to the Creator and creation in all six hymns, along with allegorical interpretations. For example, he presents the Sunday hymn *Lucis creator optime* as follows:

> On Sunday evening, the new series of hymns begins by invoking the Creator in the first line. Then it proceeds to the

creation of light on the first day. Darkness appears in the second stanza as an allegory for sin. The mind's struggle to remain faithful takes up half the poem, the last two stanzas out of four, for these new hymns are only half the length of Ambrose's model.

The hymn text for Sunday is as follows:

Lucis creator optime lucem dierum proferens primordiis lucis novae mundi parans originem	Good creator of light, bringing forth the light of days, preparing the origin of the world in the first stirrings of new light,
qui mane iunctum vesperi diem vocari praecipis: tetrum chaos illabitur audi preces cum fletibus	[you] who instruct morning-joined-to-evening to be called "day"— foul darkness descends: Hear [our] prayers with [our] wailings,

ne mens gravata crimine
Vitae sit exul munere
dum nil per enne cogitat
seseque culpis illigat.
	Nor may the mind, weighed
	  down by sin,
	be an exile from the task of life,
	while it gives no thought to what
	  is lasting
	and binds itself with faults.

caelorum pulset intimum
vitale tollat praemium
vitemus omne noxium
purgemus omne pessimum.
	Let [the mind] knock at the
	  innermost of the heavens.
	Let it take up the reward of life.
	Let us shun all that is harmful.
	Let us purge all that is worst
	  [in us].

The poem is metrical rather than rhythmic, looking back to the classical era. It makes use of assonance, a kind of vowel parallelism, that results in half-rhymes: *i* and *e* in *optime* and *originem* in the first stanza; *i* and *u* in *illabitur* and *fletibus* in the second stanza; *i* and *a* in *cogitat* and *illigat* in the third; -*imum* bracketing -*ium* in the fourth. Assonance, observable in all the hymns of this series, was not unknown in classical poetry but was very popular in the medieval period.

Jeffery also provides detailed commentary, for example the following:

> The Latin word "chaos" means more than my translation conveys with the word "darkness." It implies that nighttime threatens to undo creation itself, returning to the void and empty world that existed just before on the very first day God said, "Let there be light." The word also suggested a chasm of separation, as in Luke 16:26, especially when spelled *chaus* as it was in our manuscript before being corrected to *chaos* in the original hand. No wonder the poet fears being exiled and with prayers and wailings wells the mind (which in patristic Latin can refer to the soul) to "knock at the innermost heavens." One wonders if our poet knew that the phrase *tetrum chaos* also appears in a fifth-century north African poem about creation.[15]

This insightful commentary indicates that several things are going on in this text in addition to praising the "good creator of light." Cosmic "light" and "darkness" exemplify the classic fight between light and darkness in the soul of humans. "Chaos" is something that God ordered into creation, but it can still plague humanity. The hymn ends with such admonitions as a cosmic reference to "knock at the innermost of the heavens" and personal reference to "let us purge all that is the worst [in us]." Similar commentaries abound for all six hymns, offering richness and depth only perceived through the eyes and ears of revelation and faith in the God of creation, redemption, and covenant.

God as Creator in the Hymns of the Liturgy of the Hours

We now turn to how God is named in the hymns of the Hours by examining the present four-week cycle, the proper of time, the proper of saints and the commons.[16]

Latin	English	Associated Meanings	
Creator[17]	Creator	the one God Creator/maker of all things	*29 times*
Conditor[18]	founder	constructor	*28 times*

Continued

Rector[19]	guide	institutor, head, governor	7 times
Plasmator[20]	maker	The one who forms	2 times
Auctor[21]	author	inventor, promotor, an authority	13 times
Fons omnium[22]	font/source of all	origin	2 times
Sator[23]	the Father	first among others	8 times

A proper liturgical hermeneutic would require examining the contexts in which a liturgy is enacted,[24] which for these hymn references would be an enormous task. I single out the very first hymn for Evening Prayer during Advent (to December 16) as but one illustration of the value of noting how the Hours names the God of creation. Here, the term *conditor*, as well as several biblical and creedal references, is contextualized within the season of Advent.

Conditor alme siderum,	See John 1:3
æterna lux credentium,	John 1:9
Christe, redemptor omnium,	"redeemer" image "to buy back"
exaudi preces supplicum.	
Qui condolens interitu	
mortis perire saeculum,	Adam and Eve's fall
salvasti mundum languidum,	
donans reis remedium,	
Vergente mundi vespere,	Evening as at night and as in the Fall.
uti sponsus de thalamo,	Matt 25:1–13, wise and foolish virgins
egressus honestissima	
Virginis matris clausula.	Blessed Virgin Mary
Cuius forti potentiæ	
genu curvantur omnia;	"every knee shall bend" (Phil 2:10)
cælestia, terrestria	
nutu fatentur súbdita.	

Te, Sancte, fide quaesumus,	
venture iudex saeculi,	CR: "in glory to judge the living and the dead"
conserva nos in tempore	
hostis a telo perfidi.	
Sit, Christe, rex piissime,	Repeats last Sunday Christ the King of all Creation
tibi Patrique gloria	Trinitarian doxology
cum Spiritu Paraclito,	
in sempiterna saecula. Amen.	

1. O loving Maker of the stars,
believers' everlasting light,
O Christ, Redeemer of us all,
with kindness hear our humble prayer.

2. With pity, you beheld the fate
that death imposed on ages past;
you gave the guilty healing grace
and saved a weak and fallen world.

3. When evening fell upon the earth,
as bridegroom from the bridal room,
from honored cloister forth you came,
born from the Virgin Mother pure.

4. Before your strong and steadfast might,
on earth and in the heavens above
all knees bend low, all hearts confess
submission to your sovereign will.

5. With faith we beg you, Holy Lord,
the Judge of ages still to come,
that in our time you keep us safe
from snares of our deceitful foe.

D. To you, O Christ, most loving King,
and to the Father, glory be,

143

one with the Spirit Paraclete,
from age to age for evermore. Amen.

God is named as Creator, attributes are identified, actions are commemorated, and intercessions are made. These various theological meanings articulated in poetry, meter, and song are among the reasons why GILH says in 173,

> A very ancient tradition gives hymns the place in the office that they still retain [Matt 11:25ff. and Luke 10:21ff.]. By their mystical and poetic character, they are specifically designed for God's praise. But they also are an element for the people; in fact, more often than the other parts of the office the hymns bring out the proper theme of individual hours or feasts and incline and draw the spirit to a devout celebration. The beauty of their language often adds to this power. Furthermore, in the office hymns are the main poetic element created by the Church.

LITURGY OF THE HOURS— PASCHAL TRIDUUM

The presentation of Liturgy of the Hours for the whole Triduum is offered here as an essential complement to what was argued above in terms of the Paschal Vigil (baptism) and the Evening Mass of the Lord's Supper (Eucharist). The Paschal Triduum is celebrated from Holy Thursday evening through Evening Prayer on Easter day. This presentation of the Hours is meant to complement and to draw out that there are many ways to interpret liturgy, in general, and the sacraments, in particular. The principle has been and is sustained here that we engage the church's liturgy itself as the basis on which we appreciate what participation in the liturgy means. It is also intended to contextualize this treatment of liturgy and sacraments by presuming that the Paschal Triduum is the center of the church's faith and the heart of our celebrating this mystery of faith in the privileged liturgies of these three days. It also underscores that an ecological understanding of liturgy and the sacraments is also a paschal understanding.

Holy Thursday

The Paschal Triduum begins with the evening liturgy, thus making the Hours up to evening prayer still part of Lent. Evening Prayer for Holy Thursday is given after the heading "Easter Triduum of the Passion and Resurrection of the Lord," and the direction for this Hour states, "Evening Prayer is said only by those who do not participate in the evening Mass of the Lord's Supper."

The antiphons speak of Jesus as the "firstborn of the dead," who "will be the champion of the helpless" and who "will free the poor from the grip of the powerful." The third antiphon uses Johannine language (from Revelation and the Gospel of John) when it clearly states that "the saints won their victory over death through the blood of the Lamb and the truth to which they bore witness." The Scripture reading from Hebrews 13:12–15 speaks about Jesus's death as the means through which his people are sanctified, particularly through his blood. The responsory is not in the usual form; instead, the tradition of using the section from Philippians 2 about Christ's humiliation as a responsory here and throughout the Triduum is retained. Hence, we affirm that it was for our sakes that Christ was obedient to the point of accepting death on a cross.

Both the antiphon to the canticle of the Blessed Virgin and the introduction to the intercessions refer to the Eucharist. This is complemented in the petitions this evening that ask that we might have a greater share in both the Lord's passion and resurrection, and that as Christ humbled himself by being obedient even to accepting death, we who seek to imitate him might be given the gifts of obedience and patient endurance. The prayer to conclude this Hour is not from the eucharistic liturgy of the Lord's Supper. The prayer for evening prayer speaks of the priesthood of Christ and the paschal mystery; through the liturgy we are drawn into them.

Good Friday

Because evening prayer of Holy Thursday is said only by those who do not participate in the Evening Mass of the Lord's Supper, for most the Hours for Triduum begin with the office of readings on Good Friday. The first reading at the office of readings is from Hebrews 9:11–28, about Christ's shedding his own blood as High Priest who entered the sanctuary once for all. The text ends, "Christ was offered up once to take away the sins of the world [and] will appear a second time not to take away sin but to bring salvation to those who eagerly await him" (Heb 9:28). The responsory from Isaiah 53:7, 12 picks up on the theme of blood and the lamb led to slaughter, given up to death "to give his people life." This text is particularly important on this day because it is part of the first reading at the afternoon liturgy of the Lord's passion.

The second reading is from the *Catecheses* of St. John Chrysostom, an important collection of texts that refer to the meaning of the Christian life and the sacraments of initiation. This text takes up the theme of the import and power of blood in salvation history, drawing from the Book of Exodus and Jesus's crucifixion in the Gospel of John, which is the Gospel for the liturgy of the Lord's passion. Also, the author develops some of the eucharistic symbolism derived from this understanding of the place of blood in the act of redemption. This section can well be understood to indicate the bridge that the liturgy establishes between the Triduum and the season of Easter, for the Eucharist is traditionally understood as the paschal sacrament, the continuing renewal of the redemption won by Christ.

The psalms used at the office of readings have been specially selected to coincide with the focus on suffering and death of Good Friday. Psalm 2 has often been used in Christian liturgy because of an obvious messianic interpretation. "You are my son. It is I who have begotten you this day" (Ps 2:7) has clear christological overtones when acclaimed in the Christian liturgy of Good Friday. In addition, there is an oblique but nonetheless interesting reference that can be applied to the passion: "I myself have set up my king on Zion, my holy mountain" (Ps 2:6). It is Jesus who ascends the mount of Calvary to endure his passion, through which he reveals his kingship and rule over all creation. The antiphon helps set up these possible lines of interpretation: "Earthly kings rise up in revolt; princes conspire together against the Lord and his Anointed." Again, the title of Christ (anointed) used here is significant; his kingship is implied here since he is set in contrast to "earthly kings."

The second psalm selected for this hour, Psalm 22:2–23, reflects the cry of Jesus from the cross recounted in the Synoptics: "My God, my God, why have you forsaken me?" (Ps 22:2). The reality of suffering ignominy as people mock Jesus can be seen in the statement "all who see me deride me" (Ps 22:8). Yet the psalm also offers another important notion about Jesus's commitment from birth to do the will of his Father

(Ps 22:10–11). The section of the psalm beginning with verse 23, the last verse used, has been used in Christian liturgy as a psalm of praise for redemption, specifically Christ's victory because of the humiliation and suffering described in the psalm.

The final psalm of the office of readings, Psalm 38, is the plea of one who suffers and is afflicted.

At Morning Prayer, the customary psalms of Friday of the second week of the Psalter are used. The familiar Psalm 51 is the first psalm, with the poignant reminder that we would have no sacrifice to offer God if we did not join in Christ's: "For in sacrifice you take no delight, burnt offering from me you would refuse, my sacrifice, a contrite spirit, a humbled, contrite heart you will not spurn" (Ps 51:19). The antiphon that precedes the text indicates its christological implications: "God did not spare his own Son, but gave him up to suffer for our sake." The antiphon for the canticle (Heb 3:2–4, 13a, 15–19) states, "Jesus Christ loved us, and poured out his own blood for us to wash away our sins." This is another clear reminder of the graciousness of the act of redemption and the enduring result for all generations. The antiphon for Psalm 147:12–20 is a careful summation of much of what is contained in the Good Friday liturgy: "We worship your cross, O Lord, and we praise and glorify your holy resurrection, for the wood of the cross has brought joy to the world."

The Scripture text for Morning Prayer is taken from the same section of Isaiah as that used at the afternoon liturgy, Isaiah 52:13–15. Instead of a proper responsory, the first half of the *Christus factus est* (from Phil 2) is used. The canticle of Zechariah is introduced with an antiphon taken from the passion according to St. John asserting the accusation against Jesus as "king" of the Jews. The intercessions at Morning Prayer are particularly well written and are aimed at incorporating our needs and present situation with aspects of Christ's suffering and death. In the introduction we are invited to imitate Jesus's obedience to the Father's will, and we are reminded that through him we shall inherit eternal glory. The humility of Jesus is used as a model for our striving for this same virtue; his love is the perfect example for us to imitate as we seek to love each other. The image of Jesus's outstretched arms is a particularly graphic and poignant foundation for the prayer that God unite the scattered children into his kingdom of salvation.

Since Evening Prayer is celebrated only by those who do not attend the afternoon liturgy of the passion of the Lord, the following brief mention of its salient points is offered merely to reiterate the theology of the paschal mystery that is celebrated on Good Friday. The antiphons to the psalms carefully reflect the anguish and suffering of Jesus (first and second) as he went to death for our salvation. The third is taken from the Synoptic account of the death of Jesus: "When Jesus had taken the vinegar he said, 'It is accomplished.' Then he bowed his head and died." Interestingly, the Johannine version of the death of Jesus is not used here. Rather, the Synoptic account is used, which stresses the reality of Jesus's suffering more than does John. Clearly, the church does not want to ignore the reality of the suffering of Jesus as an essential part of the paschal mystery, hence this statement is important. Still, the overall emphasis on Good Friday relates it to the kingship and final victory of Jesus.

The psalms chosen for evening prayer continue this emphasis on suffering. The first psalm, Psalm 116:10–19, speaks of the affliction of Jesus and of our reaction to suffering when confronted with it in our lives. Yet, like Jesus we are invited to acclaim that we are servants (Ps 116:16) and that we will fulfill our vows to the Lord (Ps 116:18). The second psalm, Psalm 143:1–11, confidently asserts that the Lord will listen to our prayer (Ps 143:1–2) because of his constant faithfulness and love:

> Lord, listen to my prayer:
> turn your ear to my appeal.
> You are faithful, you are just; give answer.
> Do not call your servant to judgment for no one is just in your
> sight.

The final section of Evening Prayer psalmody is the full text of the Christ canticle from Philippians 2, of which verse 8 takes on special significance this evening: "For our sake Christ was obedient, accepting even death, death on a cross."

The Scripture passage is the same as that used on the previous Friday, 1 Peter 2:21–24, and which has been used at Sunday Evening Prayer during Lent. It is significant that the liturgy here reiterates what is obviously a most appropriate way of interpreting and appreciating the sacrificial death of Jesus on our behalf. The antiphon to the canticle of Mary states, "When we were his enemies, God reconciled us to himself by the death of his Son." Significantly, this text begins to draw out some of the effects of Christ's death, thus underscoring the important role the liturgy plays in guiding our appreciation of the paschal mystery as more than an objective event. It is the unique means through which God granted us union with him and access to heaven. The separation and estrangement we inherited from sinful Adam is here overcome in the reconciliation that is ours through Christ.

Holy Saturday

The instruction in the Roman Missal about Holy Saturday that "the Church waits at the Lord's tomb in prayer and fasting, meditating on his Passion and Death and on his Descent into Hell, and awaiting his Resurrection" appropriately reflects what is contained in the Liturgy of the Hours today. The invitatory states, "Come, let us worship Christ, who for our sake suffered death and was buried." The psalms for the office of readings have been specially selected for use today. The first is Psalm 4, a traditional night prayer (Compline) psalm, which confidently prays "in peace, I will lie down and sleep" (antiphon) and "I will lie down in peace and sleep comes at once for you alone, Lord, make me dwell in safety" (Ps 4:9). Clearly, the inference here is that Christ rested in the peace of his Father in death, but we pray in the sure hope that both his death and resurrection to new life give us a foretaste of what life eternal will be in union with God. The second psalm, Psalm 16, is introduced by the antiphon "my body shall rest in hope," and its text speaks of an attitude of trusting in the Lord:

> And so my heart rejoices, my soul is glad;
> even my body shall rest in safety.
> For you will not leave my soul among the dead,
> nor let your beloved know decay. (Ps 16:9)

On a more triumphant note, the third antiphon states, "Lift high the ancient portals. The King of glory enters." The familiar Psalm 24 takes on added significance when prayed today, for it unites our situation with the triumph of the Lord:

> Who shall climb the mountain of the Lord?
> Who shall stand in his holy place?
> Who is the king of glory!
> The Lord, the mighty, the valiant,
> The Lord, the valiant in war. (Ps 24:8)

The war waged by Jesus was against Satan and the powers of darkness and death. At the Easter Vigil we celebrate his triumph over Satan and his coming as light and life.

The first reading at this hour is taken from the letter to the Hebrews 4:1–13, which contains the significant association between ourselves in and through Christ and the Father. Through Christ we gain access to the Father (Heb 4:1) and we thus enter into the Lord's rest. This reading also refers to God's word as "living and effective, sharper than any two-edged sword. It penetrates and divides soul and spirit, joints and marrow; it judges the reflections and thoughts of the heart" (Heb 4:12). This verse sets up the important place meditating on the Lord's word will have at the Easter Vigil. That the paschal context (specifically the death of Jesus) is not lost even here is clear since the responsory to this text is from Matthew 27 (vv. 66, 60, 62) about the burial of Jesus.

The second reading is taken from an ancient homily on Holy Saturday whose place in this liturgy is most fitting and welcome. The "great silence and stillness" over the whole earth experienced today is due to the fact that "the King is asleep." "God has fallen asleep in the flesh and he has raised up all who have slept ever since the world began." In death we are told "he has gone after our first parents, as for a lost sheep." He awakens Adam with the words, "Awake, O sleeper, and rise from the dead, and Christ will give you light." Fittingly, this text relies on the account of the fall of all humanity in Adam and the symbolism of darkness as that which called for Christ to come as the light of the world. It is this light we await today, especially in the darkness in which we begin the Vigil liturgy. In associating ourselves with Christ the author admonishes us, "Rise, let us leave this place. The enemy led you out of the earthly paradise. I will not restore you to that paradise, but I will enthrone you in heaven." Our association with Christ in his paschal victory is thus expressed here and reiterated in the prayer that concludes this hour:

> All-powerful and ever-living God,
> your only Son went down among the dead
> and rose again in glory.
> In your goodness
> raise up your faithful people,
> buried with him in baptism,
> to be one with him
> in the eternal life of heaven.

At morning prayer the antiphons to the psalms reflect the attitude of the church at prayer before the tomb of the Lord: "Though sinless, the Lord has been put to death. The world is in mourning as for an only Son" (first). Our prayer would seem to reflect the cry of Jesus when we pray, "From the jaws of hell, Lord, rescue my soul" (second). The third antiphon reflects both aspects of the death and resurrection when it states, "I was dead, but now I live for ever, and I hold the keys of death and of hell." The forces of death and hell no longer have power over us who confidently meditate on and experience anew the paschal mystery of Christ.

The short Scripture passage from Hosea 5:15b—16:2 has been chosen to reflect the situation of Jesus in the tomb, lying in death: "He will revive us after two days; on the third day he will raise us up, to live in his presence." As has been customary since the beginning of the Triduum, the *Christus factus est* text of Philippians 2 is used as the responsory following this reading, but this time the whole verse is used: "For our sake Christ was obedient, accepting even death, death on a cross. Therefore God raised him on high and gave him the name above all other names." The salvation won for us in Christ is also reflected in the antiphon to Zechariah's canticle: "Save us, O Savior of the world. On the cross you redeemed us by the shedding of your blood; we cry out for your help, O God."

The intercessions at Morning Prayer refer to Christ as "our Redeemer" who "suffered and was buried for us in order to rise again." Aspects of the passion are used here to reflect our need for redemption: the sorrowing Mother represents us as we grieve over our sins and share Christ's sufferings. Like the seed buried in the ground, Christ is buried in order to bring forth the "harvest of grace." Christ, the good shepherd, lay hidden in death from which we pray that he will "teach us to live a life hidden with you in the Father." Christ is also acclaimed as the "new Adam" and as the "Son of the living God" whom we beg to raise us up to walk in newness of life with him forever.

Evening Prayer is celebrated only by those who do not attend the liturgy of the Easter Vigil. The psalmody is the same as that used at Evening Prayer on Good Friday, which is itself an indication that the note of triumph and joy at Christ's resurrection is not celebrated until the Vigil Eucharist. The antiphons speak of the paschal mystery. The first states, "Death, you shall die in me; hell, you shall be destroyed by me." The victory of Christ over sin and death is noted but in a restrained way.

The second antiphon relates the three days Jonah spent in the belly of the whale to Jesus's three days "in the heart of the earth." The third antiphon is taken from John's Gospel, where Jesus speaks about the destruction of the temple of his body and that "in three days I will rebuild it." Hence, the notion of the liturgy commemorating the paschal mystery spanning the three days of the Triduum is expressed clearly.

The Scripture text is from 1 Peter 1:18–21, which verses precede those used last evening for Good Friday. This text speaks about our being delivered from our former way of life through the blood of Christ "the blood of a spotless, unblemished lamb chosen before the world's foundation and revealed for your sake in these last days" (1 Pet 1:19–20). The antiphon from Philippians 2 follows this reading, which itself reiterates the emphasis placed here on the passion and death of Christ, endured by the Savior in obedience to his Father's will. The antiphon to the canticle of the Blessed Virgin is taken from John's Gospel, where the theme of glory dominates: "Now is the Son of Man glorified and God has been glorified in him."

The intercessions are addressed to Christ where aspects of his dying and rising are used to base petitions about our present needs. We pray that the Lamb of God will draw all humanity to himself, that he who laid in a tomb would free humanity from the powers of darkness, and that the Savior who opened the gates of paradise to the repentant thief would gather all the dead into the glory of his resurrection.

For those who do not celebrate the Easter Vigil this hour of prayer is reflective of the sufferings and death of Jesus.

Easter Sunday

The introductory comment for the office of readings states that the Easter Vigil takes the place of this office. However, those who do not participate in the Vigil "should read at least four readings with canticles, psalms and prayers from the Easter Vigil." What follows are called the four "preferred readings" of Exodus 14:15—15:1, Ezekiel 36:16–28, Romans 6:3–11, and Matthew 28:1–10. It is significant that this is the only office of readings of the liturgical year that does not contain a text from a nonscriptural source.

For Morning Prayer, the Latin edition contains the hymn *Aurora lucis rutilat*, which capitalizes on the dawn of Easter day, the exultation of heaven and earth at the Lord's resurrection, and the definitive victory over sin and death accomplished in Christ.

The psalms of week one (from the four-week Psalter) are accompanied by proper antiphons, which are used through the octave. The first antiphon states that the "splendor of Christ risen from the dead has shone on the people redeemed by his blood." This text is appropriately exultant and reiterates a positive notion of the passion by recalling that the blood used to shield Israel from death at Passover is now transferred to specify Christ's blood as that which redeems us. The second antiphon uses the term *redeemer* to acclaim Christ "risen from the tomb." The antiphon invites us to "sing a hymn of praise to the Lord our God." This text is an especially appropriate introduction to the canticle of creation from Daniel 3:57–88. The third antiphon begins and ends with the Easter acclamation "alleluia," between which is the acclamation that the Lord is risen as he promised.

After a short Scripture reading from Acts 10:40–43, a proper responsory is taken from Psalm 118: "This is the day the Lord has made, let us rejoice and be glad, alleluia." It is also used for this Sunday's Responsorial Psalm and will be used throughout the Easter octave following the Scripture reading at both Morning and Evening Prayer. This replacement indicates the importance of the theology of the octave of Easter as our liturgical experience of Easter as an eternal "day."

The antiphon to Zechariah's canticle—"very early on the morning after the sabbath, when the sun had just risen"—recalls the Gospel accounts that assign the resurrection to the morning of the first day of the week. The references to early morning and the sun's rising should not be lost as these form part of the cosmic symbolism associated with Easter. The intercessions appropriately begin by asserting that Christ was raised by the Father and that we now pray that "he will raise us up by his power." The first of the petitions reflects the cosmic symbolism of the morning ("light shining in the darkness"), the second fittingly recalls Jesus having walked "the way of suffering and crucifixion," the third recalls our baptism whereby we became members of Christ's royal priesthood, and the last appropriately orients us toward the eschatological day and asks that "we may see you face to face, and be transformed in your likeness."

The Latin edition of Evening Prayer contains the hymn *Ad cenam Agni providi*, a text that draws freely on the crossing of the Red Sea as a type to describe our passing from death to life in Christ and on Christ's victory over death and our participation in it. The antiphons recall the Synoptic accounts, which specify the presence at the tomb of "Mary Magdalene and the other Mary" (first), the invitation to "come and see the place where the Lord was buried" (second), and Jesus's postresurrection admonition not to be afraid (Matt 28:5) because he will be seen in Galilee. The Scripture reading from Hebrews 10:12–14 is part of the longer text used on Passion Sunday at the office of readings. Ritual and liturgical prescriptions of the old covenant are reiterated here acclaiming Christ's one, unique offering for our salvation.

The antiphon for the canticle of the Blessed Virgin capitalizes on the evening hour since it derives from John 20:19: "on the evening of the first day of the week." This same verse introduces the Gospel to be proclaimed the following Sunday from John 20:19–31. The introduction to the intercessions calls our attention to Christ the Lord, who "lives always to intercede for us." Significantly, the first petition asks that the Lord send "into our hearts the fire of your Spirit" because the earliest evidence of the Easter feast commemorated both the resurrection and the sending of the Spirit. The last petition is also significant theologically since it recalls Christ's being "obedient even to accepting death," a motif seen repeatedly throughout the Triduum, and his being exalted to the right hand of the Father. We pray that this mystery may be fulfilled in the eternal life of those who have died.

CONCLUSION

All liturgy is paschal.

T. S. Eliot wrote, "April is the cruellest month, breeding Lilacs out of the dead land, mixing Memory and desire, stirring Dull roots with spring rain." The battle between winter and spring is played out annually, hard ground and winter's snows give way to spring planting, rains, and first harvest. For that to take place the tasks of early spring must take place clearing, digging, planting, and nurturing so that harvest can occur once more. April is the "cruellest month" because it sees the battle between winter and spring played out once again.

Easter is the cruelest feast because it causes a similar battle within us. The annual Lenten spring requires that we probe, examine, and deal with those things that hinder us from living the life of Christ. Why Easter is so demanding is that for us to make the faith profession in Christ risen from the dead means two things: that we embrace cross as well as resurrection and that we renounce firmly and definitively Satan, evil, and sin. Often those things that separate us from God are the things that we have grown accustomed to and comfortable with. Thus, our lives in Christ require cleansing, rooting out vices and sins, and allowing the life of Christ to overtake us once more.

Easter is cruel because it requires that we view all of life from the perspective of what Easter victory, triumph, and joy implies, namely, that the central tenet of the Christian faith is an unfathomable paradox. What many fear the most in life, limitation, suffering, and death are the very things that bring us a new and everlasting life begun here on earth principally through the liturgy.

CHAPTER EIGHT

RESPONSIBILITY FOR FELLOW CREATURES ON "OUR COMMON HOME"

This chapter addresses the responsibility that worshipers share in caring for the creation that they have raised up in praise and thanksgiving in the very enactment of liturgy and sacraments. Of the possible rites and prayers/texts in liturgy that could be utilized to frame the parameters of this chapter, we choose two from the missal: the presentation of the gifts and the dismissal.[1]

At the very start of the Liturgy of the Eucharist, the Roman Missal states, "It is desirable that the faithful express their participation by making an offering, bringing forward the bread and wine for the celebration of the Eucharist and perhaps other gifts to relieve the needs of the Church and the poor" (Order of Mass 22). The GIRM indicates three times that gifts are brought forward by the faithful. In 73, "The offerings are then brought forward. It is praiseworthy for the bread and wine to be presented by the faithful," and "Even money or other gifts for the poor or for the Church, brought by the faithful or collected in the church, are acceptable." Most notably, in 69, "the faithful express their participation by making an offering." This last underscores what the laity's participation in the Eucharist means in virtue of their baptismal priesthood. It is significant that this act of presentation at the offering stands along with the act of procession at the beginning of the liturgy and the act of communion by the faithful.

The dismissal in the *Missale Romanum*—both in texts mandated after Trent and in the third edition of the *Missale Romanum* presently in use—includes the pithy text *Ite missa est*. In the Tridentine Missal, there are six musical notations to accompany this text with more or less complexity to match the feast or season being celebrated.[2] Admittedly, the exact meaning of *missa* has been matter for serious debate among scholars and catechists. A certain consensus has built around the notion that this is an admonition to live life in accord with what is celebrated.[3] The Roman Missal currently in use for the United States offers four options for the dismissal:

> Go forth, the Mass is ended.
>
> Go and announce the Gospel of the Lord.
>
> Go in peace, glorifying the Lord by your life.
>
> Go in peace.

Other vernacular translations offer similar texts. For example, the Italian provides seven:

> Go in peace.
>
> The Mass is ended go in peace.
>
> Go and announce the Gospel of the Lord.
>
> Glorify the Lord with your life.
>
> May the joy of the Lord be your strength.
>
> Go in peace in the Name of the Lord.
>
> Share with all people the joy of the risen Lord. Go in peace.[4]

With regard to the Concluding Rites, the General Instruction on the Roman Missal simply states, "so that each may go back doing good works, praising and blessing God" (90.d).[5] What this means can be understood in light of the important spiritual challenge offered at the beginning of *Laudato Si'* 8, where Pope Francis cites Patriarch Bartholomew on *ecological sin*:

> Patriarch Bartholomew has spoken in particular of the need for each of us to repent of the ways we have harmed the planet, for "inasmuch as we all generate small ecological damage,"

we are called to acknowledge "our contribution, smaller or greater, to the disfigurement and destruction of creation." He has repeatedly stated this firmly and persuasively, challenging us to acknowledge our sins against creation: "For human beings...to destroy the biological diversity of God's creation; for human beings to degrade the integrity of the earth by causing changes in its climate, by stripping the earth of its natural forests or destroying its wetlands; for human beings to contaminate the earth's waters, its land, its air, and its life— these are sins." For "to commit a crime against the natural world is a sin against ourselves and a sin against God."

Attention to sins against creation includes a consideration of how we relate to primal elements and manufactured elements. The "fellow creatures" on "our common home" should no longer be regarded as "things," and the goodness of "the work of human hands" holds responsibilities for how we relate to manufactured elements and to one another.

The plan for this chapter is to reflect on the primal and manufactured elements of our common home, including those involved in "making," as described in the previous four chapters and in light of the moral teachings and imperatives of Pope Francis in *Laudato Si'*. (What this chapter accomplishes from a Catholic perspective can also be done by raising up evidence from recent Orthodox statements, those of the World Council of Churches, and from countless other religious sources about the environment.) Thus, this chapter first provides texts of Pope Francis's encyclical *Laudato Si'* concerning care for primal elements— including their protection, cultivation, and distribution—with implications for how we raise up and revere these elements in liturgy. Then, a similar treatment is given for manufactured elements—similarly including processes for manufacture and distribution, as well as human working conditions. A final section addresses examples of food distribution and just wages, which are characteristic of the Catholic social justice teaching. In effect, the contents and structure of this chapter draw on three key phrases of the encyclical: "everything is connected,"[6] "this document, addressed to people of good will,"[7] and "dialogue with all people about our common home."[8] This last phrase is elaborated on much more fully Pope Francis encyclical *Fratelli Tutti*.[9]

The actions we perform and the words we articulate in the liturgy have regularly been called "enacted theology."[10] These have been given appropriate and due respect in what has preceded. The implications for engaging them in human life always deserves attention *theologically* (what do they "say" about God, the cosmos, the human person, etc.), *spiritually* (what do they mean in terms of leading the spiritual life in light of what celebrated), and *pastorally* (in terms of how the liturgy shapes the church community and how the church community understands themselves in relation to each other).

PRIMAL ELEMENTS

Earth and Air

Key terms: sister; abuse of goods; sickness in soil, water, air, and all forms of life; indispensable

> 2. This <u>sister</u> now cries out to us because of the harm we have inflicted on her by our irresponsible use and <u>abuse of the goods</u> with which God has endowed her. We have come to see ourselves as her lords and masters, entitled to plunder her at will. The violence present in our hearts, wounded by sin, is also reflected in the symptoms of <u>sickness evident in the soil, in the water, in the air and in all forms of life</u>. This is why the earth herself, burdened and laid waste, is among the most abandoned and maltreated of our poor; she "groans in travail" (Rom 8:22). We have forgotten that we ourselves are dust of the earth (cf. Gen 2:7); our very bodies are made up of her elements, <u>we breathe her air</u> and we receive life and refreshment from her waters.

While some have argued against the use of "brother" and "sister" terminology here, Pope Francis is true to authentic Franciscan roots. The most "primal" liturgy we celebrate is the Easter Vigil, which begins outside of the church building in the open air and the flames from the new fire. The last sentence reminds us of the foundational truth spoken as ashes are placed on our foreheads on Ash Wednesday: "Remember you are dust and unto dust you shall return."[11]

Key terms: sins against creation; biological diversity; forests; wetlands

> 8. Patriarch Bartholomew has spoken in particular of the need for each of us to repent of the ways we have harmed the planet, for "inasmuch as we all generate small ecological damage," we are called to acknowledge "our contribution, smaller or greater, to the disfigurement and destruction of creation." He has repeatedly stated this firmly and persuasively, challenging us to acknowledge our sins against creation: "For human beings…to destroy the biological diversity of God's creation; for human beings to degrade the integrity of the earth by causing changes in its climate, by stripping the earth of its natural forests or destroying its wetlands; for human beings to contaminate the earth's waters, its land, its air, and its life—these are sins." For "to commit a crime against the natural world is a sin against ourselves and a sin against God."[12]

That Pope Francis introduces us to a wealth of biblical and ecclesial teaching on ecology and the environment with the teachings of Patriarch Bartholomew is a stunning example of ecumenical respect and cooperation. This is the only paragraph of the encyclical that mentions "sins against creation." Yet its pastoral effect should have a wide-ranging impact for generations to come. This is especially true given the authentic teaching found in 66 about the meaning of human life as grounded in three relationships: with God, our neighbor, and the earth itself—in effect theologically, anthropologically, and ecologically.[13] As will be seen below, "biological diversity" will be noted again and again by Pope Francis, a reflection of his thesis that "everything is connected."

Key terms: atmospheric pollution; pollution caused by transport, industrial fumes, etc.

> 20. Some forms of pollution are part of people's daily experience. Exposure to atmospheric pollutants produces a broad spectrum of health hazards, especially for the poor, and causes millions of premature deaths. People take sick, for example, from breathing high levels of smoke from fuels used in cooking or heating. There is also pollution that affects

everyone, <u>caused by transport, industrial fumes, substances which contribute to the acidification of soil and water, fertilizers, insecticides, fungicides, herbicides and agrotoxins</u> in general. Technology, which, linked to business interests, is presented as the only way of solving these problems, in fact proves incapable of seeing the mysterious network of relations between things and so sometimes solves one problem only to create others.

Key terms: natural resources; warming; extinction of part of the planet's biodiversity; forests and woodlands; (critique of unregulated) business interests

22. Other indicators of the present situation have to do with the depletion of <u>natural resources</u>. We all know that it is not possible to sustain the present level of consumption in developed countries and wealthier sectors of society, where the habit of wasting and discarding has reached unprecedented levels. The exploitation of the planet has already exceeded acceptable limits and we still have not solved the problem of poverty.

24. <u>Warming</u> has effects on the carbon cycle. It creates a vicious circle which aggravates the situation even more, affecting the availability of essential resources like drinking water, energy and agricultural production in warmer regions, and leading to the <u>extinction of part of the planet's biodiversity</u>.

32. The <u>earth's resources</u> are also being plundered because of <u>short-sighted approaches to the economy, commerce and production</u>. The loss of <u>forests and woodlands</u> entails the loss of species which may constitute extremely important resources in the future, not only for food but also for curing disease and other uses. Different species contain genes which could be key resources in years ahead for meeting human needs and regulating environmental problems.

33. It is not enough, however, to think of different species merely as potential "resources" to be exploited, while overlooking the

fact that they have value in themselves. Each year sees the disappearance of <u>thousands of plant and animal species</u> which we will never know, which our children will never see, because they have been lost for ever. The great majority become extinct for reasons related to human activity. Because of us, thousands of species will no longer give glory to God by their very existence, nor convey their message to us. We have no such right.

34. It may well disturb us to learn of the extinction of <u>mammals or birds</u>, since they are more visible. But the <u>good functioning of ecosystems also requires fungi, algae, worms, insects, reptiles and an innumerable variety of microorganisms</u>. Some less numerous species, although generally unseen, nonetheless play a critical role in maintaining the equilibrium of a particular place. Human beings must intervene when a geosystem reaches a critical state. But nowadays, such intervention in nature has become more and more frequent. As a consequence, serious problems arise, leading to further interventions; human activity becomes ubiquitous, with all the risks which this entails. Often a vicious circle results, as human intervention to resolve a problem further aggravates the situation. For example, many birds and insects which disappear due to synthetic agrotoxins are helpful for agriculture: their disappearance will have to be compensated for by yet other techniques which may well prove harmful. We must be grateful for the praiseworthy efforts being made by scientists and engineers dedicated to finding solutions to man-made problems. But a sober look at our world shows that the degree of human intervention, often in the service of <u>business interests and consumerism</u>.

35. In assessing the environmental impact of any project, concern is usually shown for its effects on soil, water and air, yet few careful studies are made of its impact on <u>biodiversity</u>, as if the loss of species or animals and plant groups were of little importance. Highways, new plantations, the fencing-off of certain areas, the damming of water sources, and similar developments, crowd out natural habitats and, at times,

break them up in such a way that animal populations can no longer migrate or roam freely. As a result, some species face extinction. Alternatives exist which at least lessen the impact of these projects, like the creation of biological corridors, but few countries demonstrate such concern and foresight. Frequently, when certain species are <u>exploited commercially</u>, little attention is paid to studying their reproductive patterns in order to prevent their depletion and the consequent imbalance of the ecosystem.

The issue of the depletion of natural resources and species on the earth in the oceans has only grown in geometric proportions since the issuance of *Laudato Si'*. The poignant theological assertion that "everything is connected" is also a poignant truism in ecology and abut interdependence. In effect there is no such thing as "just a tree" or "only a creek." The ecological health of every single resource and species means that doing damage to one element of our common home always has consequences for the whole. That multinational business interests have raped the earth and caused death and destruction is not only in our past. Shockingly it is still in our present. It continues to destroy, so we do need to ask what are we passing on to the next generations.

Water

Key terms: fresh drinking water; water poverty; quality of water available to the poor

28. <u>Fresh drinking water</u> is an issue of primary importance, since it is indispensable for human life and for supporting terrestrial and aquatic ecosystems. <u>Sources of fresh water</u> are necessary for health care, agriculture and industry. Water supplies used to be relatively constant, but now in many places demand exceeds the sustainable supply, with dramatic consequences in the short and long term. Large cities dependent on significant supplies of water have experienced periods of shortage, and at critical moments these have not always been administered with sufficient oversight and impartiality. <u>Water poverty</u> especially affects Africa where large sectors of the population have <u>no access to safe drinking water</u> or experience droughts which impede agricultural

production. Some countries have areas rich in water while others endure drastic scarcity.

29. One particularly serious problem is the <u>quality of water available to the poor</u>. Every day, unsafe water results in many deaths and the spread of water-related diseases, including those caused by microorganisms and chemical substances. Dysentery and cholera, linked to inadequate hygiene and water supplies, are a significant cause of suffering and of infant mortality. Underground water sources in many places are threatened by the pollution produced in certain mining, farming and industrial activities, especially in countries lacking adequate regulation or controls. It is not only a question of industrial waste. Detergents and chemical products, commonly used in many places of the world, continue to pour into our rivers, lakes and seas.

Pride of place among the "natural" "primal" elements in *Laudato Si'* goes to water, spanning from everyone's right to water, to the privatization of water to political factors involved in water rights (e.g., in the Middle East, where "water is the new oil"). Allied issues concern, among other things, the division in society of the rich from the poor.

Key terms: privatization; basic human right; a right to life consistent with their inalienable dignity

30. Even as the quality of available water is constantly diminishing, in some places there is a growing tendency, despite its scarcity, to <u>privatize this resource</u>, turning it into a commodity subject to the laws of the market. Yet access to <u>safe drinkable water is a basic and universal human right</u>, since it is essential to human survival and, as such, is a condition for the exercise of other human rights. Our world has a grave social debt towards the poor who lack access to drinking water, because they are denied the <u>right to a life consistent with their inalienable dignity</u>. This debt can be paid partly by an increase in funding to provide clean water and sanitary services among the poor. But water continues to be wasted, not only in the developed world but also in developing countries which possess it in abundance. This shows that

the problem of water is partly an educational and cultural issue, since there is little awareness of the seriousness of such behaviour within a context of great inequality.

Key terms: urgent action; large multinational businesses

31. Greater scarcity of water will lead to an increase in the cost of food and the various products which depend on its use. Some studies warn that an <u>acute water shortage</u> may occur within a few decades unless <u>urgent action</u> is taken. The environmental repercussions could affect billions of people; it is also conceivable that the control of water by <u>large multinational businesses</u> may become a major source of conflict in this century.

Key terms: indispensable resource; common plan; consensus; genuine integral development; fundamental right

2. We have forgotten that we ourselves are dust of the earth (cf. Gen 2:7); our very bodies are made up of her elements, we breathe her air and we receive <u>life and refreshment from her waters</u>.

164. Interdependence obliges us to think of one world with a <u>common plan</u>. Yet the same ingenuity which has brought about enormous technological progress has so far proved incapable of finding effective ways of dealing with grave environmental and social problems worldwide. <u>A global consensus</u> is essential for confronting the deeper problems, which cannot be resolved by unilateral actions on the part of individual countries. Such a consensus could lead, for example, to planning a sustainable and diversified agriculture, developing renewable and less polluting forms of energy, encouraging a more efficient use of energy, promoting a better management of marine and forest resources, and ensuring universal access to drinking water.

185. In any discussion about a proposed venture, a number of questions need to be asked in order to discern whether or not it will contribute to <u>genuine integral development</u>. What

will it accomplish? Why? Where? When? How? For whom? What are the risks? What are the costs? Who will pay those costs and how? In this discernment, some questions must have higher priority. For example, we know that <u>water is a scarce and indispensable resource and a fundamental right</u> which conditions the exercise of other human rights. This indisputable fact overrides any other assessment of environmental impact on a region.

Key terms: sustainable use

140. We need only recall how ecosystems interact in dispersing carbon dioxide, purifying water, controlling illnesses and epidemics, forming soil, breaking down waste, and in many other ways which we overlook or simply do not know about. Once they become conscious of this, many people realize that we live and act on the basis of a reality which has previously been given to us, which precedes our existence and our abilities. So, when we speak of "<u>sustainable use</u>," consideration must always be given to each ecosystem's regenerative ability in its different areas and aspects.

Key terms: throwaway culture; natural ecosystems; cycles of production

22. These problems are closely linked to a <u>throwaway culture</u> which affects the excluded just as it quickly reduces things to rubbish. To cite one example, most of the paper we produce is thrown away and not recycled. It is hard for us to accept that <u>the way natural ecosystems work</u> is exemplary: plants synthesize nutrients which feed herbivores; these in turn become food for carnivores, which produce significant quantities of organic waste which give rise to new generations of plants. But our industrial system, at the end of its cycle of production and consumption, has not developed the capacity to absorb and reuse waste and by-products. We have not yet managed to adopt a <u>circular model of production</u> capable of preserving resources for present and future generations, while limiting as much as possible the use of non-renewable resources, moderating their consumption,

maximizing their efficient use, reusing and recycling them. A serious consideration of this issue would be one way of counteracting the throwaway culture which affects the entire planet, but it must be said that only limited progress has been made in this regard.

Key terms: warming; drinking water; marine food chain; rise in sea levels

24. Warming has effects on the carbon cycle. It creates a vicious circle which aggravates the situation even more, affecting the availability of essential resources like drinking water, energy and agricultural production in warmer regions, and leading to the extinction of part of the planet's biodiversity. The melting in the polar ice caps and in high altitude plains can lead to the dangerous release of methane gas, while the decomposition of frozen organic material can further increase the emission of carbon dioxide. Things are made worse by the loss of tropical forests which would otherwise help to mitigate climate change. Carbon dioxide pollution increases the acidification of the oceans and compromises the marine food chain. If present trends continue, this century may well witness extraordinary climate change and an unprecedented destruction of ecosystems, with serious consequences for all of us. A rise in the sea level, for example, can create extremely serious situations, if we consider that a quarter of the world's population lives on the coast or nearby, and that the majority of our megacities are situated in coastal areas.

Key terms: scarcity of water; cost of food

31. Greater scarcity of water will lead to an increase in the cost of food and the various products which depend on its use. Some studies warn that an acute water shortage may occur within a few decades unless urgent action is taken. The environmental repercussions could affect billions of people; it is also conceivable that the control of water by large multinational businesses may become a major source of conflict in this century.[14]

Key terms: short-sighted approaches to the economy;
food; biodiversity

32. The earth's resources are also being plundered because of short-sighted approaches to the economy, commerce and production. The loss of forests and woodlands entails the loss of species which may constitute extremely important resources in the future, not only for food but also for curing disease and other uses. Different species contain genes which could be key resources in years ahead for meeting human needs and regulating environmental problems.

Key terms: oceans, depletion of species,
ocean food chain

40. Oceans not only contain the bulk of our planet's water supply, but also most of the immense variety of living creatures, many of them still unknown to us and threatened for various reasons. What is more, marine life in rivers, lakes, seas and oceans, which feeds a great part of the world's population, is affected by uncontrolled fishing, leading to a drastic depletion of certain species. Selective forms of fishing which discard much of what they collect continue unabated. Particularly threatened are marine organisms which we tend to overlook, like some forms of plankton; they represent a significant element in the ocean food chain, and species used for our food ultimately depend on them.

MANUFACTURED ELEMENTS

Key terms: daily experience; cooking, heating;
network of relations

20. Some forms of pollution are part of people's daily experience. Exposure to atmospheric pollutants produces a broad spectrum of health hazards, especially for the poor, and causes millions of premature deaths. People take sick, for example, from breathing high levels of smoke from fuels used in cooking or heating. There is also pollution that affects everyone, caused by transport, industrial fumes, substances

which contribute to the acidification of soil and water, fertilizers, insecticides, fungicides, herbicides and agrotoxins in general. Technology, which, linked to business interests, is presented as the only way of solving these problems, in fact proves incapable of seeing the mysterious <u>network of relations</u> between things and so sometimes solves one problem only to create others.[15]

Key terms: population density; a third of all food produced is discarded; wasted food is stolen from the poor

50. To blame <u>population growth</u> instead of extreme and selective consumerism on the part of some, is one way of refusing to face the issues. It is an attempt to legitimize the present model of distribution, where a minority believes that it has the right to consume in a way which can never be universalized, since the planet could not even contain the waste products of such consumption. Besides, we know that approximately a <u>third of all food produced is discarded</u>, and "<u>whenever food is thrown out it is as if it were stolen from the table of the poor.</u>" Still, attention needs to be paid to imbalances in <u>population density</u>, on both national and global levels, since a rise in consumption would lead to complex regional situations, as a result of the interplay between problems linked to environmental pollution, transport, waste treatment, loss of resources and quality of life.

Key terms: employment; business creativity; small-scale food production systems; business a noble vocation

129. In order to continue providing <u>employment</u>, it is imperative to promote an economy which favours <u>productive diversity and business creativity</u>. For example, there is a great variety of <u>small-scale food production systems</u> which feed the greater part of the world's peoples, using a modest amount of land and producing less waste, be it in small agricultural parcels, in orchards and gardens, hunting and wild harvesting or local fishing. Economies of scale, especially in the agricultural sector, end up forcing smallholders to sell their land or

to abandon their traditional crops. Their attempts to move to other, more diversified, means of production prove fruitless because of the difficulty of linkage with regional and global markets, or because the infrastructure for sales and transport is geared to larger businesses. Civil authorities have the right and duty to adopt clear and firm measures in support of small producers and differentiated production. To ensure economic freedom from which all can effectively benefit, restraints occasionally have to be imposed on those possessing greater resources and financial power. To claim economic freedom while real conditions bar many people from actual access to it, and while possibilities for employment continue to shrink, is to practise a doublespeak which brings politics into disrepute. <u>Business is a noble vocation</u>, directed to producing wealth and improving our world. It can be a fruitful source of prosperity for the areas in which it operates, especially if it sees the creation of jobs as an essential part of its service to the common good.

Key terms: (papal teachings from John XXIII onward about) food security and peace; protection of the environment and regulation of migration

175. As Benedict XVI has affirmed in continuity with the social teaching of the Church: "To manage the global economy; to revive economies hit by the crisis; to avoid any deterioration of the present crisis and the greater imbalances that would result; to bring about integral and timely disarmament, <u>food security and peace</u>; to guarantee the <u>protection of the environment and to regulate migration</u>: for all this, there is urgent need of a true world political authority, as my predecessor Blessed John XXIII indicated some years ago" [*Caritas in Veritate* n. 67]. Diplomacy also takes on new importance in the work of developing international strategies which can anticipate serious problems affecting us all.

Key terms: environmental assessment; working conditions; honesty and truth; scientific and political discussions

183. <u>Environmental impact assessment</u> should not come after the drawing up of a business proposition or the proposal of a particular policy, plan or programme. It should be part of the process from the beginning, and be carried out in a way which is interdisciplinary, transparent and free of all economic or political pressure. It should be linked to a study of <u>working conditions</u> and possible effects on people's physical and mental health, on the local economy and on public safety. Economic returns can thus be forecast more realistically, taking into account potential scenarios and the eventual need for further investment to correct possible undesired effects. A consensus should always be reached between the different stakeholders, who can offer a variety of approaches, solutions and alternatives. The local population should have a special place at the table; they are concerned about their own future and that of their children, and can consider goals transcending immediate economic interest. We need to stop thinking in terms of "interventions" to save the environment in favour of policies developed and debated by all interested parties. The participation of the latter also entails being fully informed about such projects and their different risks and possibilities; this includes not just preliminary decisions but also various follow-up activities and continued monitoring. <u>Honesty and truth</u> are needed in <u>scientific and political discussions</u>; these should not be limited to the issue of whether or not a particular project is permitted by law.

Key terms: low quality of food; depletion of resources

194. Frequently, in fact, people's quality of life actually diminishes—by the <u>deterioration of the environment, the low quality of food or the depletion of resources</u>—in the midst of economic growth. In this context, talk of sustainable growth usually becomes a way of distracting attention and offering excuses. It absorbs the language and values of ecology into the categories of finance and technocracy, and the social and environmental responsibility of businesses often gets reduced to a series of marketing and image-enhancing measures.

Key terms: Eucharist; food; bread; Sunday;
rest, relaxation

236. It is in the Eucharist that all that has been created finds its greatest exaltation. Grace, which tends to manifest itself tangibly, found unsurpassable expression when God himself became man and gave himself as food for his creatures. The Lord, in the culmination of the mystery of the Incarnation, chose to reach our intimate depths through a fragment of matter. He comes not from above, but from within, he comes that we might find him in this world of ours. In the Eucharist, fullness is already achieved; it is the living centre of the universe, the overflowing core of love and of inexhaustible life. Joined to the incarnate Son, present in the Eucharist, the whole cosmos gives thanks to God. Indeed the Eucharist is itself an act of cosmic love: "Yes, cosmic! Because even when it is celebrated on the humble altar of a country church, the Eucharist is always in some way celebrated on the altar of the world" [quoting John Paul II, *Ecclesia de Eucharistia* n. 8]. The Eucharist joins heaven and earth; it embraces and penetrates all creation. The world which came forth from God's hands returns to him in blessed and undivided adoration: in the bread of the Eucharist, "creation is projected towards divinization, towards the holy wedding feast, towards unification with the Creator himself" [Benedict XVI Homily for Corpus Christi, June 15, 2016]. Thus, the Eucharist is also a source of light and motivation for our concerns for the environment, directing us to be stewards of all creation.

237. On Sunday, our participation in the Eucharist has special importance. Sunday, like the Jewish Sabbath, is meant to be a day which heals our relationships with God, with ourselves, with others and with the world. Sunday is the day of the Resurrection, the "first day" of the new creation, whose first fruits are the Lord's risen humanity, the pledge of the final transfiguration of all created reality. It also proclaims "man's eternal rest in God." In this way, Christian spirituality incorporates the value of relaxation and festivity. We tend to demean contemplative rest as something unproductive and unnecessary,

but this is to do away with the very thing which is most important about work: its meaning. We are called to include in our work a dimension of receptivity and gratuity, which is quite different from mere inactivity. Rather, it is another way of working, which forms part of our very essence. It protects human action from becoming empty activism; it also prevents that unfettered greed and sense of isolation which make us seek personal gain to the detriment of all else.

FOOD DISTRIBUTION AND *DIAKONIA*

In *Laudato Si'*, Pope Francis links a theology of ecology with food distribution, especially for the poor. In a very poignant section of the encyclical the pope offers a piercing challenge, not to say condemnation: "We know that approximately a third of all food produced is discarded, and 'whenever food is thrown out it is as if it were stolen from the table of the poor'" (50).[16] This phrase is reminiscent of the challenge offered by some Latin American (liberation) theologians when they state that you cannot celebrate the Eucharist with stolen bread. This reference to food brings us back to the celebration of the Eucharist, where the presentation of gifts of bread and wine on the altar represent the collecting of gifts to be distributed to the poor. The first summary description of the way the early Christians celebrated the Eucharist comes to us from St. Justin the Martyr in the middle of the second century. He notes that the wealthy offer gifts for the poor at the time of the presentation of the eucharistic gifts. The custom of having deacons collect and distribute these gifts is attested in liturgical literature through the time when the (permanent) diaconate faded from the practice of the Roman Church.

In some countries the contributions of the restored permanent diaconate are evident in the relationship of the deacon's service at the altar and in a life of service outside of Mass, especially to the poor, marginalized, imprisoned, and disenfranchised. What the deacon does in liturgy connects with what he does outside liturgy. This very ministry images for us the kind of ministerial life that eucharistic participation presumes. The Eucharist as the body of Christ unifies the church, and it should challenge us to abandon some of the selfishness in life in favor of self-giving and surrender of the self so that others may eat and be cared for by the same Lord. Christ's paschal victory began with his humble acceptance of suffering and death. The deacon's ministry reflects the Lord when it is humble service at the altar and in all of life as a consequence of what occurs at the altar table. Like all good church ministry, the deacon's ministry is meant to show all of us how we should live our lives—in service both in the liturgy celebrated in church and in the living out of that liturgy in the liturgy of life. In effect, this is to say that the deacons are the permanent personification of the intrinsic relationship of liturgy and life, and the Eucharist specifically as the "summit and source" of the Christian life.

The presentation of gifts for the poor has been restored as an important part of the celebration of the Eucharist at the Evening Mass of the Lord's Supper on Holy Thursday. It is both a traditional practice and a reminder of how the celebration of the Eucharist links sanctuary and marketplace, altar and dining at home, consecration of bread and wine, and feeding and sheltering the poor and the homeless. Indeed, taking and collecting of gifts for the Eucharist always implies the sharing of some of those gifts with the poor and needy. To share one's talents and offerings at the Eucharist reflects one's talents and generosity to others outside the celebration of the Eucharist. From the perspective of "sacramentality," we can say that there is a keen interrelationship between preparing and sharing food at the Eucharist with sharing food in everyday life, especially at the daily and domestic "ritual" of taking meals together.

The articulation of the phrase "work of human hands" is a constant reminder that the eucharistic liturgy derives from creatures on the earth and that human work is noble and part of human self-expression. At the same time, it can also be an important reminder that all humans share in the dignity of being daughters and sons of God and deserve both humane working conditions and a living wage for their work. As early as Pope Leo XIII's encyclical *Rerum Novarum* (1891) the official magisterium of the Catholic Church has insisted on just wages and working conditions. Because these teachings have never been fully implemented, to our widespread shame, more recent papal teachings reiterate and deepen what Leo taught. These include Pope Paul VI in 1972 (*Octogesima Adveniens*), Pope John Paul II in 1991 (*Centesimus Annus*), and Benedict XVI in 2009 (*Caritas in Veritate*). This relationship is at the heart of Pope John Paul II encyclical in 1981 on human work (*Laborem Exercens*).

In addition to human suffering caused by human action, unfair work practices can also impoverish the earth itself. Again, our Holy

Father cites pollution, deforestation, and ecological imbalances that result from unjust practices. For example, the pope speaks this way about pollution in *Laudato Si'* 20 (see above). This leads to his now often-used phrase "the throwaway culture." The pope combines a critique of unchecked free market approaches to the economy that destroy this good earth with a challenge to us all personally about the ways we "use and abuse" our companions on the earth—plants, animals, and the earth itself.

Another aspect of the Holy Father's concern for humanity regards leisure in general and the Sabbath in particular.[17] In fact, this concern reaches back to when he was archbishop in Buenos Aires, as reflected in the Latin American Bishops' Conference document on evangelization in 2007.[18] The requirement of the Sabbath observance derives from the Old Testament and is a hallmark of Jewish observance to this day. That it begins at table in the evening by invoking "Lord, God of all creation" is, again, poignant and rich for us Jews and Christians theologically. But as we all know, the Sabbath rest is not that simple, especially in a "24/7" Internet culture. I wonder whether the sweatshops where mass produced goods result in a dehumanization of too many of our brothers and sisters are replaced in other cultures with the "electronic sweatshops" of our Internet machines that lead to an equally dehumanized society.

As Joseph Pieper asked in his book *Leisure, the Basis of Culture,* what is the basis of our culture without the presumption of leisure, which led to personal integration and societal cohesion? Prophetically and poignantly, Pope Francis takes this to another level when he speaks of the Internet in *Laudato Si'* 47, and the quality of human relationships. The Sunday celebration of the Eucharist is meant to be framed by leisure, the kind of sacred leisure that the Sabbath prescriptions insured. To celebrate the Eucharist with and for each other is integral to the kind of "human" ecology popes have called for since St. John Paul II and the integral ecology so forcefully argued by Pope Francis in *Laudato Si'*.

CHAPTER NINE

INTEGRAL ECOLOGY, LITURGY, IMPLEMENTATION

In this final chapter, I address three issues that I judge deserve particular attention from the method and arguments in this book. They are three "works in progress" from my expertise. The first concerns the ongoing debate about the meaning of "integral ecology" as coined and used by Pope Francis. The second concerns the role liturgy and sacraments can play in supporting integral ecology. The third offers some indications of possible venues for implementing a liturgical integral ecology.

INTEGRAL ECOLOGY

In *Laudato Si'* Pope Francis coined the phrase "integral ecology."[1] This moved the papal rhetoric beyond "human ecology," which John Paul II coined in his encyclical *Centesimus Annus* 38:

> In addition to the irrational destruction of the natural environment, we must also mention the more serious destruction of the *human environment*, something which is by no means receiving the attention it deserves. Although people are rightly worried—though much less than they should be—about preserving the natural habitats of the various animal species threatened with extinction, because they realize that each of these species makes its particular contribution

to the balance of nature in general, too little effort is made to *safeguard the moral conditions for an authentic "human ecology."* Not only has God given the earth to man, who must use it with respect for the original good purpose for which it was given to him, but man too is God's gift to man. He must therefore respect the natural and moral structure with which he has been endowed. In this context, mention should be made of the serious problems of modern urbanization, of the need for urban planning which is concerned with how people are to live, and of the attention which should be given to a "social ecology" of work.[2]

John Paul reiterates it in his encyclical *Evangelium Vitae* 42, in which he also mentions other beings on the earth:

It is the *ecological question*—ranging from the preservation of the natural habitat of the different species of animals and of other forms of life to "human ecology" leading to a solution which respects the great good of life, of everyday life.[3]

Not unlike much of Catholic teaching, the phrase *integral ecology* cannot be confined to a single definition or summary. The signature phrase, which is also the title of the fourth chapter of *Laudato Si'*, has fascinated many, including theologians who are working to try to describe its full range of meanings. For example, Anthony Kelly and Vincent Miller offer several ways of exploring what the pope says and means by this phrase.[4] The collection of essays *Integral Ecology for a Sustainable World* contains a rich and diverse panoply of ways to understand the phrase.[5] The documents surrounding the Synod of Bishops on the Amazon and Francis's post-synodal apostolic exhortation *Querida Amazonia* employed this phrase fully and thoroughly.[6] At the same time, there is more to mine in terms of what the phrase really entails and what can be expected from the kind of conversion of mind and heart to which we are called.

Since there is no one definition or summary description of *integral ecology* in these documents, we will review all the texts that contain or refer to it by citing the key terms that Pope Francis has associated with it in these documents. In what follows I will indicate what I judge to be keywords and phrases from the documents and then cite the document itself. My sense is that each of the terms indicated below deserves its own explication that could contribute to a more fully elaborated sense of what this phrase can and might mean. Put differently, I judge that Pope Francis has offered an important new avenue to dialogue about as we most forward.

Primary Source: *Laudato Si'*

Pope Francis has offered us much to "dialogue" about regarding integral ecology, as he suggested in *Laudato Si'* (3), and directs our attention to St. Francis of Assisi, who "helps us to see that an integral ecology calls for openness to categories which transcend the language of mathematics and biology and take us to the heart of what it is to be human" (11). The dialogue to which the pope calls us includes Catholics bringing the phrase *integral ecology* to the table in working with all people of "good will" (62).

Key terms: full development of humanity; dialogue

62. Why should this document, addressed to all people of good will, include a chapter dealing with the convictions of believers? I am well aware that in the areas of politics and philosophy there are those who firmly reject the idea of a Creator, or consider it irrelevant, and consequently dismiss as irrational the rich contribution which religions can make towards an integral ecology and the <u>full development of humanity</u>. Others view religions simply as a subculture to be tolerated. Nonetheless, science and religion, with their distinctive approaches to understanding reality, can enter into an intense <u>dialogue</u> fruitful for both.

Key terms: labour; keep; till

124. Any approach to an integral ecology, which by definition does not exclude human beings, needs to take account of the value of <u>labour</u>, as Saint John Paul II wisely noted in his Encyclical *Laborem Exercens*. According to the biblical account of creation, God placed man and woman in the garden he had created (cf. Gen 2:15) not only to <u>preserve it ("keep")</u> but also to <u>make it fruitful ("till")</u>. Labourers and craftsmen thus "maintain the fabric of the world" (Sir 38:34). Developing the

created world in a prudent way is the best way of caring for it, as this means that we ourselves become the instrument used by God to bring out the potential which he himself inscribed in things: "The Lord created medicines out of the earth, and a sensible man will not despise them" (Sir. 38:4).

Key terms: interrelated; human and social dimensions

137. Since everything is closely interrelated, and today's problems call for a vision capable of taking into account every aspect of the global crisis, I suggest that we now consider some elements of an integral ecology, one which clearly respects its human and social dimensions.

Key terms: (new) humanism

141. We urgently need a humanism capable of bringing together the different fields of knowledge, including economics, in the service of a more integral and integrating vision. Today, the analysis of environmental problems cannot be separated from the analysis of human, family, work-related and urban contexts, nor from how individuals relate to themselves, which leads in turn to how they relate to others and to the environment. There is an interrelation between ecosystems and between the various spheres of social interaction, demonstrating yet again that "the whole is greater than the part."

Key terms: common good

156. An integral ecology is inseparable from the notion of the common good, a central and unifying principle of social ethics. The common good is "the sum of those conditions of social life which allow social groups and their individual members relatively thorough and ready access to their own fulfilment" (which definition is taken from the *Compendium of the Social Doctrine of the Church*, 482).

Key terms: common good; justice; future generations.

Section: Justice between the Generations

159. The notion of the common good also extends to future generations. The global economic crises have made painfully

obvious the detrimental effects of disregarding our common destiny, which cannot exclude those who come after us. We can no longer speak of sustainable development apart from intergenerational solidarity.

Key terms: harmony; contemplation

225. An integral ecology includes taking time to recover a serene harmony with creation, reflecting on our lifestyle and our ideals, and contemplating the Creator who lives among us and surrounds us, whose presence "must not be contrived but found, uncovered.

Key terms: simple daily gestures; against violence, exploitation, selfishness

230. Saint Therese of Lisieux invites us to practise the little way of love, not to miss out on a kind word, a smile or any small gesture which sows peace and friendship. An integral ecology is also made up of simple daily gestures which break with the logic of violence, exploitation and selfishness. In the end, a world of exacerbated consumption is at the same time a world which mistreats life in all its forms.

Primary Source: *Querida Amazonia*[7]

Key terms: education; new habits

58. In this regard, we can take one step further and note that an integral ecology cannot be content simply with fine-tuning technical questions or political, juridical and social decisions. The best ecology always has an educational dimension that can encourage the development of new habits in individuals and groups. Sadly, many of those living in the Amazon region have acquired habits typical of the larger cities, where consumerism and the culture of waste are already deeply rooted. A sound and sustainable ecology, one capable of bringing about change, will not develop unless people are changed, unless they are encouraged to opt for another style of life, one less greedy and more serene, more respectful and less anxious, more fraternal.

Key terms: integrate social and spiritual; dignifies persons and peoples

76. At the same time, the inculturation of the Gospel in the Amazon region must better <u>integrate the social and the spiritual</u>, so that the poor do not have to look outside the Church for a spirituality that responds to their deepest yearnings. This does not mean an alienating and individualistic religiosity that would silence social demands for a more dignified life, but neither does it mean ignoring the transcendent and spiritual dimension, as if material development alone were sufficient for human beings. We are thus called not merely to join those two things, but to connect them at a deeper level. In this way, we will reveal the true beauty of the Gospel, which <u>fully humanizes, integrally dignifies persons and peoples, and brings fulfilment to every heart and the whole of life</u>.

ECOLOGICAL PRESUPPOSITIONS OF AND IN THE LITURGY

Recent Ecumenical Initiatives

As noted (above in chapter 3) in retrospect, 1989–1990 was a watershed moment. The Ecumenical Patriarchate of Constantinople, the World Council of Churches (WCC), and the Roman Catholic Church issued statements and either began or continued to address ecology with initiatives that have had long lasting effects both within communions and ecumenically.[8]

In 1989, Patriarch Dimitrios, with the approval of the Holy Synod consisting of a dozen patriarchs from around the world, issued the first of what have become (almost) annual brief encyclical letters. The letters contain the seeds of the fundamental theological and spiritual principles that guide the ecological vision of the Ecumenical Patriarchate. This vision includes the celebration of the liturgy, emphasizing its inherent theological and spiritual meanings. In the 1989 message *The Church Cannot Stand Idle*, Dimitrios declares that the Orthodox churches would from then on celebrate a World Day of Prayer for the Protection of the Environment on September 1st, the first day of their liturgical year.[9]

In March 1990 the World Council of Churches sponsored a meeting entitled "Justice, Peace and the Integrity of Creation" in Seoul, South Korea, whose final document contained the affirmations that "the creation is beloved of God" and "the earth is the Lord's."[10]

On January 1, 1990, Pope John Paul II issued the customary annual Message for the World Day of Peace, entitled *Peace with God the Creator, Peace with All of Creation*.[11] The opening paragraph sets up his argument: world peace is threatened by a lack of due respect for nature, by the plundering of natural resources, and by a progressive decline in the quality of life. Faced with the widespread destruction of the environment, people everywhere are coming to understand that we cannot continue to use the goods of the earth as we have in the past.

The intervening years have seen numerous initiatives to deepen church support for caring for the environment. The Ecumenical Patriarchate stands in pride of place for spearheading official teachings, research, writings, and seminars that concern relating liturgy with ecology (more often than not under the heading of what "sacramentality" means). The leadership of Patriarch Bartholomew, Dimitrios's successor, has been especially important in these efforts.

The work to relate liturgy with ecology has understandably not been a strong suit for the (international) World Council of Churches given the complexity of their membership, not to say the diversity of their worship traditions.[12] At the same time, books like the collection of essays by ecumenical colleagues in honor of the distinguished Anglican liturgist H. Boone Porter, a truly groundbreaking volume, deserve special and careful attention.[13] One example of a national ecumenical dialogue on ecology that uses the structure of the historic liturgy to frame its arguments about care for creation is the 2011 work of the United States Roman Catholic–United Methodist dialogue.[14]

Taking the lead from John Paul II's Message for the World Day of Peace, many Catholic episcopal conferences, theologians, and liturgists have given more and more attention to relating liturgy to ecology and to the demands the liturgy places on us in terms of correct moral living. The wealth and breadth of this material is indicated in Pope Francis's *Laudato Si'*, which cites twenty documents from episcopal conferences about ecology, including one from the United States Conference of Catholic Bishops (USCCB).[15] Among other initiatives, it is noteworthy that the Environmental Justice Office of the USCCB sponsored four seminars in the 1990s to work through many of the ways that the Catholic theological, spiritual, and liturgical tradition could contribute to environmental theology and ethics.[16] At the very same time, liturgists and church leaders have begun to devote more attention to liturgy and (social) justice. For example, Benedict XVI's post-synodal exhortation on the Eucharist, *Sacramentum Caritatis* (2007), is framed around three major themes: "A Mystery to Be Believed," "A Mystery to Be Celebrated" and "A Mystery to Be Lived."[17]

In *Laudato Si'*, Pope Francis has laid out an extraordinarily rich, profound, and far-reaching teaching on ecology from the depths of the Catholic theological, moral, spiritual, and liturgical tradition that is aimed toward inviting dialogue "with all people about our common home."[18] Toward the end of the encyclical he speaks specifically about a number of interrelated issues that include the sacraments, the Eucharist, the Sabbath rest, and concern for others, ending with the insightful summary, "And so the day of rest, centered on the Eucharist, sheds its light on the whole week, and motivates us to greater concern for nature and the poor."[19]

The phrase and practice of a "season of creation" was established by the Lutheran pastor Norman Habel in Victoria, Melbourne (Australia) in 2000. It has become a phenomenon in many Christian church calendars (official and unofficial). Three months after issuing *Laudato Si'* (2015) Pope Francis declared that Catholics would join the Orthodox in observing September 1st as a Day "For the Care for Creation," following the path laid out by Patriarch Dimitrios in 1989.[20] The pope's document that instituted the *day* was specifically addressed to Cardinal Turkson (then the head of the Pontifical Council for Justice and Peace [subsequently subsumed under the Dicastery for Integral Human Development]) and Cardinal Koch (president of the Pontifical Council for Christian Unity) issuing specific directives to them to publicize this decision.[21] It was to be an ecumenical initiative about the earth and care for the earth.

Liturgical celebrations at St. Peter's in the Vatican on this theme and on that day were celebrated in 2015 and in 2016. They were subsequently discontinued in the Vatican. Some say because part of the intended assembly, the Orthodox, could not attend because of their own celebrations at the beginning of their liturgical year; others said it was still simply too hot in Rome to gather in the basilica. Nevertheless Pope Francis has issued statements annually since 2015 on the environment.

With specific regard to the *season* of creation, in his 2019 statement Pope Francis stated,

> For this reason, I strongly encourage the faithful to pray in these days that, as the result of a timely ecumenical initiative, are being celebrated as a *Season of Creation*. This season of increased prayer and effort on behalf of our common home begins today, 1 September, the World Day of Prayer for the Care of Creation, and ends on 4 October, the feast of Saint Francis of Assisi.[22]

He then went on to say how this should be done: by "letting our prayer be inspired anew by closeness to nature," "to reflect on our lifestyles," and "to undertake prophetic actions."[23] Notably, he says nothing about the liturgy although this is a main focus of "day of creation" celebrations many in other Christian denominations.[24] There is a veritable cottage industry of books and articles on what to add to the liturgy to reflect the "season of creation." Not surprisingly, my refrain is that the very doing of liturgy engages us in the rhythms of the cosmos through sight, sound, smell, taste, and touch. If anything, I judge that we have flattened out the liturgy in such a way that it is focused on being informed and that we emphasize that we understand what is going on.[25] Once more, my basic principle is that we collectively revere, acknowledge, and raise up fellow creatures of our common home in the very act of worship.

Selected Examples

At Sunday Morning Prayer the use of the canticle from Daniel 3 is significant in this connection (Dan 3:57–88 on Sunday of weeks I and III; Dan 3:52–57 on Sunday of weeks II and IV). The opening verse—"Bless the Lord, all you works of the Lord praise and exalt him above all forever" (Dan 3:57)—is followed by a series of acclamations citing various facets of creation and redemption as motives for praising God. These include verses about praise for creation and praise for redemption, with praise for redemption ending the canticle. These same motives for praising God are found in much of the Psalter. In the present arrangement of the Hours, "praise psalms" are used as the third psalm at

Morning Prayer, and many of the psalms contain explicit praise of God for creation (e.g., Pss 19, 65, 147, 148, and 150).[26]

That the Hours classically begins with Psalm 95, paralleling the combined themes of praising God for creation and redemption, which is an additional illustration of acclaiming the God of creation.[27] Further, two phrases from the *Te Deum*, used at the conclusion of the office of readings on most Sundays and solemnities, capture and summarize this theology:

> All creation worships you...
> Holy, holy, holy, Lord, God of hosts,
> heaven and earth are full of your glory.

Fittingly, the last two lines are repeated in the Preface acclamation (Sanctus) in the Eucharistic Prayers. These prayers praise God for the *mirabilia Dei*, especially in creation and redemption.[28] They are derived from the "blessing" (*berakah*) and "thanksgiving" (*todah*) traditions of Jewish prayer.[29] This acclamation combines praise for creation with praise for redemption, and it specifies the obedient life, death, and resurrection of Jesus. This combination of themes is part of the "classical" shape of eucharistic anaphoras, even though this motif is all too briefly expressed.[30]

The theology operative in the fourth Eucharistic Prayer in the present Roman Missal concerns praising God who has made all things and who is the source of all life.[31] It brings out the universal need for the paschal mystery and the universal effects that flow from it. The Preface to this prayer refers to the entire creation and to the Father as the ultimate source of creation and the one who is manifested in creation. Human beings fulfill the purpose of creation in giving voice to creation's praise of God by joining in the praise that is voiced in liturgy, in particular the Eucharist.[32] This prayer is a worldview in a capsule form.

At the very beginning of the (Preface to the) Roman canon, the Roman liturgy has traditionally used the title *Domine, sancte Pater, omnipotens et aeternae Deus*, containing the three dominant names for God found in most contemporary prayers.[33] Fittingly, the last part of the Preface contains the phrase (from Isa 6:3) and leads to naming God in the following way: *Sanctus, sanctus, sanctus Dominus Deus sabaoth. Pleni sunt caeli et terra gloria tua.*

The mediating function of creation is exemplified in a specifically christological sense in the liturgical use of such Scripture texts as the

Johannine Prologue (John 1:1–14, used in the West on Christmas day) and the christological hymn in the Letter to the Colossians (Col 1:15–20, specifically Col 1:15–18, used as one of the New Testament hymns at Evening Prayer). According to the Johannine Prologue, God's creative idea is the Logos, the second divine person. The "high" Christology of the preexistent Logos in the Prologue combined with the introductory words of the Prologue, "in the beginning" (recalling the first words of Genesis proclaimed at the Easter Vigil), underscore how Christ was present and active at the creation of the world. John 1:3 summarizes this idea: "Through him all things came into being, and apart from him nothing came to be." The re-creation of the world was accomplished through the same Christ, cited at the Prologue's end: "The Word [who] became flesh, and made his dwelling among us, and we have seen his glory, filled with enduring love" (John 1:14).

Similarly, the Colossians hymn emphasizes Christ's preexistence. The purpose of all creation consists in our union with Christ and through him with the Father, the origin and fulfillment of all creation, including humanity. Of note is Colossians 1:16: "In him everything in heaven and on earth was created, things visible and invisible....All things were created through him." Thus, we can assert that the stated motivation for liturgical praise is creation and redemption, and that the dynamic of Christian liturgy is to offer back creation to the Creator through Christ, the cocreator.[34]

This emphasis on the christological axis of liturgy, specifically the paschal mystery, has recently been appropriately supplemented by a pneumatologically rich emphasis on liturgy and sacraments as experiences through and in which the church is drawn into the life of the Triune God. All liturgy is triune. It is the Triune God who makes it occur.

Choices in the Roman Missal

There are prayers in the Roman Missal that refer directly to the earth in its various phases and crises that can be chosen whenever it is judged they are warranted (except on Sundays). One of the Prefaces in the third edition of the *Missale Romanum* is entitled "Creation" (*De Creatione*[35]) and states,

> For you laid the foundations of the world
> and have arranged the changing of times and seasons;

you formed man in your own image
and set humanity over the whole world in all its wonder,
to rule in your name over all you have made
and for ever praise you in your mighty works,
through Christ our Lord.

Texts from the Masses for various needs and occasions (discussed in chapter 6) are in some cases of ancient origin while others give voice to the teaching of Vatican II.[36]

Masses and Prayers for Various Needs and Occasions

FOR THE SANCTIFICATION OF HUMAN LABOR

ENTRANCE ANTIPHON (CF. PSALM 90:17)

May your favor, O Lord, be upon us,
and may you give success to the work of our hand.

COLLECT (B)

O God, who through human labor
never cease to perfect and govern the vast work of creation,
listen to the supplications of your people
    and grant that all men and women
    may find work that befits their dignity,
    joins them more closely to one another
    and enables them to serve their neighbor.

AT SEEDTIME

COLLECT

Pour out your gracious blessing on your people, Lord God,
so that through your generosity
our land may yield its fruits
for us to enjoy with ever-grateful hearts,
to the honor of your holy name.

PRAYER OVER THE OFFERINGS

Look with favor on our offerings, O Lord,
so that we, who bring you grains of wheat made into bread
to be changed into the Body of your Son,
may find joy in the blessing you bestow
on the seed to be sown in the earth.

PRAYER AFTER COMMUNION

Grant to your faithful, almighty God,
abundance of the earth's fruits,
that, nourished by these in the present age,
they may also grow in spiritual things
and so obtain the good things of eternity,
of which they have received a pledge in this Sacrament.

AFTER THE HARVEST

ENTRANCE ANTIPHON (PSALM 67:7)

The earth has yielded its fruit;
may God, our God, bless us.

COLLECT (FIRST OPTION)

O Lord, good Father, who in your providence
have entrusted the earth to the human race,
grant, we pray, that with the fruits harvested from it
we may be able to sustain life
and, with your help, always use them
to promote your praise and the well-being of all.

COLLECT (SECOND OPTION)

We give you thanks, O Lord,
for the fruits that earth has given to benefit the human family
and we pray
that, as the working of your supreme providence
has produced them,
so you may cause the seed of justice and the fruits of charity
to spring up in our hearts.

PRAYER OVER THE OFFERINGS

Sanctify, O Lord, the offerings
we bring to you with thanksgiving from the fertile earth
and, as you give us a rich harvest of the earth's produce,
so make our hearts abound with heavenly fruitfulness.

COMMUNION ANTIPHON (CF. PSALM 104:13–15)

The earth is replete with the fruits of your work, O Lord;
you bring forth bread from the earth,
and wine to cheer the heart.

PRAYER AFTER COMMUNION

Grant, we pray, O Lord,
that, as we give you thanks in this saving mystery
for the crops harvested from the earth,
we may, through the same mystery working within us,
be worthy to receive still greater blessings.

IN TIME OF FAMINE OR FOR THOSE SUFFERING HUNGER

COLLECT

O God, who, being both good and almighty,
provide for all creatures,
give us, we pray, an effective love
for our brothers and sisters who suffer hunger,
so that famine may be banished
and that they may have strength to serve you
with free and untroubled hearts.

PRAYER OVER THE OFFERINGS

Look, O Lord, on the oblation we present to you
from among your wonderful gifts,
so that the offering which signifies abundance of divine life
and unity in charity
may impel us to share all things justly
and to care for one another as brothers and sisters.

189

COMMUNION ANTIPHON (MATTHEW 11:28)

Come to me, all who labor and are burdened,
and I will refresh you, says the Lord.

PRAYER AFTER COMMUNION

O God, almighty Father,
we humbly ask you that the living Bread,
which has come down from heaven,
may give us strength
to relieve our brothers and sisters in their need.

In Time of Earthquake

COLLECT

O God, who set the earth on its firm foundation,
spare those who are fearful
and show favor to those who implore you,
so that, with all dangers of earthquake entirely gone,
we may continue to experience your mercy
and serve you in thankfulness,
safe under your protection.

For Rain

COLLECT

O God, in whom we live and move and have our being,
grant us sufficient rain,
so that, being supplied with what sustains us in this present life,
we may seek more confidently what sustains us for eternity.

For Fine Weather

COLLECT

Almighty ever-living God,
who heal us through correction
and save us by your forgiveness,
grant to those who seek your favor
that we may rejoice at the good weather for which we hope

and always use what in your goodness you bestow
for the glory of your name and for our well-being.

FOR AN END TO STORMS

COLLECT

O God, to whose commands all the elements give obedience,
we humbly entreat you,
that the stilling of fearsome storms may turn a powerful menace
into an occasion for us to praise you.

Reviving Rogation and Ember Days

The GIRM states, "In the drawing up of the calendar of a nation, the Rogation and Ember Days should be indicated, as well as the forms and texts for their celebration and other special measures should also be taken into consideration" (396). The *Universal Norms on the Liturgical Year and the Calendar* states,

> 45. On rogation and ember days the church is accustomed to entreat the Lord for the various needs of humanity, especially for the fruits of the earth and for human labour, and to give thanks to him publicly.
>
> 46. In order that the rogation days and ember days may be adapted to the different regions and different needs of the faithful, the conferences of Bishops should arrange the time and manner in which they are held. consequently, concerning their duration, whether they are to last one or more days, or be repeated in the course of the year, norms are to be established by the competent authority, taking into consideration local needs.
>
> 47. The Mass for each day of these celebrations should be chosen from among the Masses for various needs, and should be one which is more particularly appropriate to the purpose of the supplications.

The United States bishops have, so far, chosen not to adapt the Roman Rite's customs related to Rogation and Ember Days.[37] It should not be forgotten that in the evolution of the liturgical movement in the United

States, there was a very close connection with the National Catholic Rural Life Conference.[38]

There is nothing to prevent, and cogent reasons to encourage, the USCCB to move forward with reestablishing Rogation and Ember Days. These days were and should be marked by processions on the earth of the entire assembly, as well as verbal and musical engagement in the liturgy. This restoration could be a source of hope and support as the United States continues to see the sad demise of the family farm, once more, because of corporations and monopolies that take over land, sometimes at severely reduced prices, which had been a farm family for generations.

PROPOSED INITIATIVES TO IMPLEMENT *LAUDATO SI'*

Theological Curricula

Chapter 6 of *Laudato Si'* is entitled "Ecological Education and Spirituality." That many Catholic colleges and universities are offering courses in ecology in increasing numbers is highly laudable and to be encouraged. However, there is a parallel here with the way ecumenism was addressed after Vatican II. While some theological curricula began to offer courses on ecumenism, others evolved to the laudable position of ensuring that there are ecumenical and interreligious components to the existing theology and religious studies courses. The same should be done regarding the environment. In my own writing, the first chapter in my book *Models of the Eucharist* entitled "Cosmic Mass" is just such a contribution.[39]

Franciscans and Other Orders

St. John Paul II named St. Francis the patron of ecology in 1979. Certainly, Pope Francis has catapulted the *Poverello* and his followers to front row status in implementing his ecological agenda. I would hope that the many branches of Franciscans would take up this opportunity and challenge in a sustained way. In addition, the encyclical *Fratelli Tutti* deserves no less attention and care among Franciscans.

At the same time, there are other orders and religious communities in the church whose rules and charisms include ecology: for example, the Benedictines. In *Laudato Si'* 126, Pope Francis himself says,

> We can also look to the great tradition of monasticism. Originally, it was a kind of flight from the world, an escape from the decadence of the cities. The monks sought the desert, convinced that it was the best place for encountering the presence of God. Later, Saint Benedict of Norcia proposed that his monks live in community, combining prayer and spiritual reading with manual labor (*ora et labora*). Seeing manual labour as spiritually meaningful proved revolutionary. Personal growth and sanctification came to be sought in the interplay of recollection and work. This way of experiencing work makes us more protective and respectful of the environment; it imbues our relationship to the world with a healthy sobriety.

I hope that salient points of the *Rule of St. Benedict* might be raised up, synthesized, and elaborated on as part and parcel of today's Benedictine *labora*. That some monastic communities are even now self-sustaining would be a powerful witness of the value of the monastic life for the whole church.

Postpandemic Ecumenical Initiatives

In my opinion there will likely be serious financial "belt tightening" in the budgets of the Catholic Church in the United States once the pandemic is no longer a daily threat to life itself. In anticipation of shrinking resources, it is not inconceivable that Catholic parishes may continue to be consolidated and pastoral services reduced. One possibility regarding the Catholic Church's teaching on ecology would be that local religious leaders sponsor joint seminars and events based, for example, on documents such as *Ecumenical and Interreligious Guidebook: Care for Our Common Home*. Both St. John XXIII and the World Council of Churches many years ago said that churches ought not do separately what they can do together. Attention to the environment would be a perfect example of adopting this premise. This might be the basis for a wholesale restructuring of social justice initiatives and some elements of Christian formation that churches can and should do in common.

Liturgy and Sacraments Are Integral Ecology

From my own specialization in liturgy and sacraments, articles 233–37 in *Laudato Si'*, on "Sacramental Signs and the Celebration of Rest," have little resonance in subsequent magisterial and other teachings on making the obvious and necessary link among ecology, liturgy, and sacraments. If the liturgy is the "summit and source" of the church's life, it should be part and parcel of what integral ecology means. In my judgment, there are two intrinsically connected corollaries of this phrase.

Integral to the Christian Life

No other prayer in and for the church has such a central and defining role as sacred liturgy. No other prayer can come close to the unique, central role that believers have devoted to the liturgy from time immemorial. This unique reality, reflected in the texts and rites of the liturgies themselves, deserve to have a pivotal role as we seek to develop what integral ecology means. This is the basis of my argument for developing such a theology as a particular contribution that Catholicism can make to a religiously based "integral ecology."[40]

Integrative of the Christian Life

"Summit and font" means that the celebration of the liturgy derives from daily life and returns us to daily life. In more theological language, the principle of sacramentality is always part of the Catholic worldview that informs us in every way. It gives us hope when we might otherwise judge that all is hopeless. It grants us forgiveness even when we have sinned seriously. It shapes us by the proclamation of the word, lest we have no framework in which to view the world with all its joys, hopes, sorrows, and despair. The liturgy collects all the fragments of our often-fragmented life and makes of them an offering to the Triune God.

The Triune God acts among us again and again so we can reenter again and again "the work of our redemption." There is a continuum in the spiritual life that means we live in a world created, sustained, and graced by the living God, "in whom we live and move and have our being," before during and after the celebration of what we call "sacred mysteries." The celebration of liturgy and sacraments is less a "door to the sacred" than a focused and profound experience of the utterly transcendent God here and now. In effect, the liturgy enacts a "liturgical, sacramental, integral ecology" for the church and for all to see and appreciate. This is a chief element of Catholic identity that must always be in the forefront of our dialogue and action about ecology. The celebration of any liturgy cannot be regarded as a discrete part of the separable from the rest of the day. The celebration of the liturgy derives from and leads to the continuum of life. After the arguments about ideas and practices from the liturgy concerning creation, ecology, sacramentality, and the work of human hands (among many others) it will come as no surprise that I will argue that a (major) missing factor in almost all discussions about integral ecology as a characteristic Catholic element to future work in this area.

In sum, the task is not to uncover or recover the ecological aspect of the liturgy. Rather, it is to rediscover what the liturgy has always been and is: the raising up of fellow creatures of our common home in their many and diverse ways so that we on this good earth can experience Christ's paschal victory through the activity of the Trinity as ritualized in and through the givenness of the liturgy even as we yearn for its fulfillment in a new heaven and a new earth (see 2 Pet 3:30).

Deep Conversion for Deep Ecology

As I conclude, one major lingering question for me is how well the teachings of *Laudato Si'* have been received and welcomed by the American lay faithful. A study of publications from American arch/bishops since 2015 indicates nothing but failing marks in terms of the hierarchy's work to include climate change in pastoral letters and newspaper columns.[41] More specifically, I wonder to what extent the mainline Catholic principles (e.g., common good, universal destination of goods), now joined with concern for all "fellow creatures" who share "our common home," are raised up as examples in homilies as applications of the good news.

There may well be a parallel with the church's teaching on the death penalty. As far back as the Holy Year 2000, St. John Paul II asked that the lights on and around the Coliseum in Rome be left burning when a planned execution was halted. This was cause for real celebration. A life was not lost. At the time, however, the majority of American Catholics opposed the church's position, most recently and forcefully affirmed in *Fratelli Tutti* 263–70.[42] Since then, there has been a steady reaffirmation of the church's position in papal statements, in the *Catechism of the Catholic Church*, and in statements from bishops' conferences that seem to have had an impact on American Catholics. Now, the majority do not favor the death penalty. On March 24, 2021, the legislature of the state of Virginia voted to outlaw the death penalty.

It is more than notable that the final document of the Synod on the Amazon begins with chapter on "From Listening to Integral Conversion."[43] Conversion of mind and heart takes time for us all, in this case those who preach from pulpits and those who preach by their daily lives in light of what they have heard in church. I would hope and pray that the superlative initiative taken on the official levels of church life might truly "trickle down" to formation programs, parishes, and homes. Things take time. But there is an urgency and moral imperative that cause some scientists to say that we are too late in saving the planet. My own sense is that this urgency is not felt by far too many American Catholics. My hopeful sense suggests, "at least not yet."

CONCLUSION

Simply put, this methodological contribution to ecological and liturgical-sacramental studies has been to link them, to reunite them in a systematic way, and to remind ourselves that they always have been interconnected realities. In our own day, this interconnectedness in the liturgy should also raise up concern for the earth and all aspects of "our common home." We live in one graced and sacramental world where reverence and respect are due to the earth and all its inhabitants. The liturgy is a daily reminder of and engagement in the beauty of the earth by engaging our senses in a formalized way to rediscover this beauty again and again. I acknowledge that what I have offered is very traditional because communities of faith have always given voice to words and raised up elements from the earth to celebrate the action of God among them. These have been central elements of worship revered from the ancient and present Jewish liturgy to today's multitudinous rites across the world. The phrase *ever ancient ever new* comes to mind and heart.

A "sound bite" to describe this project might be *ecology is liturgy* and *liturgy is ecology*. The God we worship is found before any liturgical celebration begins because of the holiness of the sacramental world in which we live. This includes all creatures on "our common home," whom we experience through our senses—sight, sound, smell, taste, touch—not only through our minds. Then, God calls us to assemble for the liturgy to engage many elements from this common home in texts and rites that form and re-form, create and re-create us in accord with the paschal mystery. Then we are sent forth back to the same sacramental world to care for all fellow creatures and the earth itself so that it not be destroyed by the destruction brought through human sin. The sacramental cycle of worship begins in our daily lives, 24/7; it is deepened in the regular celebration of the Hours, sacraments, and all liturgy; it is continued when we are sent to live a holy and self-giving life in and on our common home.

For me, writing this book about the ecology and liturgy has been a daily exercise in revering and relishing the discovery of "ever ancient and ever new" elements in the liturgy by the daily celebration of the liturgy. There can be many ways of appreciating the liturgy and various aspects of the liturgy through books like these. But no book can ever substitute for the daily celebration of the liturgy itself. The liturgy in its many forms and structures raises up texts and rites that the churches judge are central to experiencing and understanding the paschal mystery in all its truly mysterious fullness as accomplished once and for all in Palestine and experienced in its fullness today "where two or three are gathered" in the Lord's name. A cosmic way of saying how important the daily liturgy is, is the fact that every day the sun shines (rises and sets) at a slightly different time. The same sun and the same earth. But the light in the cosmos is always (slightly) different. Similarly in the liturgy. The liturgy one day is never repeated again. The texts and rites may be engaged in again, but the coincidence of contents and context will never be the same. The liturgy is so profound that we can never comprehend or understand it all. The fact that it is a ritual with rites and texts is a gift so that each day one or another of the elements of the liturgy can engage our imaginations in ever new ways, even as we need to engage our minds, hearts, and imaginations to work as we must to "save" our common home.

I pray that the end of this book will cause us to begin again, and again to revere, not just value, the earth and all God's creation raised up in the liturgy, the sacraments and in the one graced sacramental world in which we live.

NOTES

INTRODUCTION

1. Pope Francis, Encyclical Letter *Laudato Si'* On Care for Our Common Home (May 24, 2015), http://www.vatican.va/content/francesco/en/encyclicals/documents/papa-francesco_20150524_enciclica-laudato-si.html.

2. Among others, see my own *Context and Text: A Method for Liturgical Theology*, rev. ed. (Collegeville, MN: Liturgical Press, 2018).

3. "The American Response to *Laudato Si*'," commissioned by the (Vatican) Dicastery on Integral Human Development, https://www.humandevelopment.va/en/progetti.html; "Sacramental Theology after *Laudato Si*'," in *Heaven and Earth Are Full of Your Glory* (Collegeville, MN: Liturgical Press, 2019), 245–61; "Ecology," in *Oxford Dictionary of Ecumenism*, ed. Paul McPartlan and Geoffrey Wainright, https://global.oup.com/academic/product/the-oxford-handbook-of-ecumenical-studies-9780199600847?cc=us&lang=en&; "Liturgy and Ecology," in *Worship and Church: An Ecclesial Liturgy; Essays in Honor of Gerard Austin, OP*, ed. Sallie Latkovich and Peter Phan (Mahwah, NJ: Paulist Press, 2019), 202–26; "Our Common Home," *The Heythrop Journal* 59, no. 6 (2018): 873–86; "Background to and Contributions to *Laudato Si'*, On Care for Our Common Home," in *All Creation is Connected: Voices in Response to Pope Francis' Encyclical on Ecology*, ed. Daniel DiLeo (Winona, MN: Anselm Academic, 2017), 15–30; *A Commentary on Laudato Si': Examining the Background, Contributions, Implementation, and Future of Pope Francis's Encyclical* (Mahwah, NJ: Paulist Press, 2016); "God's Icon: Creation, Sacramentality and Liturgy," in *Environmental*

Justice and Climate Change: Assessing Pope Benedict XVI's Ecological Vision for the Catholic Church in the United States, ed. Jamie Schaefer and Tobias Winwright (Lanham, MD: Lexington Books, 2013), 149–72; "Sacramentality: The Fundamental Language for Liturgy and Sacraments," in *Per Ritus et Praeces: Sacramentalita della Liturgia*, Analecta Liturgica 28 (Rome: Studia Anselmiana, 2010), 131–60; "Discovering the Sacramentality of Sacraments," *Questions liturgiques* 81 (2000): 171–83; "Sacramentality and the Theology of Creation: A Recovered Paradigm for Sacramental Theology," *Louvain Studies* 23 (1998): 159–79; "Environmental Theology—a Review Discussion," *The Thomist* 60 (April 1996): 301–16; "The Sacramentality of Creation and the Role of Creation in Liturgy and Sacrament," in *Preserving the Creation: Environmental Theology and Ethics*, ed. Kevin W. Irwin and Edmund D. Pellegrino (Washington, DC: Georgetown University Press, 1994), 67–111.

4. See my own *Liturgy and Sacraments in a COVID World: Renewal Not Restoration* (Mahwah, NJ: Paulist Press, 2021).

5. That there are several prevailing cultural attitudes that can mitigate against the celebration of the liturgy is indicated in many articles, books, and op-ed pieces that appeared during the coronavirus pandemic. For one nonscientific summary about American "culture," see my own "Introduction" in *Liturgy and Sacraments in a COVID World*, xx–xxiii.

6. See especially my own *A Commentary on* Laudato Si', "Ecology," and "Background to and Contributions to *Laudato Si', On Care for Our Common Home*," and "Our Common Home" (cited above).

7. This is largely the thesis of Alexander Gerken, *Theologie der Eucharistie*, 2nd ed. (Munich: Kosel-Verlag, 1976). Classics in this regard are the fulsome and subtle arguments from history and theology in *Handbuch der Dogmeneschite*, vol. 4, *Sakramente-Eschatologie* (Vienna/Basel: Herder Freiburg, 1980). One of the most helpful in this regard is *Die Lehre von den Sakramenten im allgemeinen Von der Reformation bis zur Gegenwart.*

8. See Leo the Great, *Sermon 74.*

9. The most influential of her catechetical works is *The Religious Potential of the Child* (Chicago: Liturgy Training Publications, 1992) and *Living Liturgy: Elementary Reflections* (Chicago: Catechesis of the Good Shepherd Publications, 1998).

10. See the very important and highly insightful books by Marva Dawn, *Reaching Out without Dumbing Down* (Grand Rapids: Eerdmans, 1995) and *A Royal Waste of Time* (Grand Rapids: Eerdmans, 1999).

11. See Benjamin Stewart, *A Watered Garden: Christian Worship and Earth's Ecology* (Minneapolis: Augsburg Fortress, 2011).

12. See Bryan Spinks, *The Worship Mall: Contemporary Responses to Contemporary Culture* (New York: Church Publications, 2011).

13. Maksimilijan Zitnik, *Sacramenta, Bibliographia International-ist*, 4 vols. (Rome: Pontificia Universitas Gregoriana, 1992).

14. *L'Eglise en prière: Introduction à la liturgie*, ed. A. G. Martimort, 4 vols. (Paris: Desclée, 1983–1984), trans. Matthew J. O'Connell as *The Church at Prayer: An Introduction to the Liturgy*, 4 vols. (Collegeville, MN: Liturgical Press, 1986–1992); *Gottesdienst der Kirche: Handbuch der Liturgiewissenschaft*, ed. Bernard Meyer et al. (Regensburg: Pustet, 1983–1989); *Anàmnesis: Introduzione storico-teologica alla Liturgia*, ed. Salvatore Marsili et al, 7 vols. (Turin: Marietti, 1974–1992); *Handbook for Liturgical Studies*, ed. Anscar Chupungco, 4 vols. (Collegeville, MN: Liturgical Press, 1997–2000); *La celebración en la Iglesia*, ed. J. M. Canals et al., dir. Dionisio Borobio, 2nd ed. (1st ed., 1985; Salamanca: Siguemi, 1988).

15. An interesting study along these lines is provided by the Institute of Pastoral Liturgy in Padua, Italy. Edizioni Messaggero Padova has published three series of books (Caro Salutis Cardo) reflecting an interdisciplinary, praxis approach to liturgy and sacraments. The first series includes explorations of the experience of God in worship and liturgy as an act of communication, studies of how the proclaimed word is interpreted in the act of liturgy, and studies of specific topics such as Eucharist and ecumenism, the theology of confirmation, and the role of the ordained minister in liturgy. This first series is Contributi and a full listing of publications, with indices, is available at http://www.ist-liturgiapastorale.net/pubblicazioni.

The second and most comprehensive series, Studi (with a full listing also available at http://www.ist-liturgiapastorale.net/pubblicazioni), includes two volumes by Pelagio Visentin entitled *Culmen et Fons* comprising a veritable encyclopedia of liturgical study: *Culmen et fons: Raccolta di studi liturgia e spiritualita*, 2 vols., Caro Salutis Cardo 3–4 (1986–1995). The first volume (subtitled *Mysterium Christi ab ecclesia celebratum*) describes in detail how the paschal mystery of Christ is celebrated in the church through the sacraments, the liturgical year, and the Hours. Methodologically, the liturgy itself serves as the fundamental theological source for this exposition. This guides the work of the second volume (subtitled *"Lex orandi" e "Lex credendi"*) concerning the process and progress of the reform of the liturgy (especially in Italy) and how the liturgy enlivens the inner dynamic of the Christian life. A complement to this magnum opus describes the praxis method of the Santa Giustina Institute: P. Visentin, A. N. Terrin, and R. Cecolin, eds., *Una liturgia per Uomo: La liturgia pastorale e i suoi compiti* (1986). This series also includes P. Visentin, A. N. Terrin, and R. Cecolin, eds., *Una liturgia per l'uomo: La liturgia pastorale e i suoi compiti* (1986). It contains essays by distinguished Italian liturgical scholars such as Salvatore Marsili, Luigi Sartori, Franco Brovelli, and Domenico Sartore. These authors deal with the relationship between liturgy and contemporary theological discourse, pastoral theology, the interdisciplinary approach to the study of liturgical celebration, and the relation of liturgy to catechesis.

16. Among others, see Susan Ross, *Extravagant Affections: A Feminist Sacramental Theology* (New York: Continuum, 2001). Also notable in this connection is her more comprehensive book *Anthropology: Seeking Light and Beauty*, in the series Engaging Theology: Catholic Perspectives, ed. Tatha Wiley (Collegeville, MN: Liturgical Press, 2012), which illustrates the "disciplinarity complexity" involved in evolving sacramental theologies today.

17. See the dated but important foray into this area in David N. Power, "Sacramental Theology: A Review of Literature in Feminist Theology and Asian and African Contributions," *Theological Studies* 55, no. 4 (December 1994): 693–704.

18. Among others, see my own *Context and Text*.

19. Kenan Osborne, *Christian Sacraments in a Postmodern World: A Theology for the Third Millennium* (Mahwah, NJ: Paulist Press, 1999).

20. See *Laudato Si'* 16, 20, 22 and 43. Pope Francis adjusted the phrase to "a throwaway world" in *Fratelli Tutti* 18–20: Encyclical Letter *Fratelli Tutti* on Fraternity and Social Friendship (3 October 2020), http://www.vatican.va/content/francesco/en/encyclicals/documents/papa-francesco_20201003_enciclica-fratelli-tutti.html.

CHAPTER ONE: OFFICIAL CHURCH TEACHING ON SACRAMENTS FROM TRENT TO THE TWENTIETH CENTURY

1. Among others, see Andre Duval, *Des sacrements au concile de Trente* (Paris: Les Editions du Cerf, 1985); Josef Finkenzeller, *Handbuch der Dogmengeschichte*, vol. 4, *Die Lehre von den Sakramenten*

im allgemeinen Von der Reformation bis zur Gegenwart (Freiburg: Herder, 1981), especially 50–67.

2. The term *fathers* is used rather than *bishops* because of the number of others, such as (superior) generals of religious orders, were involved in the deliberations of the council including the votes. See, among others, John O'Malley, *Trent: What Happened at the Council* (Cambridge, MA: Belknap Press, 2013).

3. See Bernard J. Leeming, *Principles of Sacramental Theology* (London: Longmans, Green and Co., 1956), 553–89.

4. It is notable that the creation account of Gen 1:1—2:2 is the first reading proclaimed at the Easter Vigil.

5. See Denzinger-Schonmetzer, *Enchiridion Symbolorum Definitionum et Declarationum de rebus fidei et morum*, 36th ed. (Rome: Herder, 1965), no. 1601; henceforth, Denzinger-Schonmetzer is cited as DS with item number. In *Trent*, John O'Malley provides very rich and insightful commentary on the "nuts and bolts" of what happened at Trent (as well as Bologna when the bishops could not meet in Trent).

6. See Piet Fransen, "Sacraments, Signs of Faith," in *Hermeneutics of the Councils*, ed. H. E. Mertens and F. De Graeve (Leuven: University Press, 1985), 418ff. Fransen states, "The assembled Fathers never delineate a *complete* exposition of the doctrine of the sacraments.... They aimed only at condemning the heretical positions of the Lutherans and the Calvinists, deliberately dropping whatever question, however important, was still under discussion among Catholic theologians."

7. One of the best treatments in English is George Worgul, *From Magic to Metaphor* (Mahwah, NJ: Paulist, 1980).

8. See my own *Pope Francis and the Liturgy: The Call to Holiness and Mission* (Mahwah, NJ: Paulist Press, 2020), chap. 3 ("Participation of Laity and Clergy in the Liturgy," 38–57).

9. Second Vatican Council, Constitution *Sacrosanctum Concilium* on the Sacred Liturgy (4 December 1963), https://www.vatican.va/archive/hist_councils/ii_vatican_council/documents/vat-ii_const_19631204_sacrosanctum-concilium_en.html.

10. Alexander Ganoczy, "'Splendors' and 'Miseries' of the Tridentine Doctrine of Ministries," in *Office and Ministry in the Church*, ed. Roland Murphy and Bazs van Iersel, 75–86, Concilium 80 (New York: Herder and Herder, 1972); Herve-Marie Legrand, "The 'Indelible' Character and the Theology of Ministry," in *Office and Ministry*, 54–62.

11. See my own *Serving the Body of Christ* (Mahwah, NJ: Paulist Press, 2013), 10–16, 71–75.

12. Among many others in various languages, see *Catechism of the Council of Trent for Parish Priests, issued by order of Pius V*, trans. with notes by John A. McHugh and Charles J. Callan (New York: Joseph F. Wagner, 1934), xxxixff.

For example, for the First Sunday of Advent, the following "program" is given: "1. Dogmatic Subject: The Second Coming of Christ.—*They shall see the son of man coming in a cloud with great power and majesty* (Luke xxi. 27). Pages 80 ff., 519. 2. Moral Subject: The Sixth Commandment.—*Let us walk honestly, as in the day: not in rioting and drunkenness, not in chambering and impurities* (Rom. xiii. 13). Pages 473, 534, 535, 565 ff."

13. Christian Initiation: General Introduction 22, in *Roman Ritual Revised by Decree of the Second Vatican Ecumenical Council and Promulgated by Authority of Pope Paul VI, Order of Baptism of Children*, 2nd typical ed. (Collegeville, MN: Liturgical Press, 2020); Introduction [to the Order of Baptism of Children] 18.2, in *Order of Baptism of Children*; "Third Step: Celebration of the Sacraments of Initiation [for the Rite of Christian Initiation of Adults] 212, in *Roman Ritual Revised by Decree of the Second Vatican Ecumenical Council and Promulgated by Authority of Pope Paul VI, Rite of Christian Initiation of Adults*, typical ed. (Collegeville, MN: Liturgical Press, 1988). The General Introduction provides the strongest indication: "Both the rite of immersion, which more suitably signifies participation in the Death and Resurrection of Christ, and the rite of pouring can lawfully be used.

14. Pierre Pourrat, *Theology of the Sacraments: A Study in Positive Theology*, 4th ed. (St. Louis: B. Herder, 1930).

15. Prior to becoming Pope Pius X, Giuseppe Melchiorre Sarto was patriarch of Venice. There, he had already taken initiatives related to active participation and Gregorian chant.

16. See *Pope Francis and the Liturgy*, 41–56. The review here includes Pius XII's *Mediator Dei* (1947), Congregation for Rites' *De musica sacra et sacra liturgia ad mentem litterarum encyclicarum Pii Papae XII 'Musica Sacrae Discipolina" et "Mediator Dei"* (1958), and Vatican II's *Sacrosanctum Concilium* (1963).

17. In brief, an encyclical from the pope is the highest-ranking document that a pope can issue on his own having to do with church teaching, faith, morals, and discipline. The genre of papal encyclical

began (only) with Benedict XIV (r. 1740–1756). While almost all encyclicals are addressed to bishops, priests, and the lay faithful of the Catholic church, two notable exceptions are *Pacem in Terris* by John XXIII (1963) and *Laudato Si'* by Francis (2015). These are also addressed to all people of good will.

CHAPTER TWO: ISSUES OF METHOD FOR CONTEMPORARY SACRAMENTAL THEOLOGY

1. See my own *The Sacraments: Historical Foundations and Liturgical Theology* (Mahwah, NJ: Paulist Press, 2016), 11–12.

2. See my own "Sacramental Theology," in *New Catholic Encyclopedia*, suppl. vol. 18, 447–52 (Washington, DC: Catholic University of America Press, 1988), especially 447–52. For a summary of the church's context prior to the Reformation, see Irwin, *The Sacraments*, pt. 1 (entitled "History," chap. 1–7, pp. 21–127).

3. See my own *A Commentary on "Laudato Si'": Examining the Background, Contributions, Implementation and Future of Pope Francis's Encyclical* (Mahwah, NJ: Paulist Press, 2016), 59–71.

4. I have chosen the following authors because over the years of teaching and writing about sacraments I have found their contributions to be profound and long lasting. In fact, I have worked with some of them and interviewed others. At the same time, I acknowledge a predilection for American, European, and Latin authors. It is my hope that others may fill in their own summaries of those from whom I have learned a great deal but whose writings I judge I would be unable to summarize adequately. These include the important works by Susan Ross, Lisette Larsen Miller, and Gail Ramshaw, among many others.

5. Edward Schillebeeckx, *De Sacramentele Heilseconomie: Theologische bezinning op S. Thomas' sacramentenleer in het licht van de traditie en van de hedendaagse sacramentsproblematiek* (Antwerp: H. Neiissen Bilthoven, 1952). Unfortunately, the 1952 Dutch original was never translated into English, but a (very) abridged version appeared subsequently in Dutch, entitled Christus, *Sacrament van de Godsontmoeting*. The third edition was published in Dutch (Antwerp: H. Neiissen Bilthoven, 1960) and translated into English as the highly influential *Christ, the Sacrament of the Encounter with God*, trans. Paul Barrett, Mark Schoof, and Laurence Bright (New York: Sheed and Ward, 1963).

An example of the "staying power" of Schillebeeckx's contribution in *Christ, the Sacrament* is in David Fagerberg's comment, "Still in print after forty years, this classic book took the scholastic categories in Thomas and refreshed them for modern readers by means of language about personal encounter." David Fagerberg, "The Sacramental Life," in *The Oxford Handbook of Catholic Theology*, ed. Lewis Ayres and Medi Ann Volpe, 249–62 (Oxford: Oxford University Press, 2019).

At the same time, this article by Fagerberg and those in *The Oxford Handbook* by Pamela Jackson ("The Liturgy"), Frederick Bauerschmidt, ("The Eucharist"), and Kimberly Hope Belcher ("Sacramental and Liturgical Theology 1900–2000") are dated, and repetitions of old frameworks for their respective topics. A glance at the index of this book of fifty-six articles yields no reference to "ecology," "environment," or "sacramentality," not to mention in these critical pieces. While editors are free to invite authors for specific topics granted their expertise, why a Jesuit would contribute an article on "Monastic Theology" is curious. Despite some interesting and informative articles, such as Paul McPartlan's "The Church," the volume as a whole is deeply disappointing.

6. See especially Odo Casel, *Das christliche Kultmysterium*, ed. Burkhard Neunheuser, 4th ed. (1st ed., 1932; Regensburg: Pustet, 1960), newly trans. and ed. Aidan Kavanagh, *The Mystery of Christian Worship* (New York: Crossroad, 1999); Casel, "Mysteriengegenwart," *Jahrbuch für Liturgiewissenschaft* 8 (1929): 10–224; Casel, "Glaube, Gnosis und Mysterium," *Jahrbuch für Liturgiewissenschaft* 15 (1941): 155–305. Also see Simon Striker, "Der Mysteriengedanke des hl. Paulus nach Römerbrief 6.2–11," *Liturgisches Leben* 1 (1943): 285–96; Theodore Filthaut, *Die Kontroverse über die Mysterienlehre* (Warendorf, 1947); Burkhard Neunheuser, "Odo Casel in Retrospect and Prospect," *Worship* 50 (1976): 489–503; Arno Schilson, ed., *Odo Casel: Mysterientheologie; Ansatz und Gestalt* (Regensburg: Pustet, 1986).

7. See Teresa Koernke, "Mystery Theology," in *The New Dictionary of Catholic Worship*, 885–86 (Collegeville, MN: Liturgical Press, 1990).

8. The description that sacraments "cause" grace in the life of the participants is a characteristic of Catholic sacramental theology. There were and are many approaches to this reality, and this exemplifies the richness of the Catholic theological tradition. At the same time, when the fathers at the Council of Trent described what happens in

sacraments, they asserted that "sacraments *contain*" and "*confer* grace" (DS 1606).

9. Schillebeeckx, *De sacramentele heilseconomie*, 641–55.

10. Participation on the part of the "recipient" was a standard feature of Catholic sacramental theory and practice. See Colman O'Neill, "The Role of the Recipient and Sacramental Signification," *The Thomist* 21 (1958): 257–301, 508–40.

11. In addition to the primary sources cited above, see the very fine distillation of his thought on sacraments by Schillebeeckx himself, "The Sacraments: An Encounter with God," in *Christianity Divided: Protestant and Roman Catholic Issues*, ed. Daniel Callahan et al., 145–75 (New York: Sheed and Ward, 1961).

12. I say this despite the fine *Grundkurs des Glaubens: Einführung in den Begriff des Christentums*, trans. William V. Dych as *Foundations of the Christian Faith: An Introduction to the Idea of Christianity* (New York: Seabury Press, 1978).

13. Karl Rahner, "The Theology of the Symbol," in *Theological Investigations*, vol. 4, trans. Kevin Smyth, 221–52 (Baltimore: Helicon, 1966).

14. Karl Rahner, *Kirche und Sakramente*, Quaestiones Disputatae 10 (Freiburg: Herder, 1961), trans. *The Church and the Sacraments* (New York: Herder and Herder 1963).

15. For example, see the vast number of articles on the sacrament of Penance in Rahner's *Schriften der Theologie*, as well as the following available in English: "Considerations on the Active Role of the Person in the Sacramental Event," *Theological Investigations*, vol. 14, trans. David Bourke, 161–84 (New York: Seabury, 1976); "The Concept of Mystery in Catholic Theology," *Theological Investigations*, vol. 4, 36–76; "How to Receive a Sacrament and Mean It," *Theology Digest* 19 (Fall 1971): 227–34; "Introductory Observations on Thomas Aquinas' Theology of the Sacraments in General," *Theological Investigations*, vol. 14, 149–60; "On the Theology of Worship," *Theological Investigations*, vol. 19, 141–49 (New York: Crossroad, 1983); "The Presence of Christ in the Sacrament of the Lord's Supper," *Theological Investigations*, vol. 4, 287–311; "The Presence of the Lord in the Christian Community," *Theological Investigations*, vol. 10, 71–83; "The Theology of the Symbol," in *Theological Investigations*, vol. 4, 221–25; "What Is a Sacrament?" *Theological Investigations*, vol. 14, 135–48. Also see Kimberly Hope Belcher, "Karl Rahner's Theology of the Symbol—Sacraments and Worship lecture 4,"

YouTube (21 June 2013), https://www.youtube.com/watch?v=yayZn -mUzSc.

16. See Rahner, *The Church and the Sacraments*, 11–19.

17. Rahner, *The Church and the Sacraments*, 20–23.

18. Rahner, *The Church and the Sacraments*, 25.

19. This is an especially helpful way to understand the sacramentality of matrimony and penance, which have no visible symbol attached to their celebration.

20. From Rahner, "What Is a Sacrament?," 135–48.

21. Otto Semmelroth, *Wirkendes Wort* (Frankfurt am Main, 1962), trans. John Jay Hughes as *The Preaching Word: On the Theology of Proclamation* (New York: Herder and Herder, 1965).

22. Semmelroth, *The Preaching Word*, 89–134.

23. Semmelroth, *The Preaching Word*, 136–78.

24. Semmelroth, *The Preaching Word*, 179–244.

25. See Raymond Vaillancourt, *Vers un renouveau de la théologie sacramentaire* (Montreal: Fides, 1978), trans. Matthew J. O'Connell as *Toward a Renewal of Sacramental Theology* (Collegeville, MN: Liturgical Press, 1979), 36–64.

26. Kenan Osborne, *Sacramental Theology: An Introduction* (Mahwah, NJ: Paulist Press, 1988), 69–99.

27. Edward J. Kilmartin, "A Modern Approach to the Word of God and Sacraments of Christ," in *The Sacraments: God's Love and Mercy Actualized*, ed. Francis A. Eigio, 59–109 (Villanova, PA: Villanova University Press, 1979).

28. Hans Urs von Balthasar, *Herrlichkeit*, 3 pts. (Einsiedeln: Johannes-Verlag, 1961–1985); *Theodramatik*, 5 vols. (Einsiedeln: Johannes-Verlag, 1961–1985).

29. Thomas Aquinas begins his teaching on the sacraments (in general) by asserting, "Now that we have completed our consideration of the mysteries of the Incarnate Word, our next field of investigation is the sacraments of the Church, seeing that it is from this same Incarnate Word that these derive their efficacy." Thomas Aquinas, *Summa Theologiae*, IIIa q. 60, trans. David Bourke (New York: McGraw Hill, 1974), 3.

30. See Catherine M. LaCugna, *God for Us: The Trinity and Christian Life* (San Francisco: HarperSanFrancisco, 1991), especially 111–42 on liturgical connections.

31. Edward Kilmartin, *Christian Liturgy: Theology and Practice, 1. Systematic Theology of Liturgy* (Kansas City, MO: Sheed & Ward, 1988),

106. Also see Kilmartin, "Theology of the Sacraments," in *Alternative Futures for Worship*, vol. 1, ed. Bernard Lee (Collegeville, MN: Liturgical Press, 1987), 123–75. Kilmartin here appeals to the thought of Irenaeus of Lyons.

32. Kilmartin, *Christian Liturgy*, 172.

33. Kilmartin, *Christian Liturgy*, 174.

34. Kilmartin, *Christian Liturgy*, 196–97.

35. For example, his work was critiqued by some as not emphasizing the local church. However, that is precisely the topic of his book *The Particular Liturgy of the Individual Church: The Theological Basis and Practical Consequences* (Bangalore: Dharmaram, 1987). The methodological point to be made is that one needs to glean insight from all of Kilmartin's sources.

36. I would suggest that combining his book *Christian Liturgy* with "A Modern Approach" are the closest we can come to a synthesis.

37. See Kenan Osborne, *The Sacraments of Initiation: Baptism, Confirmation, Eucharist* (Mahwah, NJ: Paulist Press, 1987); Osborne, *A History of Ordained Ministry in the Catholic Church* (Mahwah, NJ: Paulist Press, 1988); Osborne, *Lay Ministry in the Catholic Church* (Mahwah, NJ: Paulist Press, 1993).

38. Kenan Osborne, *Sacramental Theology: A General Introduction* (Mahwah, NJ: Paulist Press, 1988). This relies heavily on his "Methodology and Christian Sacraments" in *The Sacraments: Readings in Sacramental Theology*, ed. Michael Taylor, 39–52 (Staten Island: Alba House, 1981); Osborne, "Jesus as Human Expression of the Divine Presence: Towards a New Incarnation of the Sacraments," in *The Sacraments: God's Love and Mercy Actualized*, ed. Francis A. Eigo (Villanova, PA: Villanova University Press, 1979), 29–57.

39. Kenan Osborne, *Christian Sacraments in a Postmodern World: A Theology for the Third Millennium* (Mahwah, NJ: Paulist Press, 1999).

40. Kenan Osborne, *Sacramental Theology Fifty Years after Vatican II* (Cincinnati: Lectio Publishing, 2014).

41. See Osborne, *Sacramental Theology*, 69–99.

42. Osborne, *Sacramental Theology*, 115.

43. Osborne, *Sacramental Theology*, 49–68.

44. Osborne, *Christian Sacraments*, chap. 1 (41–53).

45. Osborne, *Christian Sacraments*, "Preface," 1.

46. Osborne, *Christian Sacraments*, 51.

47. Osborne, *Christian Sacraments*, 52.

48. Osborne, *Christian Sacraments*, 239.

49. Juan Segundo, *Los Sacramentos hoy* (Buenos Aires: Carlos Lohle, 1971), trans. John Drury as *The Sacraments Today* (Washington, DC: Pastoral Press, 1974), see 10, 32–40.

50. Segundo, *The Sacraments Today*, 15–20. In this connection, see Luis Maldonado, *Secularizacion de la Liturgia* (Madrid: Marova, 1970).

51. Segundo, *The Sacraments Today*, 98.

52. Segundo, *The Sacraments Today*, 36, 80–82, 98.

53. Leonardo Boff, *Los Sacramentos de Vida e a Vida dos Sacramentos* (Pietropolis: Vozes, 1975), trans. John Drury as *Sacraments of Life, Life of the Sacraments: Story Theology* (Washington, DC: Pastoral Press, 1987).

54. Boff, *Sacraments of Life*, 7.

55. Leonardo Boff, *Iglesia: Charisma epoder* (Pietropolis: Vozes, 1981), trans. John W. Diercksmeier, *Church: Charism and Power; Liberation Theology and the Institutional Church* (New York: Crossroad, 1985).

56. Boff, *Church*, 16.

57. Boff, *Church*, 9.

58. Boff, *Church*, 78.

59. Boff, *Church*, 78–79.

60. Antonio Gonzalez Dorado, *Los sacramentos del Evangelio: Sacramentologia fundamental y organica* (Santa Fe de Bogota: Consejo Episcopal Latinoamericano, 1991). The textbook series is entitled Teología para la Evangelización liberadora en America Latina and is published under the auspices of Consejo Episcopal Latinoamericano.

Closely aligned with this approach to sacramental theology is that of Francisco Taborda in *Sacramentos, praxis y fiesta* (Madrid: Editiones Paulinas, 1987).

61. See Gonzalez Dorado, *Los sacramentos del Evangelio*, 18–19. The Puebla conference refers to the second meeting of CELAM (1999); see the final document, 916, 940, and 942. The fifth CELAM meeting in Aparecida (2007) was a very significant advance over previous CELAM meetings, especially in areas that were points of real contention, such as liberation theology. The editor of the final text of the Aparecida document was Cardinal Jorge Bergoglio, who became Pope Francis. In almost every case where Pope Francis has placed his own stamp on the papacy, one can look to see what the Aparecida document had to say.

See the unpublished thesis by Cristobal Fones, "Latin American Episcopal Teaching on Liturgy after Vatican II" (STL thesis, The Catholic University of America, 2006).

62. Gonzalez Dorado, *Los sacramentos del Evangelio*, 89–108.

63. Gonzalez Dorado, *Los sacramentos del Evangelio*, 414–26.

64. Gonzalez Dorado, *Los sacramentos del Evangelio*, 255–56.

65. Gonzalez Dorado, *Los sacramentos del Evangelio*, 449–62.

66. Gonzalez Dorado, *Los sacramentos del Evangelio*, 464–77.

67. Gonzalez Dorado, *Los sacramentos del Evangelio*, 484–89, 577.

68. Gonzalez Dorado, *Los sacramentos del Evangelio*, 538–77.

69. Louis-Marie Chauvet, *Symbole et Sacrement: Une relecture sacramentelle de l'existence chrétienne* (Paris: Cerf, 1987), trans. Madeleine Beaumont and Patrick Madigan as *Symbol and Sacrament: A Sacramental Reinterpretation of Christian Existence* (Collegeville, MN: Liturgical Press, 1994); *Du symbolique au symbole* (Paris: Cerf, 1979), trans. as *The Sacraments: The Word of God at the Mercy of the Body* (Collegeville, MN: Liturgical Press, 2001).

70. Chauvet, *Symbole et Sacrement*, 459–548.

71. On this point, there is only a passing reference in Chauvet to Balthasar. The principal influence is that of Breton, but he draws also on Jürgen Moltmann and Eberhard Jüngel.

72. See *Questions liturgiques* 82 (2001), especially Lorelei F. Fuchs, "Louis-Marie Chauvet's Theology of Sacrament and Ecumenical Theology: Connections in Terms of an Ecumenical Hermementics of Unity Based on a Koinonia Ecclesiology," 58–68; Glenn P. Ambrose, "Chauvet and Pickstock: Two Compatible Visions," 69–79. Also see Kevin W. Irwin, "On Critiquing Liturgical Critics," *Worship* 74, no. 1 (January 2000): 2–19; *Leuven Encounters in Systematic Theology*, http://theo.kuleuven.be/en/lest/, especially *Previous Sacramental Presence in a Postmodern Context* (1999) and *Mediating Mysteries, Understanding Liturgies* (2013); Bilju F. Vazhappily, "A Theological Encounter with Louis Marie Chauvet: A Survey of Recent Anglophone Literature," *Questions liturgiques* 92 (2011): 46–85.

CHAPTER THREE: CONTEMPORARY ECUMENICAL TEACHINGS ON CREATION, ECOLOGY, ENVIRONMENT

1. James McPherson, "Ecumenical Discussion of the Environment, 1966–1987," *Modern Theology* 7, no.4 (1991): 363–71.

2. McPherson, "Ecumenical Discussion," 365.

3. McPherson, "Ecumenical Discussion," 365.

4. World Council of Churches, *Final Document: Entering into Covenant Solidarity for Justice, Peace and the Integrity of Creation*, in *Now Is the Time: Final Document and Other Texts* (Geneva: World Council of Churches, 1990), 7–34.

5. John Chryssavgis, ed., *On Earth as in Heaven: Ecological Vision and Initiatives of Ecumenical Patriarch Bartholomew* (New York: Fordham University Press, 2012), 4.

6. Chryssavgis, *On Earth*, 4–5.

7. Patriarch Dimitrios, Patriarchal Encyclical for the Day for the Protection of the Environment 1989, "The Church Cannot Remain Idle," in *On Earth as in Heaven*, 23–25.

8. Patriarch Dimitrios, Patriarchal Encyclical for the Day for the Protection of the Environment 1990, *Stewards, Not Proprietors*, in *On Earth as in Heaven*, 25–26.

9. John D. Zizioulas, *The Eucharistic Communion and the World*, ed. Luke Ben Tallon (New York: T&T Clark, 2011), 143–76.

10. Zizioulas, *The Eucharistic Communion*, 133–42.

11. Pope Paul VI, Encyclical Letter *Populorum Progressio* on the Development of Peoples (March 26, 1967), nos. 22–28, http://w2.vatican .va/content/paul-vi/en/encyclicals/documents/hf_p-vi_enc_26031967 _populorum.html.

12. Pope Paul VI, Apostolic Letter *Octogesima Adveniens* (May 14, 1971), no. 21, http://w2.vatican.va/content/paul-vi/en/apost_letters/ documents/hf_p-vi_apl_19710514_octogesima-adveniens.html, refer- encing Pope Leo XIII's groundbreaking 1891 document on social justice (*Rerum Novarum*).

13. Pope John Paul II, Encyclical Letter *Redemptor Hominis* (March 4, 1979), http://w2.vatican.va/content/john-paul-ii/en/encycli cals/documents/hf_jp-ii_enc_04031979_redemptor-hominis.html.

14. Pope John Paul II, Encyclical Letter *Laborem Exercens* on Human Work (September 14, 1981), http://w2.vatican.va/content/john -paul-ii/en/encyclicals/documents/hf_jp-ii_enc_14091981_laborem -exercens.html.

15. Pope John Paul II, Encyclical Letter *Sollicitudo Rei Socialis* (December 30, 1987), http://w2.vatican.va/content/john-paul-ii/en/en cyclicals/documents/hf_jp-ii_enc_30121987_sollicitudo-rei-socialis .html.

16. Pope John Paul II, Message for the World Day of Peace, *Peace with God the Creator, Peace with All of Creation* (Jan. 1, 1990), https://w2.vatican.va/content/john-paul-ii/en/messages/peace/documents/hf_jp-ii_mes_19891208_xxiii-world-day-for-peace.html.

17. World Council of Churches, *Minute on Global Warming and Climate Change: "Be Stewards of God's Creation!"* (2008), https://www.oikoumene.org/en/resources/documents/central-committee/2008/public-issues/minute-on-global-warming-and-climate-change.

18. World Council of Churches, *Statement on the Right to Water and Sanitation* (2011), https://www.oikoumene.org/en/resources/documents/central-committee/2011/report-on-public-issues/statement-on-the-right-to-water-and-sanitation.

19. Faith and Order Commission of the World Council of Churches, "The Unity of the Church as Koinonia: Gift and Calling. The Canberra Statement (1991)," in *Growth in Agreement II*, ed. Jeffrey Gros, Harding Meyer, and William Rusch (Grand Rapids: WCC Publications/Eerdmans, 1991), 937–38.

20. Faith and Order, "The Unity of the Church."

21. World Council of Churches, "Costly Unity (1993)," in *Koinonia and Justice, Peace and Creation*, ed. Thomas Best and Wesley Graberg-Michaelson (Geneva: World Council of Churches, 1993), 83–104.

22. World Council of Churches, *Statement on Water for Life* (2006), https://www.oikoumene.org/en/resources/documents/assembly/2006-porto-alegre/1-statements-documents-adopted/international-affairs/report-from-the-public-issues-committee/water-for-life.

23. World Council of Churches, *Climate Change* (Geneva: World Council of Churches, 2005), 77; cf. David G. Hallman, "The WCC Climate Change Programme: History, Lessons and Challenges," in *Climate Change*, 5–39, at 38.

24. World Council of Churches, *Minute on Climate Justice* (2013), https://www.oikoumene.org/en/resources/documents/assembly/2013-busan/adopted-documents-statements/minute-on-climate-justice.

25. World Council of Churches, *Statement on UN Climate Change Conference (COP21) in Paris, December 2015* (2015), https://www.oikoumene.org/en/resources/documents/executive-committee/2015-nov/statement-on-cop21.

26. World Council of Churches, *Statement on Climate Justice* (2016), https://www.oikoumene.org/en/resources/documents/executive-committee/statement-on-climate-justice.

27. See Chryssavgis, *On Earth*, 7–15.

28. Patriarch Bartholomew, Patriarchal Encyclical for the Day for the Protection of the Environment 1992, "Matter and Spirit," in *On Earth*, 26–29.

29. Patriarch Bartholomew, Patriarchal Encyclical for the Day for the Protection of the Environment 2001, "Harmony Between Matter and Spirit," in *On Earth*, 47–49.

30. Patriarch Bartholomew, *Matter and Spirit*.

31. Patriarch Bartholomew, Patriarchal Encyclical for the Day for the Protection of the Environment 1999, "Creation and Creator," in *On Earth*, 44–47.

32. Patriarch Bartholomew, Patriarchal Encyclical for the Day for the Protection of the Environment 1995, "King, Priest and Prophet," in *On Earth*, 35–36.

33. Patriarch Bartholomew, Patriarchal Encyclical for the Day for the Protection of the Environment 2014, https://www.goarch.org/-/encyclical-of-archbishop-demetrios-for-the-ecclesiastical-new-year-and-the-day-for-the-protection-of-our-natural-environme-1.

34. Patriarch Bartholomew and Pope John Paul II, Common Declaration on Environmental Ethics (2002), http://w2.vatican.va/content/john-paul-ii/en/speeches/2002/june/documents/hf_jp-ii_spe_20020610_venice-declaration.html.

35. Patriarch Bartholomew and Pope Benedict XVI, Common Declaration (2006), https://w2.vatican.va/content/benedict-xvi/en/speeches/2006/november/documents/hf_ben-xvi_spe_20061130_dichiarazione-comune.html.

36. Patriarch Bartholomew and Pope Francis, Common Declaration (2014), https://w2.vatican.va/content/francesco/en/speeches/2014/may/documents/papa-francesco_20140525_terra-santa-dichiarazione-congiunta.html.

37. Holy and Great Council of the Orthodox Church, Encyclical of the Holy and Great Council of the Orthodox Church (2016), https://www.holycouncil.org/-/encyclical-holy-council?_101_INSTANCE_VA0WE2pZ4Y0I_languageId=en_US.

38. See my own *A Commentary on* Laudato Si': *Examining the Background, Contributions, Implementation, and Future of Pope Francis's Encyclical* (Mahwah, NJ: Paulist Press, 2016), 14–27.

39. Pope John Paul II, Encyclical Letter *Centesimus Annus* (May

1, 1991), http://w2.vatican.va/content/john-paul-ii/en/encyclicals/documents/hf_jp-ii_enc_01051991_centesimus-annus.html.

40. Pope John Paul II, Encyclical Letter *Evangelium Vitae* on the Value and Inviobility of Human Life (March 25, 1995), http://w2.vatican.va/content/john-paul-ii/en/encyclicals/documents/hf_jp-ii_enc_25031995_evangelium-vitae.html.

41. Pope John Paul II, Encyclical Letter *Ecclesia de Eucharistia* on the Eucharist in Its Relationship to the Church (April 17, 2003), http://www.vatican.va/holy_father/special_features/encyclicals/documents/hf_jp-ii_enc_20030417_ecclesia_eucharistia_en.html.

42. See my own *A Commentary on* Laudato Si', 27–32.

43. Pope Benedict XVI, Encyclical Letter *Caritas in Veritate* on Integral Human Development in Charity and Truth (June 29, 2009), http://w2.vatican.va/content/benedict-xvi/en/encyclicals/documents/hf_ben-xvi_enc_20090629_caritas-in-veritate.html.

44. Pope Benedict XVI, Message for the World Day of Peace, *If You Want to Cultivate Peace, Protect Creation* (January 1, 2010), https://w2.vatican.va/content/benedict-xvi/en/messages/peace/documents/hf_ben-xvi_mes_20091208_xliii-world-day-peace.html.

45. Consejo Episcopal Latinoamericano, *Aparecida Concluding Document* (2007), http://www.celam.org/aparecida/Ingles.pdf.

46. See my own *A Commentary on* Laudato Si', 32–36.

47. Pope Francis, Encyclical Letter *Laudato Si'* on Care for Our Common Home (May 24, 2015), http://w2.vatican.va/content/francesco/en/encyclicals/documents/papa-francesco_20150524_enciclica-laudato-si.html.

48. Pope Francis, Letter for the Establishment of the World Day of Prayer for the Care of Creation (2015), https://w2.vatican.va/content/francesco/en/letters/2015/documents/papa-francesco_20150806_lettera-giornata-cura-creato.html.

49. Pope Francis, Message for the World Day of Prayer for the Care of Creation 2016, *Show Mercy to Our Common Home*, http://w2.vatican.va/content/francesco/en/messages/pont-messages/2016/documents/papa-francesco_20160901_messaggio-giornata-cura-creato.html, citing Patriarch Bartholomew.

50. Pope Francis, Message for the World Day of Prayer for the Care of Creation 2020, http://www.vatican.va/content/francesco/en/messages/pont-messages/2020/documents/papa-francesco_20200901_messaggio-giornata-cura-creato.html.

51. Pan-Amazon Synod, *Instrumentum Laboris* (2019), http://secretariat.synod.va/content/sinodoamazonico/en/documents/pan-amazon-synod--the-working-document-for-the-synod-of-bishops.html.

52. Pan-Amazon Synod, *Final Document* (2019), http://secretariat.synod.va/content/sinodoamazonico/en/documents/final-document-of-the-amazon-synod.html.

53. Pope Francis, Post-Synodal Apostolic Exhortation *Querida Amazonia* (2 February 2020), http://secretariat.synod.va/content/sinodoamazonico/en/documents/post-synodal-apostolic-exhortation--querida-amazonia-.html.

54. The quotation is from a document from the bishops of Columbia that was part of the *instrumentum laboris* for the synod.

55. Pope Francis, Encyclical Letter *Fratelli Tutti* on Fraternity and Social Friendship (October 3, 2020), http://www.vatican.va/content/francesco/en/encyclicals/documents/papa-francesco_20201003_enciclica-fratelli-tutti.html.

CHAPTER FOUR: METHOD

1. Often in theological circles the word *methodology* is often used to describe what I am undertaking here. However, my use of the term *method* is deliberate to distinguish it from *methodology*, which I judge to mean "the study of method."

2. My first introduction to realizing the vast scope of determining a method for the study of the liturgy was reading the Inaugural Lecture delivered by Cipriano Vagaggini for the opening of the Pontifical Liturgical Institute at Sant'Anselmo: *Liturgia e pensiero teologico recente: Prolusione inaugurale* (Rome: Pontificio Ateneo Anselmiano, 1961).

3. Among others, see the documentation of the Preparatory Commission in Angelo Lameri, *La "Pontifica Commissio de Sacra liturgia praeparatoria Concilii Vaticani II. Documenti, Testi, Verbali* (Rome: Edizioni Liturgiche, 2013). Without prejudicing my other professors, I would be remiss if I did not give pride of place to Cipriano Vagaggini, whose writings and teaching has had the most profound effect on me. Among others, see *Theological Dimensions of the Liturgy: A General Treatise on the Theology of the Liturgy*, trans. W. Jurgens from the 4th rev. ed. (Collegeville, MN: Liturgical Press, 1976). For but one indication of Vagaggini's lasting influence, see Elena Massimi, *Teologia*

classica e modernita in Cipriano Vagaggini: Percorso tra scritte editi e inedita (Rome: BEL Subsidia, 2013).

4. Among other times at Sant'Anselmo, I cherish having been in the lecture hall when Cipriano Vagaggini addressed his work on *coetus* (study group) 10, specifically his work on the addition of three Eucharistic Prayers to the Missal. The rationale for those additions is in *The Canon of the Mass and Liturgical Reform*, trans. Peter Coughlan (New York: Alba House, 1969). Vagaggini was known to have said to his confreres on the faculty at Sant'Anselmo that his work on the Eucharistic Prayers was done at the request of Pope Paul VI and was the most difficult assignment he had ever received. It is nothing less than a scandal that a current adjunct Benedictine professor would criticize this work by innuendo and falsehoods (Cassian Folsom, https://adoremus.org/1996/09/from-one-eucharistic-prayer-to-many-how-it-happened-and-why/).

My first meeting with Fr. Vagaggini was in his room ("cell") at Sant'Anselmo in early October 1974. After discussing courses I would take that fall, he immediately began to speak about possible topics for my dissertation. At that point he stood up, walked to his bookshelves, and took down a cardboard box. He said that this was all the documentation he had preserved from the debates about the revision of confirmation. He invited me to take the box home and review it. It was only some years later that I realized what a treasure I had been given to review for forty-eight hours!

5. *American Catholics and Lutherans in Dialogue on the Eucharist: A Methodological Critique and Proposal* (Rome: Studia Anselmiana, 1978).

6. This suggests that the theology of what happens in and through the liturgy is the theology *of* liturgy, where theology that is embedded in and drawn from the liturgy is theology *from* the liturgy.

7. "The Church, therefore, earnestly desires that Christ's faithful, when present at this mystery of faith, should not be there as strangers or silent spectators; on the contrary, through a good understanding of the rites and prayers [*per ritus et preces*] they should take part in the sacred action conscious of what they are doing, with devotion and full collaboration." Second Vatican Council, Constitution on the Sacred Liturgy, *Sacrosanctum Concilium* (December 4, 1963), no. 48, http://www.vatican.va/archive/hist_councils/ii_vatican_council/documents/vat-ii_const_19631204_sacrosanctum-concilium_en.html.

8. See my own *Context and Text: A Method for Liturgical Theology*, 2nd ed. (Collegeville, MN: Liturgical Press, 2018). The first edition was subtitled "Method in Liturgical Theology" (Collegeville, MN: Liturgical Press, 1994).

9. See my own *Models of the Eucharist*, rev. ed. (Mahwah, NJ: Paulist Press, 2020), 23–48.

10. That there a number of ways to understand "the comparative method" of liturgical study, see the collected essays in Robert Taft and Gabriella Winkler, eds., *Acts of Inter. Congress: Comparative Liturgy Fifty Years after Anton Baumstark (1872–1948)* (Rome, Sept. 25–29, 1998). For the origins and a first example of this method see Anton Baumstark, *Comparative Liturgy*, rev. Bernard Botte, trans. F. L. Cross, 3rd ed. (Westminster, MD: Newman Press 1958); Anton Baumstark, *On the Development of the Liturgy*, trans. Fritz West (orig. 1923; Collegeville, MN: Liturgical Press, 2011).

11. See the highly important and influential contemporary exposition of this position in Hans Bernhard Meyer, "Liturgische Theologie oder Theologie des Gottesdienstes," *Zeitschrift fur katholische Theologie* 86 (1964): 327–31. As we proceed, I will be fundamentally in sync with the present *Missale Romanum*, yet I will not be uncritical. My model for this approach is the excellent study by Patrick Regan in *Advent to Pentecost: Comparing the Seasons in the Ordinary and Extraordinary Forms of the Roman Rite* (Collegeville, MN: Liturgical Press, 2012).

12. An example of recent magisterial endorsement of liturgical inculturation is in *Querida Amazonia* nos. 81–96, within a larger and far-reaching section on inculturation under a number of aspects 66–108. Pope Francis, Post-Synodal Apostolic Exhortation *Querida Amazonia* (February 2, 2020), http://www.vatican.va/content/francesco/en/apost_exhortations/documents/papa-francesco_esortazione-ap_20200202_querida-amazonia.html.

13. The English-speaking world is enormously indebted to Anscar Chupungco for his highly insightful writings in this area including *Cultural Adaptation of the Liturgy* (Mahwah, NJ: Paulist Press, 1982); *Liturgical Inculturation: Sacramentals, Religiosity and Catechesis* (Collegeville, MN: Liturgical Press, 1995); *Liturgies of the Future: The Process and Methods of Inculturation* (Mahwah, NJ: Paulist Press, 1989).

14. For example, even the groundbreaking of writing on the sacraments of Karl Rahner and Edward Schillebeeckx offers not a hint of a reference to World War II and its aftermath.

15. Pope Francis, Encyclical Letter *Laudato Si'* on Care for Our Common Home (May 24, 2015), especially chap. 6 ("Ecological Education and Spirituality"), http://w2.vatican.va/content/dam/francesco/pdf/encyclicals/documents/papa-francesco_20150524_enciclica-laudato-si_en.pdf.

16. See my own *The Sacraments: Historical Foundations and Liturgical Theology* (Mahwah, NJ: Paulist Press, 2016), 211–12.

17. Clearly, Joseph Ratzinger wrote extensively on the liturgy with a certain (much debated) set of presuppositions and prejudices. However, it is more than noteworthy that the collection of his essays on the liturgy (never having written a monograph on the liturgy) contains not one reference to a liturgical source. What abound are references to (mostly German) systematic and biblical theologians. See Joseph Ratzinger, *Gesammelte Schriften: Theologie der Liturgie* (Freiburg/Basel/Vienna: Herder, 2008). The more popular iteration of Ratzinger's ideas for the English-speaking world is the translation of the first 194 pages of *Theologie* as *The Spirit of the Liturgy*, trans. John Saward (San Francisco: Ignatius Press, 2000). Here, Ratzinger lays out some of his (not illegitimate) critiques of the reformed liturgy but does nothing to suggest how to either invite dialogue about them, especially to determine whether his writing is accurate or not, or to ameliorate them. Nor does he refer to a source from the liturgy itself.

18. Among others, see the masterful study by Nicholas Denysenko, *The Blessing of Waters and Epiphany: The Eastern Liturgical Tradition* (Surrey/Burlington: Ashgate, 2012).

19. Irwin, *Context and Text*.

20. This was raised as part of the discussion period after Anne Clifford's presentation at the 2017 Meeting of the Catholic Theological Society of America: https://www.ctsa-online.org/resources/Convention%202017/CTSA2017Program3.29.17.pdf. The respondent from the floor was Franciscan sister Dr. Dawn Nothwehr of Catholic Theological Union (Chicago). In addition, see my own *A Commentary on Laudato Si': Examining the Background, Contributions, Implementation, and Future of Pope Francis's Encyclical* (Mahwah, NJ: Paulist Press, 2016), 241–42.

21. I say "Catholic position" because immediately before this in the encyclical the pope refers those who do not believe in a "creator." In the interests of fostering "dialogue" among a number of persons and

positions, I judge it important to be clear about what Catholics bring to the dialogue table.

22. See *Laudato Si'* 10, 11, 13, 18, 50, 62, 109, 112, 137, 14, 147, 156, 157, 159, 175 185, 194, 213, 224, 230.

23. My own attempt in the book *Models of the Eucharist* spans from creation and incarnation through a paschal theology of dying and rising as the substratum for gleaning bread and wine, through to the praise for all of God's good gifts, to ecologically inspired integral eucharistic theology.

24. Francis is citing Bartholomew's "Global Responsibility and Ecological Sustainability," Closing Remarks, Halki Summit I, Istanbul (June 20, 2012).

25. It is most notable that in the encyclical *Fratelli Tutti*, Francis refers specifically to his visit to Abu Dhabi in 2019 where he visited with the Grand Imam Ahmad Al-Tayyeb and so has broadened ecumenical to interreligious.

26. See my own "The Sacramental World—the Primary Language for Sacraments," *Worship* 76, no. 3 (May 2002): 197–211. That the notion of sacramentality is receiving a growing sphere of influence in other Christian churches, see the important works by Lisette Larsen-Miller, *Sacramentality Renewed: Contemporary Conversations in Sacramental Theology* (Collegeville, MN: Liturgical Press, 2016); Graham R. Hughes, *Reformed Sacramentality*, ed. Stefan Losel (Collegeville, MN: Liturgical Press, 2017).

27. Irwin, *A Commentary on "Laudato Si,"* 59–72.

28. See my own "The Sacramentality of Creation and the Role of Creation in Liturgy and Sacrament," in *Preserving the Creation: Environmental Theology and Ethics*, ed. Kevin W. Irwin and Edmund D. Pellegrino, 67–111 (Washington, DC: Georgetown University Press, 1994).

29. See my own "Ecology," in *Oxford Handbook of Ecumenical Studies* (publ. online, October 2017); "Background to and Contributions to *Laudato Si'*, On Care for Our Common Home," in *All Creation is Connected: Voices in Response to Pope Francis' Encyclical on Ecology*, ed. Daniel DiLeo (Winona, MN: Anselm Academic, 2017), 15–30; "Our Common Home," *The Heythrop Journal* 59, no. 6 (November 2018): 873–86; "Liturgy and Ecology," in *Worship and Church: An Ecclesial Liturgy: Essays in Honor of Gerard Austin, OP*, ed. Sallie Latkovich and Peter Phan (Mahwah, NJ: Paulist Press, 2019), 202–26; "Sacramental Theology after

Laudato Si'," in *Full of Your Glory: Liturgy, Cosmos, Creation*, ed. Teresa Berger (Collegeville, MN: Liturgical Press, 2019), 245–61.

30. See the now classic commentary on Tertullian's phrase by Cipriano Vagaggini, *Caro Salutis est Cardo: Corporeta, eucaristia e liturgia*, introduction by Andrew Grillo and postscript by Fiorgio Bonaccorso, new ed. (1st ed., 1966; Arezzo: Edizioni Camaldoli, 2009). An interesting contemporary approach is in Frank Senn, *Embodied Liturgy: Lessons in Christian Ritual* (Philadelphia: Fortress Press, 2016).

As we expound some ideas and principles from this important text it is important to make distinctions among the ways biblical and other authors (myself included) use the same word to mean different things. With regard to the word *flesh* as used here, I will use it in the fulsome Johannine meaning from John 1:14: "And the Word became flesh and lived among us, and we have seen his glory." The importance of the Prologue to John's Gospel in the church's understanding of the mysteries of salvation is that it is proclaimed ion Christmas Day in the Roman Church and on Easter in many Eastern rites. Keywords in this text include, "In the beginning was the Word....All things came into being through him, and without him not one thing came into being.... The Word became flesh and lived among us, and we have seen his glory, the glory as of a father's only son, full of grace and truth" (John 1:1, 2, 14). I am not using the word *flesh* in the Pauline sense.

31. See my own, "Liturgy as Mediated Immediacy: Sacramentality and Enacted Words," *Josephinum Journal of Theology* 19, no. 1 (Winter/Spring 2013): 129–40.

32. See *Context and Text*, 126–27.

33. See my own method with fuller nuances in *Context and Text*, chap. 1 ("Tradition") and chap. 2 ("Method").

Similarly, the Colossians hymn (Col 1:12–20) emphasizes Christ's preexistence. The purpose of all creation consists in our union with Christ and through him with the Father, the origin and fulfillment of all creation, including humanity. Of particular note is Col 1:16: "In him all things in heaven and on earth were created, things visible and invisible...all things have been created through him." Thus, we can assert that the stated motivation for liturgical praise is creation and redemption, and that the dynamic of Christian liturgy is to offer back creation to the Creator through Christ, the cocreator.

This emphasis on the christological axis of liturgy, specifically the paschal mystery, has recently been appropriately supplemented by a pneumatologically rich emphasis on liturgy and sacraments as experiences through and in which the church is drawn into the life of the Triune God. All liturgy is triune. It is the Triune God who makes it occur. Just as Jürgen Moltmann can rightly argue that creation is the result of the power and life of the Spirit, thus ending what perhaps can be regarded as too christological an approach to creation, so we can emphasize that the liturgy is dependent on the dynamism of the Trinity (particularly when understood both immanently and economically). Explicit faith in the Trinity is also illustrated in the Creed:

> *Credo in unum Deum,*
> *Patrem omnipotentem, factorem caeli et terrae*
> *visibilium omnium et invisibilium*
> *Et in unum Dominum Iesum Christum...*
> *per quem omnia facta sunt....*
> *Et in Spiritum Sanctum, Dominum et vivificantem.*

Thus, the act of creation is not limited to the Father; it is equally christological and pneumatological.

34. See Joseph Ratzinger, *Gesammelte Schriften: Theologie der Liturgie* (Freiburg, Basel, Vienna: Herder, 2008).

35. It is by no means a coincidence that this phrase was taken from the title of a book by Leonardo Boff, *Cry of the Earth, Cry of the Poor*, trans. Phillip Berryman (Maryknoll, NY: Orbis, 1997).

36. Pope Francis cites the "Christmas Message" from bishops of the Patagonia-Comabue region in Argentina (December 2009). In addition to raising up this teaching about pollution and the environment, this stands as another example of the way the pope has invited a number of other voices to support and fill out his teachings.

37. See, among others, Timothy Fry, ed., *RB80. The Rule of St. Benedict in Latin and English* (Collegeville, MN: Liturgical Press, 1981), 203–17. Also see the excellent exploration of what the text means in pt. 3, app. 3, "The Liturgical Code in the Rule of St. Benedict," 379–414.

CHAPTER FIVE: BAPTISM

1. See Pope Francis, Apostolic Letter given *motu proprio Traditionis Custodes* on the Use of the Roman Liturgy prior to the Reform of 1970, https://www.vatican.va/content/francesco/en/motu_proprio/

documents/20210716-motu-proprio-traditionis-custodes.html. For an articulation of why I will not engage the previous editions of these rites except by way of comparison and study see my own, *Context and Text: A Method for Liturgical Theology*, rev. ed. (Collegeville, MN: Liturgical Press), xxxvi–lvii.

2. It is important to note that General Instruction of the Roman Missal states, "The Diocesan Bishop, the prime steward of the mysteries of God in the particular Church entrusted to his care, is the moderator, promoter, and guardian of the whole of liturgical life" (22, quoting the Constitution *Sacrosanctum Concilium* on the Sacred Liturgy 41 and the Decree *Christus Dominus* on the Pastoral Office of Bishops 15). This a most important principle for understanding the liturgy presided over by the diocesan bishop as the liturgy's premier expression.

3. An example of a rite for exceptional circumstances is "Chapter V: Order of Baptism of Children in Danger of Death, or at the Point of Death, to Be Used in the Absence of a Priest or Deacon," *Order of Baptism of Children* (Washington, DC: United States Conference of Catholic Bishops, 2020). In this rite, baptism can be administered by "a minister or some suitable member of the faithful" and "the water need not be blessed" (83).

4. I offered a critique of Aidan Kavanagh's approach in *On Liturgical Theology* (New York: Pueblo, 1984): see my own *Liturgical Theology: A Primer* (Collegeville, MN: Liturgical Press, 1990), 46–48. Also, that Alexander Schmemann had an enormous influence on Kavanagh is not surprising: Alexander Schmemann, *The Eucharist: The Sacrament of the Kingdom* (Crestwood, NY: St. Vladimir's Seminary Press, 1988); *Introduction to Liturgical Theology* (London: The Faith Press, 1966); "Liturgy and Theology," *The Greek Orthodox Theological Review* 17 (1972); *Theology and Liturgical Tradition*, ed. Masey Shepherd (New York: Oxford University Press, 1963), 165–78. Since the focused topic of his doctoral dissertation subsequently published as *Theologia Prima: What Is Liturgical Theology*, 2nd ed. (Chicago: Hillenbrand Books, 2004), David Fagerberg has deepened these seminal insights in his *On Liturgical Asceticism* (Washington DC: The Catholic University Press, 2013).

5. See my own *The Sacraments: Historical Foundations and Liturgical Theology* (Mahwah, NJ: Paulist Press, 2016), 11–12.

6. For example, "Order of Baptism of Children in Danger of Death."

7. The title of Anscar J. Chupungco's doctoral dissertation at the Pontifical Liturgical Institute at Sant'Anselmo (Rome) was *The Cosmic Elements of the Christian Passover* (Rome: Analecta Anselmiana, 1997). He argues that despite the difference is the solstices between the Northern and Southern Hemispheres, the fact that Christ's passion, death, and resurrection happened historically in the Northern Hemisphere in the spring and the imperative that the whole church celebrate feasts and seasons at the same time makes any change in the calendars inadvisable. Parts of this book shaped two other of his books, *Cultural Adaptation of the Liturgy* (Mahwah, NJ: Paulist Press, 1982) and *Liturgies of the Future* (Mahwah, NJ: Paulist Press, 1989).

8. A classical and masterful liturgical study of these primal elements in A. J. MacGregor, *Fire and Light in the Western Tradition: Their Use at Tenebrae and at the Paschal Vigil*, Alcuin Club Collection 71 (Collegeville, MN: Liturgical Press, 1992). An interesting, though not theologically profound work is Christina Z. Peppard, *Just Water: Theology, Ethics and the Global Water Crisis* (Maryknoll, NY: Orbis Books, 2014).

9. Among others, see the masterful study by Nicholas Denysenko, *The Blessing of Waters and Epiphany: The Eastern Liturgical Tradition* (Burlington, VT: Ashgate, 2012).

10. See the comprehensive study by Valentina Angelucci, *Ad collectam e sacrario: I riti d'ingresso nella liturgia romana* (Zurich: LIT Verlag, 2021).

11. All translations from the former missal are from *Saint Andrew Bible Missal*, prepared by a Missal Commission of St. Andrew's Abbey (Bruges: Biblica, 1960). All translations from the present English translation of the third edition of the *Missale Romanum* are from the translation approved by the USCCB and printed in various editions in 2011.

12. This resource is available at https://www.sefaria.org.

13. Recall Tertullian's phrase, "The flesh is the instrument of salvation." For a classic commentary see Cipriano Vagaggini, *"Caro Salutis est Cardo": Corporietà, eucaristia e liturgia*, introduction by Andrea Grillo and postscript by Giorgio Bonaccorso, new ed. (1st ed., 1966; Arezzo: Edizioni Camaldoli, 2009). For a somewhat provocative contemporary discussion, see Frank Senn, *Embodied Liturgy: Lessons in Christian Ritual* (Minneapolis: Fortress Press, 2016).

14. This is to admit the "convenience" of the paschal celebrations in the springtime in the Northern Hemisphere. Arguments abound

about the suitability and shape of the paschal rites celebrated in the Southern Hemisphere. I defer to local experts for their insights and suggestions.

15. Among others, see Mircea Eliade, *Cosmos and History: The Sacred and the Profane* (New York: Harper Torchbooks, 1959); *The Myth of the Eternal Return* (Princeton, NJ: Princeton University Press, 1971).

16. See Stephen Wilbricht, "The Work of Bees and Your Servants' Hands," *Ephemerides Liturgicae* 93 (2012): 74–99. When I was assigned as director of liturgy for the North American College (NAC) in Rome in 1977, one of my annual responsibilities was to give conferences about the Paschal Triduum and to prepare the celebration of those liturgies with the faculty and students. In my first year I was disappointed that the stand for the paschal candle was hardly three feet tall. Whatever can be said about the chapel at the NAC, it is certainly large. I searched around in the bowels of the college and found a stunningly beautiful paschal candle stand that was ten feet tall, designed and executed for the chapel's size and space, made of brass. The only ornamentation on the stand are scores of bees embedded in the stand's design. I proceeded then to order a new paschal candle each year that complemented the size of the stand. The cosmic symbolism of the paschal candle as an essential part of the theology of the Vigil could not be missed.

17. At the same time, in an era of efficiency I want to raise the issue of integrity of materials in the liturgy. Several companies offer refillable liquid candles rather than beeswax candles. Is there not something to a candle that burns down and burns itself out being placed next to the altar at which the Lord's sacrifice is perpetuated? Is there not something about the custom of the Holy Father blessing real candles in St. Peter's for all the religious congregations in Rome on the Feast of the Presentation (February 2)—religious who live out vows and lives of self-surrender and self-sacrifice day in and day out just as (votive) candles burn day in and day out?

While the issue of integrity of materials concerns a number of things, e.g., the church itself and vesture, the other issue that needs evaluating is the use of cellphones, iPads, etc. In the act of worship, several ritual books can be prayed from and read from: e.g., the missal and lectionary. In accord with ancient Jewish tradition, the Torah receives great respect in jeweled coverings for fabric covers and in the way these are carried in procession. This continued in the Christian ritual books. The carrying of the Book of the Gospels at the entrance procession, for example, leads to the procession to the ambo for proclamation. In addition, there is an important theological meaning evident when the Book of the Gospels is placed on the altar. Vatican II's Constitution *Sacrosanctum Concilium* states, "The two parts which, in a certain sense, go to make up the Mass, namely the liturgy of the word and the eucharistic liturgy are so connected with each other that they form but one single act of worship" (56). The placing of the Book of the Gospels is a very significant nonverbal expression of this traditional teaching. The acts of reverence to this book also iterate the importance of the proclamation of the word at every liturgy. In my judgment there can be a "hierarchy" of books for use at Mass: Book of the Gospels, Lectionary, Missal.

The use of electronic devices like cellphones or computer tablets flies in the face of the important, though sometimes ignored, issues of the integrity and beauty of furnishings and printed books for the liturgy. Just because one can use a more convenient and smaller hand-held machines from which to read does not mean that they should ever be allowed in worship. Part of this rationale is that liturgical books are dedicated for a single purpose: e.g., to proclaim the sacred word of God. Cellphones and computer tablets can function for any number of uses, some of which are hardly of God or the things of God.

18. Antoine Dumas, "Les sources du nouveau Missel romain," *Notitiae* 7 (1971): 37–42; 74–77; 94-95; 134–36; 276–80, at 74.

19. A related adjustment is that the prayer for blessing in the rite for infant baptism is presumed to be done each time a baptism occurs, except during the Easter season, when the water blessed at the vigil is to be used.

20. Texts from the revised *Missale Romanum* in any number of editions, including *Missale Romanum*, editio typica tertia emendata (Vatican City: Libreria Editrice Vaticana, 2008).

21. See the insightful summary of this issue (up to 2015) in the doctoral dissertation of Pei Tsai, "The Importance of the Noahic Covenant and Its Function as the Basis of Creation Care" (PhD diss., University of Oregon, 1989), https://rts.edu/wp-content/uploads/2019/05/201505-Tsai-Pei.pdf.

22. When compared with the regular translation of *mereor* verbs in the revised Roman Missal as "may merit," the absence of "merit" in this translation is most notable.

23. See the very important studies by Dominic Serra about the changes made in the reformed liturgy from the original in the *Gela-*

sianum Vetus: "The Blessing of Baptismal Water at the Paschal Vigil in the Gelasianum Vetus: A Study of the Euchological Texts, Ge 444–448," *Ecclesia orans* 6 (1989): 323–44; "The Blessing of Baptismal Water at the Paschal Vigil: Its Post–Vatican II Reform," *Ecclesia orans* 7 (1990): 343–68; "The Blessing of Baptismal Water at the Paschal Vigil: Ancient Texts and Modern Revisions," *Worship* 64 (1990): 142–56.

24. The Latin text *natura* is translated here as *substance*.

25. These texts are from the "Tridentine" Missal and are found in any number of sources. Translations are from *St. Andrew Bible Missal*, cited above.

26. *Liber Sacramentorum Romanae Aeclesiae ordinis anni circuli: Sacramentarium Gelasianum; Cod. Vat. Reg. lat. 316*, ed. Leo Cunibert Mohlberg, 1960 (repr., Rome: Casa Herder, 1981), nos. 444–48 (pp. 72–73).

27. On the previous practice, see *Liber Usualis* (New York: Desclée, 1962), 10–13.

28. This phrase, which coincides with the theology of *Laudato Si'*, insists that we are all "fellow creatures." If salt is to be blessed and added to the water, it is notable that the phrase is "to bless this creature salt" (*ut hanc creaturam salis*).

29. That there were a number of rituals issued after Trent, with differences among the texts, is worth noting, and comparisons among them have been very fruitful. The Latin and English texts used here are from *The Roman Ritual*, ed. Philip T. Weller, complete ed. (Milwaukee: Bruce Publishing, 1964).

CHAPTER SIX: EUCHARIST

1. At the same time as will be indicated Holy Thursday was not always a part of the "three days" and originally meant Friday, Saturday, and Sunday. For a brief historical overviews, see my own *Context and Text: A Method for Liturgical Theology*, rev. ed. (Collegeville, MN: Liturgical Press, 2018), chap. 6–7.

2. The premier study of Holy Week in the Roman Rite is still Hermann Schmidt, *Hebdomada Sancta*, 2 vols. (Freiburg: Herder, 1956–1957).

3. The first English language translation in the *Sacramentary for Mass* contained the acclamation "Christ has died, Christ is risen, Christ will come again." It does not appear in the revised translation

of the Missal because, first, it was never in the Latin *Missale Romanum* and, second, it was not an acclamation because it described the paschal mystery and did not signal that we are incorporated into this mystery of faith again and again through the liturgy.

4. See my own *Models of the Eucharist*, 2nd ed. (Mahwah, NJ: Paulist Press, 2020), chap. 8.

5. Both priest and assembled church offer the Eucharist. The liturgy enacts this by its nature. Any preconceived notions that the priest alone offers is just that—a preconceived notion. Among others, see my own *Pope Francis and the Liturgy: The Call to Holiness and Mission* (Mahwah, NJ: Paulist Press, 2020), chap. 3.

6. Second Vatican Council, Constitution *Sacrosanctum Concilium* on the Sacred Liturgy (December 4, 1963), https://www.vatican.va/archive/hist_councils/ii_vatican_council/documents/vat-ii_const_19631204_sacrosanctum-concilium_en.html; Pope Paul VI, Apostolic Constitution *Missale Romanum* on the New Roman Missal (April 3, 1969), http://www.vatican.va/content/paul-vi/en/apost_constitutions/documents/hf_p-vi_apc_19690403_missale-romanum.html.

7. See Maurizio Barba, *La riforma conciliare dell'"ordo Missae": Il percorse storico-redazionale dei riti d'ingresso, di offertorio e di comunione*, new ed. (Rome: Edizioni Liturguche, 2008), 265–67.

8. Barba, *La riforma conciliare*, 266.

9. For example, see *Missale Romanum ex Decreto Sacrosancti Concilii Tredentini Restitutum; Editio Trigesima una juxta sextam Vaticanam post typicam* (Tours: Mame, 1960).

10. Nathan Ristuccia, "Rogationtide and the Secular Imaginary," in *Full of Your Glory: Liturgy, Cosmos, Creation*, ed. Teresa Berger, 165–85, at 166 (Collegeville, MN: Liturgical Press, 2019).

11. See M. Bradford Bedingfield, *The Dramatic Liturgy of Anglo-Saxon England* (Woodbridge: Boydell, 2002), 191–209.

12. Ristuccia, "Rogationtide," 166.

13. *Missale Romanum* (1960).

14. *Sacramentary for Mass* (New York: Benzinger Brothers, 1994).

15. Ristuccia, "Rogationtide," 184–85.

16. See Michael Foley, "Rogationtide," *The Latin Mass* 17, no. 2 (2008): 39. Foley continues, "On the one hand, we fret over the barbaric or hazardous treatment of livestock, commercial pesticides, genetically modified foods, the demise of the family farm, and the rise of food

cartels....On the other hand, at no point in American history have so many of us lived away from the farm."

17. Vincent Miller, *Consuming Religion: Christian Faith and Practice in a Consumer Culture* (London: Continuum, 2005), 3.

18. Among others, see Thomas J. Talley, *The Origins of the Liturgical Year*, rev. ed. (Collegeville, MN: Liturgical Press, 1991).

19. I cannot help but note that for many living in Italy, the main meal at midday (*pranzo*) could contain several courses, while the amount of food eaten at breakfast and supper together did not equal the amount consumed at *pranzo*. The requirement to abstain from fish today often means an outlay of money that exceeds that paid for meat.

20. In the preface, I also noted the impacts of war, noting Mass formularies for the preservation of peace and justice and in time of war and civil disobedience. I am indebted to Enda Murphy and Daniel McCarthy for assistance with the source information for these prayers, which follows. In the Mass *Pro pace et iustitia servanda*, the collects of set A are drawn from Matthew 5:9 (first) and *Gaudium et Spes* 24, 29, 78 (second), the prayer over the offerings from *Gaudium et Spes* 92 and *Lumen Gentium* 9, and the prayer after communion from the *Collection of the Blessed Virgin Mary* from the Mass of Mary, Queen of Peace. A second set has two collects, the first from the *Gelasianum Vetus* (first), the second, a new composition inspired by prayers of the Mozarabic tradition. In the Mass *Tempore belli vel eversionis*, the second collect is from the *Gelasianum Vetus*. For more on the latter Mass, see Thomas Whelan, "Mass in Time of War or Civil Disturbance (*Missale Romanum* 2008): Elements of a Liturgical Theology in a Collect," *Studia Liturgica* 43, no. 1 (March 2013): 155–68.

21. Here, the term *oratio* (plural, *orationes*) refers to the prayer prior to the Liturgy of the Word, that is, the collect.

22. Paul Turner, *Sacred Oils* (Collegeville, MN: Liturgical Press, 2021), 4.

CHAPTER SEVEN: LITURGY OF THE HOURS

1. See Second Vatican Council, Constitution *Sacrosanctum Concilium* on the Sacred Liturgy (December 4, 1963), no. 99, https://www.vatican.va/archive/hist_councils/ii_vatican_council/documents/vat-ii_const_19631204_sacrosanctum-concilium_en.html; Pope Paul VI, Apostolic Constitution *Laudis Canticum* (November 1, 1970), https://

www.vatican.va/content/paul-vi/la/apost_constitutions/documents/hf
_p-vi_apc_19701101_laudis-canticum.html.

2. The sense of the cosmos as delineating much of the liturgical year is found in illuminated manuscripts of calendars where the seasons are regularly depicted from agricultural and cosmic designs. Some even indicate the location of the sun at some point in the delineation of the liturgical days in a given month. For example, *The Medieval Calendar: Locating Time in the Middle Ages*, ed. Roger Wieck (New York: The Morgan Library, 2017). The front cover depicts a harvesting of wheat. In the text of ten of the months of the year, the manuscript states *sol*, two of which are of particular interest, i.e., *sol in ariete* (in March) and *sol in saggitario* (in mid-November).

Also see Jurgen Moltmann's interesting thesis, "The Sabbath: The Feast of Creation," in *God in Creation: A New Theology of Creation and the Spirit of God*, 276–95 (San Francisco: Harper and Row, 1985), as well as the appendix, "Symbols of the World," 297–328.

The important place of the Sabbath in Pope Francis's theology goes back to when he edited the *Aparecida Concluding Document* (2007): Consejo episcopal Latinoamericano, *Aparecida Concluding Document* (2007) www.celam.org/aparecida/Ingles.pdf. Also see my own *A Commentary on Laudato Si': Examining the Background, Contributions, Implementation and Future of Pope Francis's Encyclical* (Mahwah, NJ: Paulist Press, 2016), 37–39.

3. There are five Mass formulas for "VII Kalens Iulias Natale Sancti Iohannis Baptistae" in the Verona Collection: *Sacramentarium Veronense*, ed. Leo Cunibert Mohlberg, Rerum ecclesiasticarum documenta 1 (Rome: Herder. 1978), 232–56.

4. Insightful descriptions of the *lucernarium* and its influence on Christian evening prayer are found in Paul F. Bradshaw, *Daily Prayer in the Early Church* (New York: Oxford University Press, 1982), 22, 51, 57, 75–77, 80, 116, 119, 135; George Guiver, *Company of Voices: Daily Prayer and the People of God* (New York: Pueblo, 1988), 62–66, 202–3; Robert Taft, *The Liturgy of the Hours in East and West* (Collegeville, MN: Liturgical Press, 1986), 26–28, 36–38, 55–56, 211–12, 355–56.

5. See Susan Roll, *Towards the Origins of Christmas*, Liturgia Condenda 5 (Leuven: Peeters, 1995). That there is another theory about the origin of Christmas as intrinsically related to the Paschal Mystery also needs to be recalled.

6. See my own "The Sacramentality of Creation and the Role of

Creation in Liturgy and Sacrament," in *Preserving the Creation: Environmental Theology and Ethics*, ed. Kevin W. Irwin and Edmund D. Pellegrino (Washington, DC: Georgetown University Press, 1994), 67–111.

7. See Duco Vollebregt, "Night or Dawn? Easter Night in Light of Cosmos and Creation," in *Full of Your Glory: Liturgy, Cosmos, Creation*, ed. Teresa Berger (Collegeville, MN: Liturgical Press, 2019), 117–36.

8. See the appendix to *Sacrosanctum Concilium*.

9. To try to comment on the whole revised Liturgy of the Hours would be an impossible task. In addition, I realize that monastics and mendicants can have a different hymn and a different distribution of psalms in their respective monasteries and orders. Among others see Anne Field, ed., *The Monastic Hours: Directory for the Celebration of the Work of God and Directives for the Celebration of the Monastic Liturgy of the Hours*, 2nd ed. (1st ed., 1981; Collegeville, MN: Liturgical Press, 2000).

10. See my own *The Sacraments: Historical Foundations and Liturgical Theology* (Mahwah, NJ: Paulist Press, 2016), pt. 3, "Theology," 209–373, where the discussions of sacramentality, humans and human work, word enacted, prayer events, experiences of the Trinity, paschal memorial, communion, and the already and not yet are contextualized by specific and regular reference to the Easter Vigil.

11. In the previous Hours, this same narrative was assigned for the readings and responsories for the night office in Septuagesima week.

12. Among others, see Helmut Gneuss, "Zur geschichte des Hymnes," *Der latinische Hymnus im Mittelalter: Uberlieferung—Asthetik—Ausstrahlung*, ed. Andreas Haug, Chsistoph Marz, and Lorenz Welker, Monumenta Monodica Medii Aevi, Subsidia 4 (Kassel: Barenreiter, 2004), 63–86.

13. For example, for the Benedictines see *Antiphonale Monasticum pro diurnis horis juxta vota RR.DD. Abbatum congregationum confederatarum Ordinis Ssancti Benedicti, a Solesmesibus Monachis restitutum* (Tournai: Desclée, 1934); for the Dominicans, Philip Carl Smith, "The Hymns of the Medieval Dominical Liturgy, 125–1369" (BA Honors Thesis, University of Notre Dame, 2008).

14. See Peter Jeffery, "The Six Evenings of Creation in the Hymns of the Roman Breviary," in *Full of Your Glory*, 137–64.

15. Jeffery, "The Six Evenings of Creation." His reference to a north African source is to Friedrich Vollmer, ed., *Fl. Merobaudis Reliquae; Blossii Aemilii Dracontii Carmina: Eugenii Toletani Episcopi Carmoina*

et Epistulae, Monumenta Germaniae Historica, Auctores Antiquissimi 14 (Berlin: Weidmann, 1905), 24.

16. As I list the titles, I will offer the customary English translation of each word. Then I will offer some fuller explorations of what these term mean taken from Albert Blaise, *Dictionnaire Latin-Français des Auteurs Chrétiens* (Turnhout: Brepols, 1954/93).

17. *Four Week Psalter*: 83 EP I, Sun I/III; 87 EP II, Sun I/III; 96 Readings Wed I and III; 123 EP Tue II/IV; 124 Readings Wed II/IV; 126 AM Wed II/IV; 127 PM Wed II/IV; 133 Day Fri II/IV; 138 AM Sat, II/IV. *Proper of Time*: 9 Christmas before Epiphany AM; 41 Ascension EP I and II; 44 Easter Time after Ascension (?) EP I and II. *Proper of Saints*: 152 AM, St. Joseph; 154 Readings Annunciation; 171 AM Nativity and Passion of John the Baptist; 191 Readings and EP, Lawrence the deacon. *Commons*: 249 Readings, Common of BVM and on Sat; 252 Readings, Common of BVM and on Sat; 288 EP I, II Common for Holy Women for Several Saints. Citations of numbers and abbreviations are from *The Hymns of the Liturgy of the Hours*, translated from the *Liturgia Horarum*, editio typica altera (Washington, DC: International Committee on English in the Liturgy, 2019).

18. *Four Week Psalter*: 84 Readings Sun I/III; 86 AM Sun I/III; 91 EP Mon I/III; 95 EP Tue I/III; 116 Readings Mon II/IV; 117 Day Mon II/IV; 122 AM Tus II/IV; 133 Day Fri II/IV. *Proper of Time*: 1 EP Advent (*jj*); 15 AM Solemnity of Mary; 20 Readings and EP II Baptism of the Lord; 22 EP Sundays of Lent; 28 EP I and II Holy Week and Sunday of the Passion of OL and Sept 14; 29 Readings Holy Week (*Pange lingua*); 49 AM Holy Trinity; 64 Midmorning Advent after Dec 16, Christmas Time, Epiphany, thru the Year except Lent and Easter Time. *Proper of Saints*: 189 EP I, II Transfiguration; 217 Readings Guardian Angels. Commons: 252 Readings Common BVM and on Sat.

19. *Four Week Psalter*: 83 combined with *creator* EP I, Sun. I/III; 96 Readings Wed I/III. *Commons*: 269 AM Common for Pastors, one Pastor; 288 EP I, II Common of Holy Women for Several Saints.

20. *Four Week Psalter*: 107 EP Fri I/III.

21. *Four Week Psalter*: 109 Readings Sat I/III; 126 AM Wed II/IV. *Proper of Time*: 7 EP Christmas Time before Epiphany; 9 AM Christmas Time before Epiphany; 14 Readings Solemnity of Mary; 34 EP Holy Saturday; 45 Readings Pentecost; 53 EP I, II Sacred Heart of Jesus; 55 AM Sacred Heart of Jesus. *Proper of Saints*: 192 AM, Lawrence the Deacon; 243 Readings Holy Innocents.

22. *Four Week Psalter*: 111 EP I, II/IV.

23. *Four Week Psalter*: 123 EP Tues II/IV; 124 Readings Wed II/IV. *Proper of Time*: 17 Readings Christmas from Epiphany.

24. See my own *Context and Text: A Method for Liturgical Theology*, rev. ed. (Collegeville, MN: Liturgical Press, 2018), chaps. 1—2.

CHAPTER EIGHT: RESPONSIBILITY FOR FELLOW CREATURES ON "OUR COMMON HOME"

1. Other examples from the Mass are the petitions in the universal prayer and the announcements (as part of the dismissal rite).

2. See *Missale Romanum ex Decreto Sacrosanctum Concilii Tridentini Restitutum. Summorum Pontificum Cura Recognitum, editio Trigesima una juxta Sextam Vaticam post Typica* (Tours: Mame, 1960), 395–96, with the following designations: for Paschal Time, for solemnities, for feasts ranked as "double" (*duplicibus*), Virgin Mary, Sundays through the year, and "simple" feasts.

3. Among others, *Ite missa est* is translated as "Go, you are sent forth" in the pre–Vatican II English language *St. Andrew Bible Missal* (Biblica: Bruges, 1960). Immediately following this dismissal the editorial committee from the Bruges Abbey offer the following commentary: "The members of the assembly are sent out into the world to meet their challenge. They have received the message and the Body of the Lord. They are now going to show their gratitude for the great gifts by living according to the words of God with the strength which the Body of Christ has given them. The power of the Eucharist will act in them and shine through them. This is the way God wants to establish his kingdom in the world, through the personal effort of each Christian: we should try to prolong the Celebration into our daily work and dealings with our fellow-men."

4. See *Messale Romano. Riformato a norma dei Decreti del Concilio Ecumenico Vaticano II promulgato da Papa Paolo VI e Rivenduto da Papa Giovanni Paolo II*, 3rd ed. (Rome: Fondazione di Religione Santi Francsco d'Assisi e Caterina da Siena, 2020). The Italian texts follow:

> *Andate in pace.*
> *La Messa e finite: andate in pace.*
> *Andate e annunciate il Vangelo del Signore.*

Glorificate il Signore con la vostra vita. Andate in pace.
La gioia del Signore sia la vostra forza. Andate in pace.
Nel nome del Signore, andate in pace.
Portate a tutti la gioia del Signore risorto.

5. The Latin reads *ut unusque ad opera sua bona revertatur, collaudans et benedicens Deum.*

6. See *Laudato Si'* 91 and 117. Article 91 reads, "Everything is connected. Concern for the environment thus needs to be joined to a sincere love for our fellow human beings and an unwavering commitment to resolving the problems of society."

7. In article 62 of *Laudato Si'*, Francis asks, "Why should this document, addressed to all people of good will, include a chapter dealing with the convictions of believers?" He continues, "I am well aware that in the areas of politics and philosophy there are those who firmly reject the idea of a Creator, or consider it irrelevant, and consequently dismiss as irrational the rich contribution which religions can make towards an integral ecology and the full development of humanity. Others view religions simply as a subculture to be tolerated. Nonetheless, science and religion, with their distinctive approaches to understanding reality, can enter into an intense dialogue fruitful for both."

8. Francis places himself in a direct line from John XXIII when he says in article 3, "More than fifty years ago, with the world teetering on the brink of nuclear crisis, Pope Saint John XXIII wrote an Encyclical which not only rejected war but offered a proposal for peace. He addressed his message *Pacem in Terris* to the entire 'Catholic world' and indeed 'to all men and women of good will.' Now, faced as we are with global environmental deterioration, I wish to address every person living on this planet. In my Apostolic Exhortation *Evangelii Gaudium*, I wrote to all the members of the Church with the aim of encouraging ongoing missionary renewal. In this Encyclical, I would like to enter into dialogue with all people about our common home."

9. See Pope Francis, *On Fraternity and Social Friendship: The Encyclical Letter "Fratelli Tutti,"* introduction by Kevin W. Irwin (Mahwah, NJ: Paulist Press, 2020).

10. See my own *Context and Text: A Method for Liturgical Theology*, rev. ed. (Collegeville, MN: Liturgical Press, 2018), chap. 2.

11. This phrase was used for centuries with the imposition of ashes. In 1975, for the Holy Year for Renewal and Reconciliation, Pope

Paul VI offered another option: "Repent and believe in the gospel." My own sense is that the former is the far more primal, the latter useful especially for the Holy Year.

12. Pope Francis cites three statements from the Orthodox tradition. One is from the patriarch's *Statement for the Day of Prayer for the Protection of Creation* (September 1, 2021) and another, his "Address in Santa Barbara, California" (November 8, 1997). The latter is in *On Earth as in Heaven: Ecological Vision and Initiatives of Patriarch Bartholomew*, ed. John Chryssavagis (New York: Fordham University Press, 2012).

13. Also see *Laudato Si'* 66: "The creation accounts in the book of Genesis contain, in their own symbolic and narrative language, profound teachings about human existence and its historical reality. They suggest that human life is grounded in three fundamental and closely intertwined relationships: with God, with our neighbour and with the earth itself. According to the Bible, these three vital relationships have been broken, both outwardly and within us. This rupture is sin. The harmony between the Creator, humanity and creation as a whole was disrupted by our presuming to take the place of God and refusing to acknowledge our creaturely limitations. This in turn distorted our mandate to 'have dominion' over the earth (cf. Gen 1:28), to 'till it and keep it' (Gen 2:15). As a result, the originally harmonious relationship between human beings and nature became conflictual (cf. Gen 3:17–19). It is significant that the harmony which Saint Francis of Assisi experienced with all creatures was seen as a healing of that rupture. Saint Bonaventure held that, through universal reconciliation with every creature, Saint Francis in some way returned to the state of original innocence [quoting Bonaventure *The Major Legend of St. Francis*]. This is a far cry from our situation today, where sin is manifest in all its destructive power in wars, the various forms of violence and abuse, the abandonment of the most vulnerable, and attacks on nature."

14. Pope Francis quotes a greeting he delivered to the Food and Agricultural Organization in 2014. The organization is sponsored by the United Nations and centered in Rome. This is but one indication of the wideness of Francis's embrace to all "of good will" who seek to dialogue and work on ecological issues.

15. Francis continues in 21: "Account must also be taken of the pollution produced by residue, including dangerous waste present in different areas. Each year hundreds of millions of tons of waste are generated, much of it non-biodegradable, highly toxic and radioactive,

from homes and businesses, from construction and demolition sites, from clinical, electronic and industrial sources. The earth, our home, is beginning to look more and more like an immense pile of filth. In many parts of the planet, the elderly lament that once beautiful landscapes are now covered with rubbish. Industrial waste and chemical products utilized in cities and agricultural areas can lead to bioaccumulation in the organisms of the local population, even when levels of toxins in those places are low. Frequently no measures are taken until after people's health has been irreversibly affected."

16. Pope Francis cites his own Catechesis of June 5, 2013, three months into his papacy.

17. This was also a major concern of John Paul II in *Dies Domini* (1998).

18. See Consejo Episcopal Latinoamericano, *Aparecida Concluding Document* (2007), http://www.celam.org/aparecida/Ingles.pdf.

CHAPTER NINE: INTEGRAL ECOLOGY, LITURGY, IMPLEMENTATION

1. Pope Francis, Encyclical Letter *Laudato Si'* on Care for Our Common Home (May 24, 2015), http://w2.vatican.va/content/francesco/en/encyclicals/documents/papa-francesco_20150524_enciclica-laudato-si.html.

2. Pope John Paul II, Encyclical Letter *Centesimus Annus* (May 1, 1991), http://w2.vatican.va/content/john-paul-ii/en/encyclicals/documents/hf_jp-ii_enc_01051991_centesimus-annus.html.

3. Pope John Paul II, Encyclical Letter *Evangelium Vitae* on the Value and Inviolability of Human Life (March 25, 1995), http://w2.vatican.va/content/john-paul-ii/en/encyclicals/documents/hf_jp-ii_enc_25031995_evangelium-vitae.html.

4. See Anthony Kelly, *Laudato Si': An Integral Ecology and the Catholic Vision* (Adelaide: ATF Theology, 2016); *Integral Ecology and Fullness of Life: Theological and Philosophical Perspectives* (Mahwah, NJ: Paulist Press, 2018). It is curious that the contents of particularly impressive chapter on the Eucharist in the first book (2016), with the argument in the first book that Eucharist and eucharistic theology must be integral to "integral ecology," is totally neglected in the second book (2018).

Notes

See Vincent Miller, ed., *The Theological and Ecological Vision of "Laudato Si'": Everything Is Connected* (London: T&T Clark, 2017).

5. Dennis O'Hara, Matthew Eaton and Michael Ross, eds., *Integral Ecology for a Sustainable World: Dialogues with "Laudato Si'"* (Lanham, MD: Lexington Books, 2020).

6. For Pan-Amazon Synod "Amazonia: New Paths for the Church and for an Integral Ecology, see *Preparatory Document*, http://secretariat.synod.va/content/sinodoamazonico/en/documents/preparatory-document-for-the-synod-for-the-amazon.html, *Instrumentum Laboris*, http://secretariat.synod.va/content/sinodoamazonico/en/documents/pan-amazon-synod--the-working-document-for-the-synod-of-bishops.html, and *Final Document*, http://secretariat.synod.va/content/sinodoamazonico/en/documents/final-document-of-the-amazon-synod.html.

7. Pope Francis, Post-Synodal Apostolic Exhortation *Querida Amazonia* (February 2, 2020), http://www.vatican.va/content/francesco/en/apost_exhortations/documents/papa-francesco_esortazione-ap_20200202_querida-amazonia.html.

8. See my own "Ecology," in *The Oxford Handbook of Ecumenical Studies*, ed. Geoffrey Wainwright and Paul McPartlan (Oxford: Oxford University Press, 2017), http://www.oxfordhandbooks.com/view/10.1093/oxfordhb/9780199600847.001.0001/oxfordhb-9780199600847-e-23.

9. Dimitrios, "Patriarchal Encyclical for the Day for the Protection of the Environment, 'The Church Cannot Remain Idle,'" in *On Earth as in Heaven: Ecological Vision and Initiatives of Ecumenical Patriarch Bartholomew*, ed. John Chryssavgis (New York: Fordham University Press, 2012), 23–25.

10. World Council of Churches, *Now Is the Time, Final Document and Other Texts: World Convocation on Justice, Peace and the Integrity of Creation* (Geneva: WCC Publications, 1990).

11. John Paul II, Message for the World Day of Peace, *Peace with God the Creator, Peace with All of Creation* (January 1, 1990), https://w2.vatican.va/content/john-paul-ii/en/messages/peace/documents/hf_jp-ii_mes_19891208_xxiii-world-day-forpeace.html.

12. The WCC's agreed statement on the sacraments from January 1982 is all the more remarkable: Faith and Order, *Baptism, Eucharist and Ministry*, Faith and Order Paper 111 (15 January 1982), https://www.oikoumene.org/en/resources/documents/commissions/faith-and-order/i-unity-the-church-and-its-mission/baptism-eucharist-and-ministry-faith-and-order-paper-no-111-the-lima-text.

13. Ralph N. McMichael, ed., *Creation and Liturgy: Essays in Honor of H. Boone Porter* (Washington, DC: Pastoral Press, 1993). *Creation and Liturgy* contains essays by very distinguished North American liturgical scholars: Aidan Kavanagh, Thomas J. Talley, Paul F. Bradshaw, Leonel L. Mitchell, Bonnell Spencer, Marion J. Hatchett, Charles P. Price, Byron Stuhlman, Louis Weil, A. MacDonald Allchin, Ralph N. McMichael, Reginald H. Fuller, Nathan Wright, Ormonde Plater, Barbara Carey, Frank C. Senn, John Wilkinson, and Anne Perkins. It is notable that the essays are divided under the topics "Lex Orandi," "Lex Credendi," and "Lex Vivendi."

14. United States Roman Catholic–United Methodist Dialogue, Agreed Statement, *Heaven and Earth Are Full of Your Glory* (2012), https://www.usccb.org/resources/Heaven-and-Earth-are-Full-of-Your-Glory-Methodist-Catholic-Dialogue-Agreed-Statement-Round-Seven_0.pdf. The phrase "the structure of the historic liturgy" means the structures of the liturgy as prescribed and used in mainline "liturgical churches," for example, the Orthodox, Eastern Christians, Roman Catholics, Anglicans, Episcopalians, Lutherans, and Methodists.

15. See my own *A Commentary on "Laudato Si'": Examining the Background, Contributions, Implementation, and Future of Pope Francis's Encyclical* (Mahwah, NJ: Paulist Press, 2016), 40–59. The document from the bishops of the United States is United States Conference of Catholic Bishops, *Global Climate Change: A Plea for Dialogue, Prudence and the Common Good* (June 15, 2001), http://www.usccb.org/issues-and-action/human-life-and-dignity/environment/global-climate-change-a-plea-for-dialogue-prudence-and-the-common-good.cfm.

16. See Walt Grazer, "*Laudato Si*': Continuity, Change and Challenge," in *Creation Is Connected: Voices in Response to Pope Francis's Encyclical on Ecology*, ed. Daniel R. DiLeo (Winona, MN: Anselm Academic, 2018), 32–34. Some of the papers delivered at the USCCB summer seminars are in Walt Grazer and Drew Christiansen, eds., *And God Saw That It Was Good: Catholic Theology and the Environment* (Washington, DC: USCCB, 1996).

17. Benedict XVI, Post-Synodal Apostolic Exhortation on the Eucharist as the Source and Summit of the Church's Life and Mission, *Sacramentum Caritatis* (February 22, 2007), http://w2.vatican.va/content/benedict-xvi/en/apost_exhortations/documents/hf_ben-xvi_exh_20070222_sacramentum-caritatis.html. My own pathways in researching and writing about ecology began at a conference at Georgetown University

in 1993 (inspired by John Paul II's 1990 Message for the World Day of Peace), published as Edmund Pellegrino and Kevin W. Irwin, eds., *Preserving the Creation: Environmental Theology and Ethics* (Washington, DC: Georgetown University Press, 1994).

18. Notably, "dialogue" is addressed in the text nearly two dozen times: 3, 14, 15, 47, 60, 62, 63, 64, 81, 119, 121, 143, 146, 163, 164 [twice], 176, 189, 199, 201. Several initial reactions indicate the importance this encyclical will likely continue to have. For example, see the collection Vincent Miller, ed., *The Theological and Ecological Vision of Laudato Si'*, which originated from a 2015 symposium at the University of Dayton. Also see the articles devoted to *Laudato Si'* in *Theological Studies* 77, no. 2 (June 2016), whose editorial stated that Francis's encyclical is "the most important encyclical ever written in the history of the Catholic Church" (293). Notably, the Catholic Theological Society of America devoted its 2016 convention to the theme "Ecology: Theological Investigations," https://ejournals.bc.edu/ojs/index.php/ctsa/issue/view/977. Among other world class meetings on *Laudato Si'* include the invitation-only symposium "Connecting Ecologies," which gathered experts in a variety of fields (theology, ethics, philosophy, politics, science etc.) at Campion Hall, Oxford, in December 2017.

19. For one example of the way a careful reading of *Laudato Si'* can lead to relating creation to the sacraments and how the celebration of the sacraments leads to important (social) justice implications—such as just wages, working conditions, and air pollution—see the talk by Cardinal Peter Turkson, Prefect for the Dicastery of Integral Human Development, at the 2016 Eucharistic Congress in the Philippines, "The Eucharist and the Care for Creation" (January 27, 2016), http://www.iustitiaetpax.va/content/dam/giustiziaepace/presidenteinterventi/2016/2016.01.27%20Turkson-Ledesma_IEC_ENG.pdf.

20. Among many other sources, see Bert Groen, "The First of September: Environmental Care and Creation Day," in *Full of Your Glory: Liturgy, Cosmos, Creation*, ed. Teresa Berger (Collegeville, MN: Liturgical Press 2019), 307–31.

21. Pope Francis, Letter for the Establishment of the World Day of Prayer for the Care of Creation, 1st September (August 6, 2015), http://w2.vatican.va/content/francesco/en/letters/2015/documents/papa-francesco_20150806_lettera-giornata-cura-creato.html.

22. Pope Francis, Message for the 2019 World Day of Prayer for the Care of Creation (September 1, 2019), http://w2.vatican.va/

content/francesco/en/messages/pont-messages/2019/documents/papa
-francesco_20190901_messaggio-giornata-cura-creato.html.

23. In the Message for the 2019 World Day of Prayer for the Care
of Creation, Francis continues, "It is an opportunity to draw closer to
our brothers and sisters of the various Christian confessions. I think in
particular of the Orthodox faithful, who have celebrated this Day for
thirty years. In this ecological crisis affecting everyone, we should also
feel close to all other men and women of good will, called to promote
stewardship of the *network of life* of which we are part. This is *the season for letting our prayer be inspired anew* by closeness to nature, which
spontaneously leads us to give thanks to God the Creator. It is also *a
season to reflect on our lifestyles*, and how our daily decisions about food,
consumption, transportation, use of water, energy and many other
material goods, can often be thoughtless and harmful. Too many of us
act like tyrants with regard to creation. This too is *a season for undertaking prophetic actions*. Many young people all over the world are making
their voices heard and calling for courageous decisions."

24. Among many others, see Anne and Jeffery Rowthorn, *God's
Good Earth: Praise and Prayer for Creation* (Collegeville, MN: Liturgical Press, 2018). I am very concerned that these "models" will be
"add-ons" to the existing liturgy and mar its integrity. Also see https://
seasonofcreation.org. Among the most thorough resources, see those
from the USCCB Office for Justice and Peace: http://www.usccb.org/
issues-and-action/human-life-and-dignity/environment/upload/
ecology-resource-all.pdf. The recommendation to celebrate a "*Laudato
Si'* Mass" from the United Kingdom Office is severely flawed, not to say
totally out of line with the integrity of Catholic worship.

25. While I was delighted by the contents of the document *Magnum Principium*, I would have preferred an emphasis on full, conscious,
and active *participation* in the liturgy, part of which is cosmic, rather
than the focus on comprehension and understanding in the document's
opening paragraph: "The great principle, established by the Second
Vatican Ecumenical Council, according to which liturgical prayer be
accommodated to the comprehension of the people so that it might
be understood, required the weighty task of introducing the vernacular language into the liturgy and of preparing and approving the versions of the liturgical books, a charge that was entrusted to the bishops."
Pope Francis, Apostolic Letter given *motu proprio Magnum Princium*

(September 3, 2017), https://press.vatican.va/content/salastampa/en/bollettino/pubblico/2017/09/09/170909a.html.

26. The General Instruction on the Liturgy of the Hours 43, states, "The psalmody of morning prayer consists of one morning psalm, then a canticle from the Old Testament…and finally a second psalm of praise, following the tradition of the Church."

27. For example, Bernhard Anderson states, "Creation is the foundation of the covenant; it provides the setting within which Yahweh's saving work takes place. But it is equally true that creation is embraced within the theological meaning of covenant. Therefore, psalmists may regard creation as the first of God's saving deeds (Psalm 74:12–17) and in the recitation of the Heilgeschichte may move without a break from the deeds of creation to historical deeds of liberation (Psalm 136)." Bernhard W. Anderson, *From Creation to New Creation: Old Testament Perspectives* (1994, repr., Eugene, OR: Wipf and Stock, 2005), 26.

28. Anderson states, "It seems, then, that Israel's earliest traditions did not refer to Yahweh as creator in a cosmic sense but concentrated, rather, on Yahweh's 'mighty deeds' of liberation, through which the Holy God became known and formed Israel as a people out of the chaos of historical oblivion and oppression." Anderson, *From Creation to New Creation*, 23–24.

29. See Cesare Giraudo, *La struttura letteraria della preghiera eucaristica: Saggio sullagenesi letteraria di una forma; Toda veterotestamentaria Berakah giudaica*, Anafora cristiana (Rome: Biblical Institute Press, 1981); *Eucaristia per la Chiesa: Prospettive teologiche sulla l'eucaristia a partire della "lex orandi"* (Rome: Gregorian University Press, 1989).

30. The use of *classic* in "classical eucharistic anaphoras" indicates those elements that are most generally found in eucharistic prayers in the tradition. It is not meant to suggest that there is but one model for eucharistic praying. In fact, a review of these prayers discloses much variation within the commonly agreed-upon anaphoral structure. See, for example, the useful overview of the ritual and theological differences in Hans Bernhard Meyer, *Gottesdienst der Kirche: Handbuch der Liturgiewissenschaft, vol. 4, Eucharistie: Geschichte, Theologie, Pastoral* (Regensburg: Friedrich Pustet, 1989), especially chap. 3, "Vom Herrenmahl zur Eucharistiefeier," and chap. 4, "Die Ritusfamilien des Ostens und des Westens." A helpful comparison summary of the Antiochean and Alexandrian anaphoral structure is on 133. For a collection of such texts and appropriate comparisons within and among liturgical families,

see Anton Hänggi and Irmgard Pahl, *Prex eucharistica: Textus e variis liturgiis antiquioribus selecti* (Fribourg: Editions Universitaires, 1968). Also see Joseph Keenan, "The Importance of the Creation Motif in the Eucharistic Prayer," *Worship* 53, no. 4 (1979): 341–56.

31. Louis Bouyer argues that the sources for this prayer are Eastern and include the *Apostolic Constitutions*, the Liturgy of St. James and the Liturgy of St. Basil. See Bouyer, *Eucharist: Theology and Spirituality of the Eucharistic Prayer*, trans. Charles Underhill Quinn (South Bend, IN: University of Notre Dame Press, 1968), 448.

32. Anderson states, "Although all God's creatures are summoned to praise their Creator, human beings are the only earthlings in whom praise can become articulate. They are made for conversation with God, for a dialogue in an I-and-thou relation….Israel's calling is to vocalize the praise that wells up from all peoples and nations." Anderson, *From Creation to New Creation*, 34.

33. A comparison of the titles for God in the present Latin *Missale Romanum* reveals that among the most frequently used terms, *omnipotens* is used 277 times, whereas *creator* is used 5 times. See Thaddaus A. Schnitker and Wolfgang A. Slaby, *Concordantia verbalia Missalis Romani* (Westfalen: Aschendorff Munster, 1983), col. 398–99, 1704–16. In *Reviving Sacred Speech*, Gail Ramshaw states, "Thus at the beginning of the Great Thanksgiving, we pray along with Abraham who obeyed the call (Genesis 12:4), with Moses, who received the Torah (Exodus 19:20), and with Jesus, who was the Word (John 1:1). As we eat bread and wine, we recall Abraham, who shared his food with three mysterious visitors (Genesis 18:8), Moses, who ate and drank with God on Sinai and did not die (Exodus 24:11), and Jesus, who breaking bread on Sunday evening, showed forth his wounds (Luke 24:31)." Gail Ramshaw, *Reviving Sacred Speech: The Meaning of Liturgical Language; Second Thoughts on "Christ in Sacred Speech"* (Akron: OSL Publications, 2000), 44.

34. See, among others, Jürgen Moltmann, *The Future of Creation: Collected Essays*, trans. Margaret Kohl (Philadelphia: Fortress Press, 1979), 119–30.

35. The sources for the preface are the Bergamo Sacramentary (648) and the Gellone Sacramentary (2643).

36. GIRM 15 states, "For part of the new Missal orders the prayers of the Church in a way more open to the needs of our times. Of this kind are above all the Ritual Masses and Masses for Various Needs, in which tradition and new elements are appropriately brought together.

Thus, while a great number of expressions, drawn from the Church's most ancient tradition and familiar through the many editions of the Roman Missal, have remained unchanged, numerous others have been accommodated to the needs and conditions proper to our own age, and still others, such as the prayers for the Church, for the laity, for the sanctification of human labor, for the community of all nations, and certain needs proper to our era, have been newly composed, drawing on the thoughts and often the very phrasing of the recent documents of the Council."

37. It needs to be said that the exact origins and meaning of Ember Days is still debated in the liturgical literature, including Thomas Talley's (classic) doctoral dissertation, "The Development of the Ember Days to the Time of Gregory VII" (ThD diss., General Theological Seminary, 1969). For Rogation Days, see "Rogationtide and the Secular Imaginary," in *Full of Your Glory*, ed. Teresa Berger (Collegeville, MN: Liturgical Press, 2019), 165–85.

38. Among many others, see Michael J. Woods, *Cultivating Soil and Soul: Twentieth Century Agrarians Embrace the Liturgical Movement* (Collegeville, MN: Liturgical Press, 2010).

39. See my own *Models of the Eucharist*, 2nd ed. (Mahwah, NJ: Paulist Press, 2020), 23–48.

40. Few authors have taken up the challenges put forth about spirituality, education, and liturgy. An exception is Peter McGrail, "*Laudato Si'*: The Ecological Imperative of the Liturgy," in *Integral Ecology for a More Sustainable World: Dialogues with Laudato Si'*, ed. Dennis O'Hara, Matthew Eaton and Michael T. Ross (Lanham, MD: Lexington Books, 2020), 317–36.

41. See Sabrina Danielsen, Daniel R. DiLeo, and Emily Burke, "U.S. Catholic Bishops' Silence and Denialism on Climate Change," *Environ. Res. Lett.* 16, no. 114006 (2021), https://iopscience.iop.org/article/10.1088/1748-9326/ac25ba/pdf. As a note of caution, "climate change" was only part of the numerous messages in *Laudato Si'*.

42. See Pope Francis, Encyclical Letter *Fratelli Tutti* on Fraternity and Social Friendship (October 3, 2020), https://www.vatican.va/content/francesco/en/encyclicals/documents/papa-francesco_20201003_enciclica-fratelli-tutti.html.

268. The arguments against the death penalty are numerous and well-known. The Church has rightly called attention to several of these, such as the possibility of judicial error and

the use made of such punishment by totalitarian and dicta-
torial regimes as a means of suppressing political dissidence
or persecuting religious and cultural minorities, all victims
whom the legislation of those regimes consider "delinquents."
All Christians and people of good will are today called to
work not only for the abolition of the death penalty, legal or
illegal, in all its forms, but also to work for the improvement
of prison conditions, out of respect for the human dignity of
persons deprived of their freedom. I would link this to life
imprisonment....A life sentence is a secret death penalty.

269. Let us keep in mind that "not even a murderer
loses his personal dignity, and God himself pledges to guarantee this" [from John Paul II]. The firm rejection of the
death penalty shows to what extent it is possible to recognize
the inalienable dignity of every human being and to accept
that he or she has a place in this universe. If I do not deny
that dignity to the worst of criminals, I will not deny it to
anyone. I will give everyone the possibility of sharing this
planet with me, despite all our differences.

270. I ask Christians who remain hesitant on this point,
and those tempted to yield to violence in any form, to keep
in mind the words of the book of Isaiah: "They shall beat
their swords into plowshares" (2:4). For us, this prophecy
took flesh in Christ Jesus who, seeing a disciple tempted to
violence, said firmly: "Put your sword back into its place; for
all who take the sword will perish by the sword" (Mt 26:52).
These words echoed the ancient warning: "I will require a
reckoning for human life. Whoever sheds the blood of a man,
by man shall his blood be shed" (Gen 9:5–6). Jesus' reaction,
which sprang from his heart, bridges the gap of the centuries
and reaches the present as an enduring appeal.

43. For example, see Tik Root, "U.S. Is Top Contributor to Plastic
Waste, Report Shows," *Washington Post*, December 1, 2021), https://www
.washingtonpost.com/climate-environment/2021/12/01/plastic-waste
-ocean-us/. This is but one brief yet urgent and poignant about the grim
reality of ignoring the planet at our communal peril. Another excellent
source for information about the ecological disaster and human harm of
mining for gold in the Amazon see www.amazonaid.org.

INDEX

245